D1124557

NATIONAL SECURITY AND IMMIGRATION

CHRISTOPHER RUDOLPH

National Security and Immigration
Policy Development in the United States and Western Europe Since 1945

STANFORD UNIVERSITY PRESS

STANFORD, CALIFORNIA 2006

© Stanford University Press
Stanford, California

Printed in the United States of America on acid-free,
archival-quality paper

Library of Congress Cataloging-in-Publication Data

Rudolph, Christopher, date–
   National security and immigration : policy development in
the United States and Western Europe since 1945 / Christopher
Rudolph.
      p. cm.
   Includes bibliographical references and index.
   ISBN 0-8047-5377-6 (cloth : alk. paper)
      1. Emigration and immigration—Government policy.
2. Immigrants—Government policy.   3. National security.
I. Title.
JV6271.R83   2006
355′.03354—dc22   2006010317

Original Printing 2006

Last figure below indicates year of this printing:
15   14   13   12   11   10   09   08   07   06

Typeset by G & S Typesetters, Inc. in 10/14 Janson

For Lori

Contents

List of Figures

List of Tables

Acknowledgments

This book would not have been possible without the love and support of my beautiful wife, Lori, to whom I owe my greatest thanks. I am indeed fortunate to be able to share my life with such an amazing woman, and not a day goes by that I do not recognize and appreciate how lucky I am.

My family has provided the foundation of support that I have continually depended on. Thanks to my mom, Doris, who has always done so much for me and for the rest of our family—often without adequate thanks and appreciation. My dad, Woldemar, was unwavering in his confidence in me and instilled in me a desire to always try to see the positive and that all things are possible. For that, I am thankful. I miss him dearly, but he is always with me in spirit. I'd also like to thank my "new" family, Elinor and Diane, who have always made me feel like a part of the family and have given much support and encouragement. I'm also lucky to have been able to get to know Milton Luster—albeit for too brief a time. To remember him always brings a smile.

Professionally, I owe a great many thanks to teachers, mentors, colleagues, and friends. Art Stein, Jim Hollifield, Martin Heisler, and David Rapoport have all been tremendous mentors to me over the years, offering both wise counsel and much needed encouragement. I also wish to thank Mia Bloom, Rey Koslowski, Deborah Larson, Nick Onuf, Richard Rosecrance, and Henry Yu. Thanks to Elsa Arismendi for her research assistance and work on the index, and to Alexandria Giardino for her meticulous copyediting. Thanks also to Amanda Moran, Jared Smith, and Mariana Raykov at Stanford University Press for all their help in seeing the manuscript through the publication process.

Over the past few years I have been fortunate to spend time in remarkable places of research and learning. I was lucky to engage a wide array of scholars and students and to have many opportunities to share ideas and gain needed feedback. For this, I thank Kevin Middlebrook and Wayne Cornelius (Center for U.S.-Mexican Studies and the Center for Comparative Immigration Studies at the University of California, San Diego), Ann Tickner (Center for International Studies at the University of Southern California), Steve Lamy (School of International Relations at USC), and Jeff Anderson (Center for German and European Studies at Georgetown University). My sincere thanks to the fantastic staff at each for all their help, including Graciela Platero, Melissa Ince, Marisela Schaffer, Calluna Euving, Allison Hillegeist, Kim Jaeger, and Barbara Kalabinski. I also thank Louis Goodman and the faculty at the School of International Service for bringing me to American University and for providing me with such a great place to continue my research and teaching.

Financial support for this project has been received from the UCLA graduate division, UCLA Department of Political Science, the Institute for the Study of World Politics (Washington, DC), the USC Center for International Studies, the Canadian Embassy in Washington, DC, and the School of International Studies at American University. A portion of Chapter 7 appeared as "Sovereignty and Territorial Borders in a Global Age," *International Studies Review* 7, no. 1 (2005): 1–20.

CWR
Alexandria, VA

NATIONAL SECURITY AND IMMIGRATION

CHAPTER ONE

Introduction

Ahmed Ressam boarded a ferry in Victoria, British Columbia, on December 14, 1999. Ressam had carefully stowed high explosives in the trunk of his car that he intended to detonate during the worldwide millennium celebration at Los Angeles International Airport. Using a forged Canadian passport under the name of Benni Noris, he hoped that he would avoid suspicion when he entered the United States. Fortunately, U.S. border agents in Port Angeles, Washington, became suspicious of Ressam during routine questioning and decided to search his vehicle. Although he attempted to flee on foot, agents were able to apprehend the Algerian-born terrorist and thus to avert a potential millennium disaster.[1] Given that five hundred million people cross the border and enter the United States each year, and that it is extremely difficult to maintain strict security along the country's one hundred thousand miles of shoreline and six thousand miles of land borders, the fact that Ressam was apprehended could be considered quite remarkable. Unfortunately, we were not so fortunate in the fall of 2001: all of the 9/11 terrorists were foreign nationals who exploited U.S. immigration and border policy to infiltrate the country and carry out their mission.[2]

These events made two things clear: global terrorism has emerged as a central security issue the world over; and effective immigration and border control has become a necessary condition to maintain national security.[3] That national security and control of international migration are linked is now conventional wisdom. Less recognized, however, is the fact that *migration and national security have been strongly linked long before September 11 and the emergence of the global terror threat.* International migration is not simply an issue of homeland security; it affects numerous facets of governance necessary for national security.

This is a book about the complex relationship that exists between national security and international migration. International migration presents the state with important choices that impact economic production and the accumulation of wealth, manpower resources that can be drawn on to defend the country, internal security, relations with other states, and the national identity—the fabric of our sense of social belonging. Given this complex mix of implications, we face an important question: How can we explain state behavior toward international migration?

My purpose is to address this important question and to provide a theoretical model of migration and border policymaking among advanced industrial states since 1945. Two primary elements are stressed: (1) I will show how the structural security environment facing states affects their decisions regarding immigration and border policies; and (2) I will show how evolving patterns of international migration can influence the national security priorities of states, broadly defined. In the process of explaining these dynamics, the interplay between realpolitik and idealpolitik—between power and interest, and ideas and norms—emerges as a central theme of the book.

Evolving Notions of Security

It has been said that September 11 "changed everything." Indeed, the emergence of a new global "war on terrorism" has significantly affected the security priorities of many countries around the world, and homeland security interests now figure prominently in foreign-policy decisions. However, in a broader sense, the two world wars of the twentieth century and the period of economic upheaval between them would seem the more pivotal in their effect on the politics of our contemporary era. The devastation left in the wake of these wars provided important lessons for international politics that was used by the architects of the postwar world order. Beginning with Franklin Delano Roosevelt's plans for great power cooperation among the world's five powers that later evolved into key international institutions such as the United Nations and the North Atlantic Treaty Organization (NATO), emphasis was placed on facilitating cooperation among states. These efforts were not limited to regimes to foster collective security, but also included the economic realm, beginning with the establishment of the Bretton Woods monetary regime and the General Agreement on Tariffs and Trade (GATT).

Charles Kindleberger documented how the global economic and political collapse during the interwar period provided the impetus for a new postwar conventional wisdom regarding economic strategy.[4] Isolationism and protectionism were identified as factors contributing to a downward spiral of economic depression, political instability, resurgent nationalism, and ultimately, world conflict. Such lessons provided fertile ground for the adoption of a Ricardian strategy for the accumulation of material power in the emerging postwar world order and took the form of the Bretton Woods monetary regime and the GATT trade regime. Following Ricardian principles of comparative advantage, this emergent strategy was based on the notion that liberal trade policies and laissez-faire treatment of international factor flows is a Pareto-improving endeavor, one that promises to create a "rising tide that will lift all boats" that would increase global output and increase global wealth.[5] Large, powerful states, increasingly found it more advantageous to plumb the world market through the management of international trade and factor flows rather than attempting to secure resource stocks through military conquest.[6] Smaller states faced similar incentives to adopt policies favoring openness and engagement rather than isolation. Given their limited resource endowments, pursuing a strategy of autarky was not a realistic option for smaller states desiring an efficient economy. In the post–WWII era, states of all sizes faced considerable pressure to trade in order to sustain an independent national existence—in other words, security.

Richard Rosecrance characterized this emergent strategy as constituting the rise of "trading states," where state power is increasingly a function of control over a global trading system rather than one based on the accumulation of power via territorial conquest.[7] By no means does he render military affairs useless to statecraft, but he does argue that security in the trading-state world is being recast in response to long-term changes in the nature of warfare and lessons learned from the great empires of the past. As warfare has become increasingly costly, complicated, and destructive, the cost of conquering and maintaining vast empires of territorial holdings has become evident to those states with imperial or hegemonic designs.[8] Moreover, the development of increasingly sophisticated weaponry and exponential growth in their destructive capacity have made wars of territorial expansion not only more costly but also more dangerous, both economically and politically. In both economic and political terms, the development of nuclear weapons and the availability of intercontinental delivery systems have made the cost of major war unpalatable for material, political, and normative reasons.[9] Moreover, emergent international norms regarding modern laws of war place increasing emphasis on legitimacy regarding the use of force. States not deemed to be engaging in a "just war" increasingly risk being ostracized by the international community—an outcome that can have significantly deleterious political and economic effects.

American leadership and its rise to maintaining a preponderance of power in the Western sphere facilitated the emergence of this trading-state system in the post–WWII era. Although not a global hegemony, the bipolar distribution of power during the cold war established two distinct spheres, each with a dominant hegemon.[10] In the West, the United States was able to create and maintain a generally open economic structure by providing stability and offering incentives to other states to embrace openness by giving them access to its large domestic market in the form of asymmetric tariff bargains.[11] In addition, the United States also provided the confidence required for a stable international monetary system, and the strength of its currency offered the liquidity needed to maintain an increasingly open system, especially when external shocks threatened global stability. Regimes then serve to maintain such systems as the structural environment changes over time.[12]

There is certainly strong evidence to support the argument that a trading-state orientation has shaped trade policies and capital flows since 1945. Since Bretton Woods, tariffs have dropped steadily and significantly, especially among advanced industrial states, spurring increased levels of world trade.[13]

In fact, during the 1990s, world trade grew at more than three times the rate of global output.[14] Even more significant expansion has taken place in the volume of flows in international capital markets.[15] Facilitated by the deregulation of domestic financial markets, liberalization of capital flows, and advanced IT hardware and communications devices, the foreign-exchange market's daily turnover rate grew from $15 billion in 1970 to some $1.5 trillion in 1998.[16]

What about international labor mobility? Here, the evidence is less supportive of purely Ricardian explanations. Although most trading states employed more liberal and open policies regarding international migration in the early cold war period, they have generally taken a nearly opposite trajectory relative to policies governing trade and capital flows over the past thirty-five years.[17] This raises some important questions: *Why do trading states seem to favor more openness for trade and capital flows than for labor flows? More generally, how can we account for state behavior regarding international migration?*

Given current conventional wisdom, this tendency might be easily explained by suggesting that facilitating international migration in an age of global terrorism has simply become "too risky." However, such explanations do little to explain restrictivism prior to 2001. Another appealing explanation might be to suggest that immigration involves a net cost to the state and thus serves to *decrease* state power rather than increase it. Or, we might take a softer position and posit that immigration involves less *relative* gains for the state than those available through open trade or capital mobility. In fact, neither of these would seem to be supported by the available evidence.

Historical perspectives of the economic gains achieved from migration suggest that it can be of vital importance to the production and accumulation of material power. Timothy Hatton and Jeffrey Williamson found that gains from migration were higher than trade in goods in the nineteenth-century Atlantic economy.[18] When comparing gains in historical perspective, "it really looks like the 'bigger bang' was received in that period from migration—by quite a long shot—than from trade in goods."[19] Moreover, whereas the dominant economic perspective on the relationship between migration and trade has long viewed the two as *substitutes*, these more recent analyses of the empirical evidence suggest that migration and trade are, in fact, *complements*.[20] Economists and scholars of international political economy have long pointed to the importance of trade for the accumulation of material economic power. However, if migration complements trade, then it must be considered a necessary condition to achieve maximum gains through trade, especially in situations of total specialization or where locational economies of scale exist.[21]

These economic incentives for liberal immigration policies remain important even as most advanced industrial countries shift from Fordist manufacturing-based economies to knowledge- and skills-based economies. In an ever more skill-driven world economy, *knowledge* is indeed an increasingly important component of state power.[22] A 1999 OECD report surmised that "the movement toward an economy and society where knowledge is highly valued is more or less inevitable."[23] In advanced industrial states, the proportion of GDP that is generated by services—especially those in the high value category—has steadily increased during the past half-century. In the United States, the percentage of GDP that was generated by services increased from below 60 percent in 1960 to about 70 percent by 1990, with most focused in the high-value categories.[24] In 2001, the percentage of GDP attributed to services reached 80 percent. In contrast, since 1960 the percentage of U.S. GDP attributed to industry (manufacturing) decreased from 35 percent to its current level of 18 percent. The U.S. Labor Bureau forecast that the country would need 1.7 million computer technicians during the decade ending in 2008, and predicted that demand would continue to increase over time. Maximizing national wealth and power would thus be a function of attracting the best and the brightest in the global labor market and of establishing policy that facilitates their entry and retention.

The economic gains from immigration are not limited to the high-skill sector, however. The increasing returns to high-skilled labor in advanced industrial countries create incentives for a restructuring of the labor market that pushes domestic workers toward those careers where returns are higher (that is, high-skilled services). However, low-skilled jobs remain crucial to a well-functioning economy and society, including domestic labor (for example, child care) and low-skilled service labor (for example, gardening, housekeeping, maintenance, and so on). Such jobs are increasingly unappealing to the domestic labor force due to low wages, low opportunity for career advancement, and/or low social status linked to these occupations.[25] Increasingly these jobs are assumed by foreign labor in such segmented labor market economies, and demand for foreign labor can become "structurally embedded" in the economy and society.[26]

The effects that current demographic trends in advanced industrial countries have on social welfare systems also create demand for immigration. Low fertility rates among populations in most advanced industrial countries (averaging about 1.7) not only serve to decrease the pool of available "high productivity" labor but also change the age composition of the population over time. The aging population creates increased demand on social security entitlements at a time when there are fewer workers paying into the system, creating a growing problem of solvency.[27] Three remedies are commonly offered to this dilemma: (1) increase domestic birthrates (which is not only difficult for the state to manage but also will take nearly two decades to bolster the rolls of those contributing to the system); (2) increase returns on the social security fund held by the state (increasing returns invariably involves accepting increased risk); or (3) increasing the number of working-age laborers through liberalized immigration. Given the risks and limitations of the first two alternatives, there are incentives for states to pursue the third option.

Like trade, openness to immigration flows is generally associated with economic gains necessary for the creation of state wealth and power. Of course, not all domestic actors benefit. As is the case with trade flows, factor flows create short-term winners and losers in the domestic economy.[28] However, in aggregate and over the long-term, most economists agree that immigration has had favorable economic consequences for receiving countries.[29] Immigrants contribute to economic growth by increasing demand for goods and services through their consumption patterns, creating new jobs due to their generally high levels of entrepreneurship, and contributing to an economy's comparative advantage by facilitating the creation of economies of scale production.[30]

From the standpoint of the state seeking to maintain its place in international society through the accumulation of power, it would seem that liberalization of policy would be an important facet of trading-state grand strategy. Yet, policy outcomes do not consistently display the type of steady, increased liberalization over time that is evident for trade policies or openness to international capital mobility. However, this behavior is *not* because immigration is not an important element of the national interest, but rather because migration's place in the construction of state grand strategy is more complex than a purely Ricardian (or "trading state") model can capture. The model delineated in this book is intended to, among other things, "fill in the blanks" present in the trading-state model to better account of state behavior.

Plan of the Book

This study begins by examining existing models of immigration and border policy formation. A survey of the extant literature presented in Chapter 2 makes two things clear. First, although a sizeable literature exists dealing with the issue of international migration from myriad disciplinary perspectives, there are few comprehensive models of policy formation that incorporate more than a single case study. Instead, much of the focus reflected in the literature has been placed on explaining factors that can generate migration pressures, its effects on sending- and receiving-countries in terms of jobs and wages, issues of immigrant incorporation and assimilation, or the personal and social aspects of migration networks.[31] The focus of analysis is on migration processes or the migrants themselves rather than on state responses to migration through the creation of new policy. Second, most existing models of policymaking forward a conventional thinking about the context in which such processes take place. Immigration and border policy is considered to be inherently an issue of *domestic* public policy. Among political scientists, this conventional wisdom has placed (and maintained) immigration scholarship among Americanists and area studies specialists. Variables examined to explain policy outcomes are generally specific to a given case and generally conform to a "bottom-up" conception of political processes.

In contrast to these existing models, the remainder of Chapter 2 outlines a theory of policy formation where the state serves a central, rather than peripheral, role. Rather than characterizing the state as primarily inward looking (as domestic politics scholars tend to do if they include the state as an autonomous actor) or outward looking (as international relations theorists are prone to), I argue that the state figuratively resembles the mythological Roman god Janus, with one face looking out as the other looks in. In crafting an overall grand strategy that shapes the general direction of policy outcomes, policymakers must respond to perceived threats along both vectors. Policy is then modeled as primarily a function of threat perception, and whether threats are most acutely felt originating externally (geopolitics) or internally (domestic politics). However, the manner in which a state responds (the specific characteristics of policy outcomes) is *shaped* according to prevailing ideas about security and economics.

Chapters 3 through 6 present empirical evidence from four case studies since 1945, including the United States, Germany, France, and Great Britain. Each case not only shows central tendencies in the construction of a three-dimensional grand strategy—one comprised of military, economic, and societal factors—but also identifies and explains the effects of intervening variables that shape policy outcomes. These case studies show that among this set of primary trading states (those most instrumental in shaping postwar security and economic institutions based on trading-state principles), central tendencies of policy formation exist across cases that conform to a three-dimensional security logic. Although case-specific intervening variables also affect policy outcomes, an emphasis is placed on explaining how geopolitical structure and ideas interact at the state level to establish a baseline direction for immigration and border policies.

The primary purpose of the book is to present an explanation of state behavior that subsumes existing explanations within a more comprehensive analytical framework. However, international migration and policies enacted to manage it and other cross-border flows has significant social and political implications that go beyond simple explanations of policy outputs. International migration and the global mixing of peoples have a profound affect on social identities, political order and the legitimacy of the state, and the principle of sovereignty on which international order is based. Chapter 7 offers concluding remarks about these important issues and how the findings presented in the study help us to understand them better. International migration rests at the fault line between the tectonic forces that shape our world—between the forces of globalization, on the one hand, and the forces of fragmentation, on the other. Understanding the state's position relative to these forces is paramount if we are to gain a clear understanding of the factors that shape state behavior.

The globalization of international migration (as well as other flows, including trade and capital) offers a means to national wealth and power—requirements to maintain both security and sovereignty. Yet it is the globalization of migration in particular that calls into question basic ordering principles. As international migration flows have grown in scale and scope, expressions of social anxiety have manifest themselves in calls for restrictionist policies.[32] At the root of many of these expressions is the question of how the globalization of migration prompts us to continually reassess a basic question: Who are we?[33] Good governance as we move forward in our increasingly global age is dependent on the state's ability to craft policy that maintains security and order, both externally and internally. To this point, so-called trading states have been characterized solely by their focus on the material benefits of openness and globalization.[34] However, such a perspective neglects the political importance of the nationalist impulse in societies. Clearly, relative success for states in a world of cross-border flows is increasingly a function of their ability to navigate the complex political terrain between these conflicting impulses for globalization and fragmentation.

CHAPTER TWO

Explaining Immigration and Border Policy Development

Why is it important to understand the politics of immigration and border policy development? There are numerous reasons why managing international migration is among the most crucial issues facing states today. First, the total volume of international migration is considerable and continues to rise.[1] From 1975 to 2000, the number of people living outside of the country of their birth or nationality increased from 85 million to 175 million.[2] Among more developed nations, the percentage of population growth attributed to migration grew from 26.7 percent from 1985–90, to 45.0 percent from 1990–95.[3] These trends are especially acute in Europe, where the percentage of population growth due to migration has leaped from 29.6 to 87.5 percent during this period.[4] However, as Rey Koslowski notes, "The political significance of migration . . . is not simply a function of its magnitude."[5]

International migration is increasing not only in volume but also in scope.[6] Reduced transportation costs, global access to information, and the availability of social capital in the form of international migration networks contribute to the increasing volume and diversity of flows.[7] Moreover, the economic restructuring associated with the process of industrialization and globalization adds structural pressures for increased levels of international migration. Global migration pressures are not only a function of the disparity of wealth and population growth between developed and developing nations, but also on domestic economic restructuring as developing countries move from a base of subsistence agriculture to industrial production.[8] Industrialization promotes a shift in domestic labor from the agricultural sector to the industrial sector. However, because job creation usually lags behind labor supply produced through rural-urban migration, an increase in emigration is likely in the short- to medium-run time frame.[9]

In addition to added volume and diversity, several factors suggest that international migration will become increasingly politicized in the coming years, both *within* and *between* states. Within migrant-receiving states, population growth is no longer solely the result of domestic birthrates and infant mortality rates, but is increasingly a function of migration. This trend is most acutely felt in Germany, where immigration accounted for virtually all of the country's population growth since World War II, though similar patterns are evident in other European nations and the United States. While immigration accounted for only one-eighth of the nation's population increase in 1960, by 1990 it accounted for one-third.[10] Moreover, fertility rates among new immigrants tend to be significantly higher than among domestic populations. For example, U.S. Bureau of Census figures show that fertility rates of new immigrants (those immigrating since 1970) run approximately 50 percent higher than those of prior immigrants, creating a multiplier effect for immigration's impact on demographic changes. The influence of demographic changes on the politics of migration is unmistakable. Michael S. Teitelbaum and Jay Winter argue that "the three decades of roughly 1965–95 form what may be termed a generation in demographic and political history, characterized by fundamental shifts in the parameters of political and demographic life that make it distinctive and identifiable."[11] In noting the connection between such transformations and the politics of national identity, they add, "Racial, in some ways unprecedented, demographic movements intersected with highly charged debates about national identity."[12] Increased politicization is also a function of the emerging trend among new migrants for segmented assimilation rather than "melting pot" assimilation, a preference increasingly accompanied by demands for group rights, dual (or multiple) citizenship, and/or semisettlement.[13]

In terms of increased politicization *between* states, a potential divergence of interests relative to international migration exists between developing (primarily migrant-sending) states and developed (primarily migrant-receiving) states.[14] For developing states, emigration provides a safety valve to reduce unemployment pressures that can hamper economic growth, as well as significant potential inflows of foreign exchange through migrant remittances. However, their migration preferences are likely to prefer that emigration consist primarily of low-skilled labor (in abundance) rather than high-skilled (which is relatively scarce). By contrast, developed states increasingly display a distinct preference for a lower overall volume of immigration, in addition to sharp preference for high-skilled over low-skilled immigrants.[15] Increasingly, developing countries have established new institutions to promote and manage emigration abroad and have increased lobbying activities directed at receiving states.[16] Divergent interests provide fertile ground for potential conflict, and the first salvo in this exchange may have come in the form of Mexican foreign minister Jorge Castañeda's declaration in June 2001 that any immigration deal with the United States must be comprehensive, not piecemeal as U.S. policymakers suggested they preferred. In his words, Mexico demanded the "whole enchilada" or nothing at all.[17] Unfortunately for the Mexicans and the Fox administration that made migration policy the focal point of its foreign policy, the political gambit did not pay off. September 11 served to table all bilateral talks of a comprehensive new migration regime. The factors that served to escalate the political tensions between sending and receiving countries remain, however, and future negotiations are likely to remain contentious in both the domestic and international political spheres.

In addition to the increasingly politicized nature of immigration and border policy debates, human rights issues related to migration flows also make effective management a policy imperative for liberal states. On the one hand, political and natural disasters that produce large-scale refugee flows present a formidable challenge to the protection of human rights and effective governance. Numerous civil conflicts that have erupted around the world since the end of the cold war have produced significant numbers of refugees needing aid and protection. For example, ethnic conflict in the Darfur region of Sudan has engendered genocidal violence that produced some 1.4 million displaced persons. In 2004, approximately two hundred thousand refugees fled into neighboring Chad. Moreover, the World Health Organization estimated some ten thousand refugees die per month due to conditions in refugee camps since the violence began.[18] In addition to refugee crises, another recent development in international migration with significant human rights implications is the rise in the illicit migrant-smuggling industry.[19] Smuggling illegal aliens into industrial democracies has emerged as a multibillion-dollar industry. According to figures from the International Organization for Migration, smuggling undocumented workers generates some $10 billion annually for those who transport the estimated four million migrants that utilize these services each year.[20] The sophistication of these smuggling networks makes exercising control distinctly more difficult for states seeking to assert control over their borders.

These are just a few of the implications of international migration that make it among the most crucial issues on both the domestic and foreign-policy agenda. They also illustrate why it is important to understand the political factors that affect state behavior and policy development. This chapter addresses the central theoretical question of this book: How can we explain trading-state behavior regarding international migration? Given the increasing political salience of international migration to both domestic and foreign policy, the paucity of theorizing about policy formation is quite surprising.[21] Much of the work done is either policy analysis (determining the effectiveness of immigration policy on flows) or it forwards a particular normative position vis-à-vis immigration and border policy (arguments for increased liberalization or restriction).[22] Many are empirically oriented and lack a general theory of policy development.[23] Of those works that do offer a theoretical model of policy formation, most are either single-case specific and/or conform to a conventional wisdom that determinants of policy outcomes are the product of purely domestic actors, interests, and ideas.

This chapter surveys the existing scholarship of immigration and border policy development and outlines the questions left unanswered. I then offer a statist theory of policy formation applicable to advanced industrial trading states that emphasizes the role of geopolitical structure and central ideas / norms in shaping policy outcomes. The model does not suggest that domestic politics do not matter or cannot influence policy decisions. Rather, it suggests that the structural environment in which these processes take place can influence the nature and timing of such processes. Moreover, it suggests that while structural determinants and ideas manifest at the state level are influential in charting the general course of immigration and border policy, both intervening variables and / or domestic political mobilization can (and often do) result in policy adjustments along this general path.

Existing Explanations of Policy Outcomes

The existing scholarship on policy determinants can be organized within three groups, determined by the primary variables used to explain outcomes. These include studies that focus on domestic economic factors and political economy, those that focus on the role of institutions, and those that are based on ideational and / or cultural variables.

DOMESTIC POLITICAL ECONOMY

Daniel Tichenor notes, "Models of economic causation dominate popular and scholarly accounts of immigration politics and policy in the United States and Western Europe."[24] Classical economic models are based on principles of supply and demand—among migration scholars and labor economists, this is usually characterized as the push-pull model. In terms of labor mobility, this perspective suggests that migration levels respond to labor market forces, and correspondingly, state policy should attempt to match policy with labor needs.[25] A purely domestic-economics policy model suggests that policy openness should be largely a function of a robust and growing economy (stimulating demand for labor) and / or low unemployment (low supply of available labor). Policies of closure are, consequently, a function of economic stagnation and / or high unemployment rates. Although migration pressures are certainly a function of both supply side (migrant-sending state) and demand side (immigrant-receiving state) economic conditions, policy outcomes do not consistently follow the business cycle or employment trends. For example, the push-pull model cannot explain why Britain adopted an open regime for Commonwealth migration in the late 1940s at a time of high domestic unemployment. Nor can it account for restrictionism in the United States in 1917, 1924, 1929 (prior to the stock market crash) when the economy was healthy, or in 1996 at a time when the country's economy was reaching staggering new heights. James Hollifield, Daniel Tichenor, and Gary Zuk found that, in the U.S. case, since 1946 "the effects of unemployment and GNP on immigration flows weaken over time while the impact of government interventions significantly increase."[26] Another study conducted by Ashley Timmer and Jeffrey Williamson reached similar conclusions that macroeconomic circumstances, including levels and trends in real wages, GDP, or unemployment were not sufficient in explaining shifts in immigration policy.[27]

Other variants based on domestic economics focus instead on economic interests and political mobilization of domestic actors to explain policy outcomes. Marxist, class-based models posit that the interests of employers dominate the political process because of a privileged access to the capitalist state.[28] They point out that immigration serves the capitalist elite in several important ways, including (1) utilizing immigrants as labor reserves to keep wages down and confound union action; (2) providing labor for production and capital accumulation; (3) increasing profits (linked with wage control); (4) counteracting structural inflation; and (5) dividing the working class.[29] Others focusing on labor market analysis suggest that employer interests are not in conflict with other societal interests because migrant labor is localized in the secondary labor market and generally complements returns in the primary labor market.[30] Thus, political-economic tensions are ameliorated, again preferencing business interests.

Although such theories purport to explain the generally open migration policies of capitalist states, they have difficulty explaining the volatility of migration policy. If growth in immigration were a structural element of the growth of capitalism, one would expect that this "privileged" political position would result in a continuous liberalization of migration policies. Yet this has not been the case in any of the advanced industrial democracies during the past half-century. Perhaps more importantly—relative to the general argument presented herein—Marxist perspectives do not account for variance in state sensitivity regarding the ethnic or cultural composition of immigrant flows. The available empirical evidence reveals that states are acutely aware of the qualitative nature of flows and carefully shape policy in response to these characteristics. Like many current theories of migration, their myopic preoccupation with migration's economic dimensions leaves out a significant aspect of migration policymaking.

Another approach rooted in domestic political economy is the pluralist or collective action model. From this point of view, politics is seen as competition between competing societal interests, and government policy is viewed as the result of this strategic interaction at the group level.[31] An initial approach involved analyzing the lobbying efforts of employers that utilize foreign labor, focusing on their economic interests and their desire for a flexible labor supply.[32] Subsequent research has refined this approach by incorporating a collective action dynamic.[33] Gary Freeman argues that the interest-group politics of immigration policy is largely a function of the obstacles to political mobilization through collective action. Drawing on Mancur Olson's theory, Freeman suggests that because it is more difficult to organize large groups as opposed to small groups, collective action favors business interests over those of the general public (similar to a Marxist perspective).[34] Moreover, because the benefits of migration are concentrated (benefiting employers) while the costs of migration are diffuse (to the general public), those who reap its benefits have greater incentive to mobilize politically than those who bear its costs.[35] Thus, the interest-group politics associated with migration can be characterized as "clientist," and immigration politics in liberal democracies exhibits an expansionary bias.[36]

Yet another variant of the domestic political economy approach stresses the role of political geography on political processes. Increasing the level of sophistication, Jeannette Money begins by noting that international migration flows are not evenly distributed geographically within states, but are generally concentrated in distinct locales.[37] For example, 70 percent of all immigrants to the United States reside in only seven of the fifty states. Moreover, within regions, migrants generally concentrate in certain cities, and in ethnic enclaves within these cities. Money argues that this spatial concentration affects how the costs and benefits of migration are distributed, which can sharply affect the politics of migration policy on the national level if fluctuations in costs or benefits occur in key "swing" states during elections.

Although such interest-group theories present a compelling explanation for the domestic politics of migration policy, important questions remain left unanswered. First, because of the economic advantages foreign labor offers, one would expect a continual process of liberalization in policies concerning labor mobility. This has clearly not been the case in any advanced industrial state during the past half-century. Policies enacted in the past thirty years have been overtly hostile toward migrants and have stressed a strong political will to "regain control" of the national borders.[38] Moreover, if business interests truly dominated political processes, policy should not necessarily display preferences based on racial or ethno-cultural criteria in the allocation of immigrant visas or temporary work permits. From a strictly economic standpoint, "a worker is a worker," regardless of their skin color or ethnicity. Thus, we would expect preferences based solely on economic need and the skill-set an individual migrant possesses. In practice, however, migration and border policies in most advanced industrial countries have displayed an acute sensitivity to the racial, ethnic, and cultural composition of flows.

Another challenge to pluralist models concerns the interest groups themselves. The framing of "pro-" and "anti-immigration" groups by liberal theorists suggests that clear divisions exist between groups. However, interest groups do not always line up in predictable ways, and the supply of immigration policy does not always match demand, as evidenced by the mixed results of studies seeking to quantitatively gauge the effect of interest-group pressure on immigration legislation in the U.S. Congress.[39] This can be attributed to the fact that business groups have a broad array of interests and may, on occasion, engage in "strange bedfellow" coalitions that forward other dimensions of an overall business strategy.[40] These models also neglect ideational and institutional factors that can shape the goals of various interest groups. James Hollifield suggests that "policy outputs are heavily contingent on ideational, cultural, and institutional factors, which often distort the market interests of different groups, to such an extent that some groups (like organized labor, for example) may end up pursuing policies that would seem to be irrational, or somehow at odds with their economic interests."[41] How such lobbying plays out among legislators may also strongly affect the interplay of interests, for legislators are responsible for a much larger array of issues and have limited resources, which may at times divert their focus from immigration-related lobbies.

THE ROLE OF INSTITUTIONS

There are three primary variants to extant institutional analyses of immigration and border policy development: (1) those that focus on the structure of government; (2) those that focus on the role of bureaucracies associated with immigration control; and (3) those that focus on institutionalized ideas and legal principles.

One type of institutional variable that can affect the policymaking process involves governmental structures. Analyses based on this type of institutionalism argue that organizational biases of governmental structure can serve to advantage the political participation and influence of certain domestic actors and interest groups while constraining others.[42] In terms of explaining immigration policy, state strength (defined in terms of relative insularity from constituency pressures) can affect policy outcomes by either insulating decision-making processes from societal pressures and interest-group lobbying ("strong state") or by increasing the likelihood that such groups will have success in "capturing" the state ("weak state"). There is a clear link here between this type of institutionalism and the interest-group politics models already discussed. In the U.S. case, this framework has been used to suggest that, because immigration policy is in the jurisdiction of the U.S. Congress, policy outcomes are more likely to reflect interest-group dynamics resulting from congressional dominance of this issue area.[43] However, this insight in and of itself does little to unpack the dynamics that shape the domestic forces that pressure for particular types of policy responses in the congress. Moreover, this perspective must face the same questions posed to pluralist collective action models. Daniel Tichenor forwards a more stylized and elegant model stressing governmental structure.[44] In explaining why U.S. immigration policy has not conformed to the vacillations of the economy, public opinion, and political realignments, Tichenor points to four primary explanatory variables: (1) the fragmentation of power in the American governmental system that continually presents groups with changing structural opportunities and constraints; (2) continually shifting political coalitions; (3) the emergence of professional expertise in the shaping of immigration policy; and (4) international pressures. Although this approach provides a more nuanced model of government institutionalism and includes variables that extend beyond the actions of domestic interest groups, Tichenor's analysis is limited in its focus on explaining legal entry rules and quotas. Migration flows involve multiple channels, and policy explanations should also account for border policy regimes if they are to be considered comprehensive. Moreover, as with many other extant models, the analysis is single-case specific and does not argue for its application beyond the sphere of U.S. immigration policy.

Another institutionalist strategy is to focus on the role of bureaucratic agencies involved in managing migration flows. This approach suggests that individual agencies maintain their own political agenda and that these agency-centered interests can have a substantial impact on migration control strategies and policies. Moreover, the political and policy decisions of today can shape both ideas and policy in the future as they become institutionalized in the political consciousness. In her analysis of the U.S. Immigration and Naturalization Service during the Bracero period, Kitty Calavita traces the relationship between the missions of various agencies involved with migration issues and identifies a conflict of interest between the missions of the U.S. Immigration and Naturalization Service (INS) and the U.S. Department of Labor.[45] Clearly the mission of the INS preferences control and closure, and it has been successful during the 1980s and 1990s in shaping migration and border statistics to effectively lobby for increased funding to expand its control capacity.[46] It can be argued that this bureaucratic framing of immigration as beset by a "neglected" border significantly contributed to the U.S. sense of crisis during the 1980s and 1990s.[47] The strength of such an approach lies in its ability to reflect intervening variables either in the policymaking process (bureaucracies as a source of information and a generator of public discourse), or in affecting the outcome of policies (variability in the application of state policy). They do not offer a comprehensive account of immigration and border policy development.

A more expansive approach to the institutionalist perspective is what has been dubbed "rights-based liberalism."[48] Here the connection between ideas regarding human rights and political institutions is the focus of analysis. Although there are several variants of this point of view, all generally argue that ideas concerning human rights have significantly altered the relationship between the state and those that inhabit its territory.[49] On the basis of international human rights law, states are becoming accountable to all their *residents*, not just their *citizens*; thus, establishing legal protections that apply equally to both groups blurs the distinction between citizen and alien. Moreover these rights are not manifest solely at the international level, but have been subsumed within domestic law and continue to do so at a vigorous pace in many industrialized democracies. Evolving notions of human rights as applied to migration (for example, family reunification, asylum, protection against deportation, and so on) and enforced by the judiciary, constrain states from responding as vigorously as public opinion would prefer. This "rights-based" approach has been critiqued on several grounds. Whereas some proponents have suggested that these processes have instigated a transformation of state sovereignty, Christian Joppke has suggested that rights extended to noncitizens are simply examples of "self-limited sovereignty" enacted because it forwards state interests.[50] Moreover, with regard to the application of rights for noncitizens, states maintain a strong degree of sovereignty in interpreting how such rights may or may not be applied.[51]

NATIONAL IDENTITY

Another school of thought concerning the determinants of immigration policy focuses on the role of identity. The work of Rogers Brubaker is probably among the most noted of scholarship that can be collectively classified as the national identity approach.[52] The key independent variable in explaining policy outcomes is the nature of a country's national identity, or what Brubaker calls "idioms of nationhood." Utilizing a comparative case-study analysis that contrasts France and Germany, Brubaker suggests that the citizenship regime employed by each is largely determined by national identity—specifically, whether the country is based on a civic or an ethnic national principle. For these two cases the evidence seems quite compelling in explaining why France's civic republicanism favors citizenship based largely on the principle of *jus soli*, while German romanticism concerning the ethnic foundations of the German *Volk* produce a citizenship regime based on kinship, or *jus sanguinis*.[53]

Another variant of the national identity approach focuses on the role of racism in policy development. These approaches often differ in determining the source of racism as it pertains to the policymaking processes. Some emphasize societal racism and reflect policy as a governmental response to social pressures favoring racial preferences.[54] Others suggest that racist policies are the product of elites, and that the political discourse generated by elites and policies that follow from it drive (or contribute to) racial attitudes reflected among the general public.[55]

Although compelling, the limitations of this national identity approach soon become evident. First, the model attempts a rather limited explanation of policy outcomes: it seeks only to explain rules concerning citizenship. This is certainly an important component of state management of international migration, but it is not the only component. The national identity approach says little about other elements of policy such as visa issuance, labor recruitment, refugee and asylum, illegal immigration, or border enforcement. It is also unclear how useful the model is for other cases, especially those that cannot easily be categorized as distinctly "civic" or "ethnic" nations, or for those that display multiple traditions of nationhood.[56] Lastly, there is ambiguity in terms of the resilience of identity as an independent variable. On the one hand, Brubaker shows how ideas regarding national identity are formed within the context of a particular structural environment. For example, he points to the "irony of German ethno-nationalism," one based on a mythic primordialism but in truth the product of Bismarck's realpolitik in the late nineteenth century.[57] This would seem to counter the primordialist notion of static identities. Yet, it is this very notion of static identity that informs the remainder of Brubaker's argument: national identity produces a consistent effect on policy precisely because it remains fixed. National identity and the nationalism (and/or racism) it can produce can have a profound effect on politics—especially those related to the issue of international migration. However, models that incorporate this important variable must account for both complexities (and contradictions) in its construction as well as the fact that these identities are continually shaped and reshaped. The process of imagining communities is perpetual.[58]

TOWARD AN ALTERNATIVE FRAMEWORK

Although the existing scholarship is useful in explaining elements of migration policymaking, significant questions remain unanswered and a truly comprehensive theory applicable to more than one state remains elusive. It is curious that a phenomenon so intrinsically global in its dynamics and scope has so often been considered solely within the confines of a domestic level of analysis. This may partially explain why, until quite recently, scholars have not turned to international relations theory to explain the policy choices of states.[59] However, international relations theory can be useful in that it allows for the consideration of variables outside the domestic realm and provides a framework within which the dynamics of the state can be included in the policymaking process. Because of the lack of extant theorizing, such a model must be constructed from the ground up, beginning with international relations theory's core question: What is the primary function of the state? Understanding migration's place in state grand strategy reveals a great deal about policy development, but this requires a more comprehensive and nuanced framework of the underlying interests states face at the national level.

Defining National Security

Realism is the most venerable school of thought in international relations theory and often forms the baseline of theory formation.[60] For realists, the basis of state action in international politics is the concept of "interest defined in terms of power."[61] In an anarchic international system, the fundamental interest of the state is to survive—in other words, to remain sovereign. This is the common understanding of the term "national security," though more simplistic than the one used in this book. From the realist perspective, interest is defined as power because the ability to realize interests is primarily a function of power. What this baseline perspective *does not* elucidate, however, is by what means power is best maximized in order to support state interests. It also does not delineate the referent object of national security—*what exactly is being secured?* Although the connection between these points and migration policy may not be obvious at this point, they are central to the theoretical framework built herein.

National security was primarily defined in terms of military defense in scholarship produced during the cold war.[62] The dominant theories produced during this period not only emphasized military defense as the object of security but also focused on structural variables to explain state behavior—in other words, on the relative distribution of power in the international system.[63] From this one might assume a security-enabling function for migration. For centuries, population size was directly equated with military power. It stands to reason that *immigration* would be viewed positively and that only security-threatening aspect of migration would be *emigration*, as this would negatively impact population size. However, with the development of more sophisticated means of warfare, a large population is no longer the cornerstone of state power.

International political economists challenged the orthodox view of security-as-military defense by emphasizing the necessary conditions to defense buildup—state wealth.[64] Given focus on comparisons of military power that dominated what some refer to as the "golden age of security studies," this emergent emphasis on the relationship among state wealth, economic productivity, and national security may have appeared novel.[65] Although cold war security scholarship may have neglected it, Robert Gilpin points out that, "In all historical epochs, realist thinkers have focused on the economic dimensions of statecraft."[66] From as far back as Thucydides' account of the Peloponnesian War to the work of Jacob Viner, E. H. Carr, and Hans Morgenthau, it was understood that "wealth is an absolutely essential means to power, whether for security or for aggression."[67] As such, Robert Keohane has pointed out, "In the real world of international relations, most significant issues are simultaneously political and economic."[68] Trading-state policies among the Western bloc during the cold war not only suggests that the accumulation of wealth was seen as a necessary condition to secure military defense but also reveals a dominant state grand strategy for realizing that objective.

From the standpoint of national security defined in terms of military defense, this suggests that explanations of state behavior must account for security interests along two dimensions rather than one. However, even this expanded definition of national security is insufficient to explain state interests, for it focuses only on the security relationship between states and others in the international system. We must also consider, however, the security interests within states. Kenneth Waltz asks us to consider, "Which is more precarious: the life of a state among states, or of a government in relation to its subjects?"[69] The question is an important one because it asks us to reconsider our assumptions about the referent object of security (that is, what exactly is being secured). The issue of the relationship between a government and its subjects is founded on notions of national identity because this provides the vehicle for social unity within a polity that legitimizes state actions based on forwarding this collective interest. In other words, "We have to know who we are before we can know what our interests are."[70]

Realist explanations of state behavior provide no space for the consideration of identity issues relevant to security. The emergence of a constructivist perspective, however, has proven more amenable to the consideration of ideational variables, including culture and identity.[71] Admittedly, both are elusive subjects for empirical study, yet the impact of these issues on relations within and among states has become increasingly evident to pundit and layman alike. In their most virulent manifestation, culture and identity lie at the core of the rise of ethno-nationalist violence and wartime atrocities in places like the Balkans, Chechnya, the Middle East, and many African states.[72] Even in multicultural states, issues of culture and identity have proven to be extremely volatile and divisive. With constructivism's challenge to the realist and neoliberal assumptions regarding the primacy of material rationalism, the door has been opened for the (re)introduction of culture and identity as important variables in the study of world politics.[73] Yale Ferguson and Richard Mansbach have gone so far as to suggest that the emerging salience of identity warrant a complete revision of traditional ways of thinking about international society.[74] They write, "In our view, we should conceive of global politics as involving a world of 'polities' rather than states and focus on the relationships among authority, identities, and ideology."[75] How identity and culture figure prominently in the contemporary rise in ethno-nationalist conflicts—especially among small or developing nations—has been recently addressed by those scholars studying the causes and consequences of such identity-related violence.[76] How these issues figure into the security interests of advanced industrial states, as well as among these states and between developed and developing states, has received much less attention from scholars.

Considerable attention has been given to a hypothesized global struggle between the cultures of the West versus "the rest," yet the salience of identity in world politics is not necessarily limited to some grand clash between civilizations.[77] Rather, societal tensions are most commonly manifest *within* nations and are often created or exacerbated by transborder flows.[78] While concerns have been levied from certain regions (especially from China and from Muslim countries with more fundamentalist regimes in power) regarding the transmission of culture through trade and capital movements, the most volatile threat to notions of stable identity comes with the large-scale movement of people and the demographic change this can create. Such sentiments may be most acutely felt in countries where national identity is based on perceived familial or blood ties, but they are by no means limited to them.[79]

Under what conditions can demographic change be considered a security threat? Myron Weiner and Michael Teitelbaum note that if one segment of a given population—defined in terms of a socially defined category such as race, ethnicity, or religious affiliation—grows more rapidly than another, such changes may shift domestic political power balances.[80] They may also fundamentally challenge a polity's conception of national identity and long-held beliefs regarding the traditional bases of sociopolitical community.[81] Weiner and Teitelbaum add that these factors can "become problematic in political or security terms when they are unusually rapid or are driven by forces seen as unlawful or illegitimate"—in other words, when such processes are seen to violate a polity's sense of communal or "societal sovereignty."[82] Mass migration represents the most viable means of engaging processes that initiate rapid demographic and social change that can subsequently create perceptions of threat and bring identity issues to the forefront of the political agenda in receiving states. In a "worst-case" scenario, these tensions may escalate into violent civil war. Another possibility is that political pressure by diaspora communities may affect the receiving country's foreign policies and entangle it in armed conflict abroad.[83]

Combining these security perspectives provides us with a framework of "national security" with three dimensions rather than one. In addition to military defense, national security interests are also related to economic productivity (that is, wealth) and to domestic stability. The difficult question, from an analytical position, is, what promotes domestic stability? Certainly, domestic stability is at least in part a function of a well-functioning economy and as such is interrelated with that dimension of security as is military defense. But it is also about the means of determining common interests. This element is at least in part a function of national identity and culture.

Admittedly, operationalizing this variable is a bit "wooly," but its importance makes its inclusion in any explanation of state behavior nonnegotiable.

Ole Wæver offered the concept of "societal security" to capture the social-internal dimension of security. He defines societal security in terms of "the sustainability, within acceptable conditions for evolution, of traditional patterns of language, culture, association, and religious and national identity and custom."[84] Whereas change is integral to economic rationalization (increasing productivity, expanding markets, and so on), national identity is often based on a myth of primordial origins that prove enduring over time. Change is thus inherently threatening. Precisely defining "societal security" is inherently problematic, for, as the extensive literature on nationalism makes clear, social identities are often highly complex, continually evolving, and politically contested.[85] Societal security is frequently presented in solely ethno-cultural terms and is measured by public reactions to demographic changes that significantly alter a polity as an "ethnic community."[86] However, few of the world's states are ethnically homogeneous and most of today's advanced industrial states are based at least in part on including liberal ideology as a prominent component of the national identity. A more accurate use of "societal security" must acknowledge and account for the political effects such "multiple traditions" have on political discourse and policy outcomes. By introducing large numbers of people of diverse ethno-cultural and ideological backgrounds to a host-society, the globalization of migration represents a potentially significant threat to notions of stable national identities, culture, and ways of life—regardless of whether ethno-cultural or ideological criteria are emphasized.

Societal security is both a useful and necessary concept in order to understand the ideational interests that can strongly influence state grand strategy, especially when geopolitical threats are low. However, operationalizing such variables presents considerable obstacles to social-scientific analysis. I draw on four primary sources to operationalize threat perception in the area of societal security, including public opinion polls, public and policymaker discourse analysis, symbolic voting practices (for example, voter initiatives, support for Right-wing parties, and so forth), and deconstruction of the policies themselves. Immigration and border policy is much more nuanced than terms such as "open" or "closed" can capture. Although both increased border surveillance and reduction of immigrant visas can be classified as "restrictive," paying attention to where such limitation is placed can tell us important information regarding ulterior motives, as is often the case with issues of race and culture in so-called multicultural democracies. Admittedly, some of the indices used here to determine societal insecurities have weaknesses. Although numerous public opinion polls have been taken in all the case nations surveyed here, systematic and consistently worded polls across the time period examined here simply do not exist. Moreover, racialized discourse is often reflected publicly only by the extremist minority, although such ideas may strike a chord among the mainstream who are either unwilling to be publicly associated with such groups or who are experiencing cognitive dissonance with these notions and their more liberal sense of social identity. Lastly, while Right-wing political parties may present largely single-issue platforms (such as anti-immigration) mainstream voters may not mobilize on single issues. As such, using voting patterns for such parties as a proxy for societal insecurities may present a more limited indicator of public sentiments than are actually present in a given polity. However, even though no single proxy for measuring "societal insecurity" exists, careful analysis of these variables *in aggregate* provides the most tangible means of understanding the political processes involved where societal security interests are at stake.[87]

The ideational basis of societal security lies in stark contrast to the material rationalism on which the geopolitical and economic dimensions of security are based; yet all three are highly interdependent. Military security provides stability necessary for economic development and longevity for the national polity. Material security (that is, economic production) is necessary for military production and defense and contributes to social harmony. Nationalism provides the unity and cooperation necessary to mobilize against enemies and provides a sense of common ground that facilitates a well-functioning domestic economy. Moreover, not only are security's three dimensions interdependent in many ways, but also migration potentially affects all three. Consequently, we can see that it rests at the nexus of security's three dimensions (Figure 2.1). Because of this, it is reasonable to expect policies to be responsive to changes in the security environment. The challenge is to establish a model that can account for policy outcomes in response to such variation in security environment.

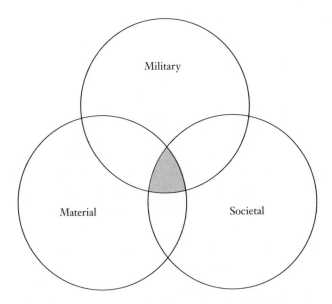

Figure 2.1.   Migration: At the Nexus of Three Dimensions of Security

Power, Interests, and Ideas: Explaining Policy Using International Relations Theory

Having posited the core interests of the state, we must then ask what prompts states to respond to their national security interests, broadly defined. Stephen Walt suggests that state behavior concerning national security is driven largely by the perception of threat(s) rather than simply on changing constellations of power in the system, and he used this observation to explain patterns of alliance formation.[88] If a geopolitical threat is the general condition that generates a response among states, we can assume that it may affect more aspects of state grand strategy than just alliance formation, including those related to migration and border control. In the present study, the structural threat environment is the primary independent variable. The dependent variable being explained is "migration policy," defined here to include all facets of state control over migration, including citizenship and naturalization, refugee and asylum, visa policy, policy regarding illegal immigration, and border management. In general, these elements vary in terms of relative openness. We can consider the basic causal pathways as follows: Geopolitical threat → State response = Policy output. Given this initial framework, we can then begin to form hypotheses regarding specific policy outcomes.

Given the three-dimensional security framework, it is reasonable to assume that different elements of security can be threatened differently. I hypothesize that, in times of high geopolitical threat, grand strategy will be dominated by policies to support defense and the economic production necessary to support defense interests. When such external threats ebb (geopolitical recessive), then security interests are likely to place a higher *relative* emphasis on internal, societal aspects of security. That states primarily respond to their security interests and that the level of response is a function of state power are both consistent with the realist perspective of international politics. However, although this notion of "modes of threat" provides a rationale for predicting shifts in overall grand strategy, it is not particularly helpful in predicting specific types of policy outcomes. What determines *how* a state responds? To address this question, I incorporate a constructivist perspective that emphasizes of the role of ideas in shaping outcomes to supplement the realist focus on power and interest. Figure 2.2 indicates that ideas serve as an intervening variable that shapes particular policy outcomes given a strategic threat environment.

Threat Hypothesis

In the post–WWII Bretton Woods era, the resurgence of classical economic ideas and principles strongly shaped policy discourse and preferred responses among trading states.[89] Figure 2.2 provides a graphic representation of how ideas shape policy outcomes in a given structural threat environment. High geopolitical threat produces security interests favoring defense and material production, and these interests are shaped by the dominance of neoclassical economic ideas. This, in turn, produces a shift in grand strategy that creates a higher probability of migration policies favoring openness, as well as conforming policy to the state's foreign-policy interests. Neoclassical economic ideas are thus a significant intervening variable. In times when

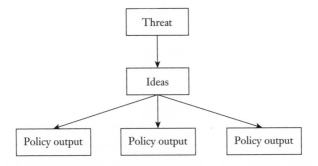

Figure 2.2.   Security Paradigm: Threat Hypothesis

economic productivity is an imperative for national security, these ideas would direct policy responses to those that favored increasing openness to international flows. This leads to the first hypothesis offered in this book: as geopolitical threats increase, policies regarding international labor mobility (migration) should become relatively more open in order to facilitate the production of wealth to support defense. Moreover, in this environment migration policies should also favor foreign-policy interests wherever possible. I refer to both aspects as the "Threat Hypothesis," in that outcomes are primarily a function of the geopolitical threat environment and ideas that shape the preferred state response to such threat.[90]

WARTIME NATIONALISM AND THE RALLY-EFFECT

A second key ideational intervening variable concerns ideas of nationalism / patriotism common during wartime. The nationalism literature reveals that external threats support group cohesion by creating an environment of common interests. This sense of common interest often begets a sense of common identity. Nowhere is this more apparent than in the nationalism associated with the decolonization movement, for example Suharto's ability to craft notions of Indonesian nationhood within the context of Dutch and Japanese occupation. In liberal democratic and/or multiethnic countries, this nationalist rally-effect in times of external threat should reduce perceptions of societal differences among members of the polity and reduce xenophobia that may press states to employ policies of closure regarding migration. From this, we can hypothesize that a high degree of external threat should result in more open migration policies and a declining emphasis on ethno-cultural entry criteria (referred to in the text as the Rally Hypothesis). One obvious exception to this rule would be if migrant flows or new immigrants are directly associated with a current military adversary. Clearly, World War II did not increase social inclusiveness for Japanese-Americans, many who were forced into internment camps.

Both the Threat Hypothesis and the Rally Hypothesis predict more open policy in structural environments of acute geopolitical threat, though these occur for different reasons. The Rally Hypothesis does not suggest that the rally-effect will generate positive social pressures for more open policy. Rather, nativist xenophobia should have less emphasis and will result in fewer calls for closure. This means that there is lower probability of nativist obstruction to neoclassical policies favoring openness predicted by the Threat Hypothesis. In terms of the policy development paradigm, the presence of a societal rally-effect (or its opposite, nationalist xenophobia) serves as a second intervening variable with ideational characteristics (Figure 2.3). In terms of which will have more effect on policy outcomes at a given point in time, the Threat and Rally Hypotheses suggest that neoclassical economic ideas will dominate under high external threats and that the nationalist ideas will gain in salience when external threats decline.

FEEDBACK LOOPS

There are additional causal mechanisms that must be taken into consideration if the model being constructed here is to accurately portray state responses to structural conditions in the context of both external and internal security interests. These involve feedback loops.[91] The framework for political systems developed by David Easton provides insight into the role feedback loops play on political processes.[92] Feedback loops involve the effects of policy outputs that are then factored into the political system at various points and can affect primary independent variables as well as intervening variables. In terms of the security paradigm constructed here, feedback loops can operate in several ways.

First, policy outcomes will have an effect on environment—in this case, on the level and composition of international migration flows. Elements of migration patterns can exacerbate perceptions of threat, particularly in times

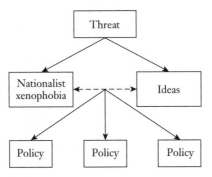

Figure 2.3.   Security Paradigm: Rally Hypothesis

of lower geopolitical insecurity, contributing to societal insecurities and domestic discord. Often this is the result of unanticipated consequences of policy choices and frequently comes in the form of xenophobic rhetoric or worse—anti-immigrant violence and/or ethnic unrest, as was seen in France in the autumn of 2005. Elements of international migration that affect societal insecurities include the perceived social proximity of migrants by receiving societies, their geographic concentration (both in terms of channel of entry and/or settlement patterns), intensity of flow (concentration in time), and attitudes about integration and/or assimilation. Each of these elements serves to increase the visibility of international migration flows and can, at times, magnify perceptions of the magnitude of flows among the general public. Moreover, if policies implemented in response to demand for border control are not deemed effective, they may confirm general fears that current levels of migration are but a trifle compared to what is yet to come. This in turn creates even more demand for policies that can establish an even higher expectation of control than previously expressed. We might refer to this as a "cycle of threat," and it can be represented by multiple iterations of feedback loops (represented in Figure 2.4 by the feedback loop connecting policy outcomes with threat environment). As these elements may increase when geopolitical threats are declining, they may have a profound effect on what is considered threatened and what response is required by the state.

Another feedback loop involves political learning (represented in Figure 2.4 by the loop connecting outcomes with ideas). Rigorous immigration

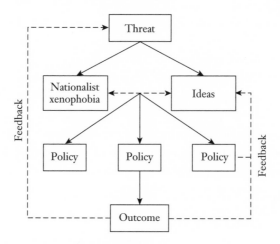

Figure 2.4. Integrated Security Paradigm

and border control as a state imperative is a relatively new phenomenon in governance if placed in historical perspective: "The successful monopolization of the legitimate means of movement by states had to await the creation of elaborate bureaucracies and technologies that only gradually came into existence, a trend that intensified dramatically toward the end of the nineteenth century."[93] Many types of new policy innovations resulted in unanticipated consequences, which then later affected policy debates and subsequent policy preferences among states. For example, the German and American experience with temporary-labor recruitment programs revealed that, in the words of Philip Martin, "nothing is more permanent than temporary workers."[94] Another example involves the U.S. extension of amnesty for undocumented workers offered through the 1986 Immigration Reform and Control Act. Rather than facilitating the creation of a "clean slate" from which undocumented migration could be better controlled, amnesty created nearly three million new immigrants that could potentially (and arguably did) contribute to increases in future migration flows, both documented and undocumented. Clearly, the 1986 legislation did little to stem the flow of unwanted illegal immigration, and amnesty has proven to be a politically untenable policy option for U.S. policymakers ever since.[95]

Policy outcomes themselves can also forge another type of feedback loop, especially when these create new institutions and/or bureaucratic structures to process such policies. Institutionalists have asserted that once policy preferences become institutionalized, they establish a form of path dependence that constrains future policy options. The Liberal State Hypothesis is one example of how this is manifest through increased legalization. In liberal democracies, if new migration policies establish new rights for migrants, these become institutionally protected through the judiciary, limiting state policy options.[96] One example is the principle of *non-refoulement*, codified in Article 33 of the Convention Relating to the Status of Refugees (1951), which prohibits the repatriation of refugees or asylum seekers if "his life or freedom would be threatened on account of his race, religion, nationality, membership of a particular social group or political opinion."[97] "Liberal State" institutionalism is better utilized as an intervening variable or feedback loop in a more comprehensive model of policy formation, than as a self-contained explanation of policy outputs.

A second type of institutional feedback loop stemming from policy outputs involves the creation of new bureaucracies or political structures. In Europe, one manifestation of this type of feedback involves the continuing process of regional integration and concomitant supranationalization of governmental structures. Similar to Liberal State theorists, neofunctionalists would argue that integration regimes and the institutions created by them establish not only new political actors but also spill-over effects.[98] Applied to migration policies in Europe, this logic would suggest that because the European Union's supranational institutions were created to promote integration and facilitate trade and factor mobility among its membership, they would serve as active proponents of continued policy liberalization among member states.[99] In the United States, the restructuring of the federal government and the relocation of immigration control from the Justice Department to the new Department of Homeland Security may have similar feedback effects on future policy discourse and policy outputs.

Taken together, these provide a comprehensive explanation of policy development with an emphasis on structural determinants and an active role for the state. The geopolitical structure provides the initial impetus for a state response, which then varies along two dimensions: (1) whether external threats are dominant; and (2) ideas concerning what the best policy response would be. At any point in time, an equilibrium exists among the three constellations of national security—defense, economic, and societal. The aggregate mix of policies used to reflect this constellation of interests defines grand strategy. Subsequent changes in state grand strategy, defined in this context of aggregate policies, are then the product of (1) the changing structural threat environment, (2) dominant ideas and the effect of feedback loops on them, and (3) institutional constraints of prior policies.

Methodology

To test these hypotheses, I examine the formation of migration and border policies in four advanced industrial states in the context of the structural threat environment from 1945 to 2001 using a comparative case-study method.[100] Although quantitative, rational-choice methodologies have gained academic currency during the past twenty years, an interpretive historiography structured by comparative case studies would seem to be a more suitable method for understanding political processes that are not easily or reliably measurable quantitatively, are characterized by high degrees of "hypocrisy" (and /or "doublespeak"), and where both statements and policy may have discreet rather than overt objectives. Qualitative, contextualized analysis allows for evaluation of both policy discourse and observable behavior. It is important to analyze the relationship between discourse and policy goals in the context of resultant policies and outcomes in cases where objectives may run contrary to the liberal norms of a given society. For example, consider the complexities of the relationship between race and the myth of the "land of immigrants" in the United States. The eugenics movement of the early twentieth century is certainly inconsistent with America's self-conception as a haven to immigrants, yet the two coexisted in time and space. The relationship between culture /ethnicity and national ethos may be even more complex today. Although extremists on both the Left and the Right take bold, overt positions, understanding the position of mainstream America requires qualitative sensitivity to the nuances of migration discourse, as well as a qualitative analysis of the relationship between political discourse and policy actions.

Because the hypothesized model is based on the economic and political interests of advanced industrial "trading states" and the political implications of immigration flows, all fit this classification, including the United States,

Germany, France, and Great Britain. Although developing states also have strong interests at stake in processes of global migration—particularly the use of emigration as an unemployment "safety valve" and the use of migrant remittances as sources of much needed foreign exchange—the security agenda of these states is sufficiently different to require separate in-depth analysis. The four cases examined here represent excellent "critical cases" for theory development not only because of common economic and geopolitical interests, but also because "societal security" is socially contested and is based on competing visions of national identity. Heterogeneous, liberal, multicultural societies represent the most difficult tests of models incorporating societal security as an explanatory variable.

To operationalize changes in the geopolitical security environment (the primary dependent variable), I draw on the existing security scholarship. In addition to differences in relative power, geopolitical threat is determined by factors such as geographic proximity, bellicosity, and the stability of security relationships (both adversarial and among alliance members).[101] This latter factor relates to issues of predictability, trust, and norms of behavior—what we might refer to as a "routinization" of the security relationship.[102] During periods of transition or where routinization remains underdeveloped, higher levels of threat are expected due to this instability. In terms of power differentials between the Soviet and Western blocs, the rebuilding of Europe and the creation and expansion of NATO collective security under the nuclear umbrella are important factors to characterizing the cold war era as one displaying a declining degree of relative threat over time. Moreover, routinization of the bipolar relationship improves understanding of why security competition between the superpowers was more intense during the early years of the conflict.[103] In this book, external threat is organized into four periods: (1) early cold war (1945–mid-1960s); (2) transition to détente; (3) post–cold war period (1990–2001); (4) post–September 11, 2001.

What patterns should be present if the hypotheses proposed here are valid? In general, high degrees of geopolitical threat stemming from early cold war instability, belligerence, and mistrust should skew grand strategy toward the military and material poles and generally result in more open and foreign-policy oriented policies; this preference for openness stems from the combination of a desire for higher aggregate economic returns, the dominance of Ricardian strategies to achieve such ends, and the societal rally-effect. As such threats decline with the emergence of détente and later the end of the cold war, societal dimensions of security should become increasingly more salient and policies should move toward increasing degrees of closure.

Conclusion

How can we measure the strength of a given theoretical model? Andrew Moravscik offers four bases on which to judge the power of a theory: (1) it should be general and parsimonious; (2) it should be rigorous and coherent; (3) it should demonstrate empirical accuracy vis-à-vis other theories; and (4) it should demonstrate multicausal consistency.[104] The model of state behavior presented here is intended to forward existing theoretical explanations along all four dimensions. First, the model provides an explanation of policy outcomes that moves beyond singular, isolated cases, as is common in the existing literature on immigration policy. It provides insight into the general core interests of the state and the way that migration control fits within this framework. The emphasis on structural variables as primary causal factors of policy outputs provides both advantages and disadvantages. On the one hand, it offers a highly parsimonious model of state behavior that captures the fundamental political processes that direct outcomes. Kenneth Waltz notes, "Within a system, a theory explains continuities. It explains recurrences and repetitions, not change."[105] The national security centered theory presented herein provides just such an explanation of outcomes within the system of advanced industrial trading states. Some may argue that the level of abstraction employed by structural theories "black-boxes" the state. In other words, it obfuscates the myriad processes internal to state politics that can produce outcomes and affect structural form. Granted, the level of descriptive detail offered by structural theories may leave some unsatisfied. However, the parsimony gained from the high-order of abstraction enables structural theories to avoid the pitfalls of "reductionist" theorizing: the proliferation of a seemingly unlimited number of "causal" variables that ultimately result in endless debate, none of which can be considered conclusive.[106]

Instead of focusing on adding precision in the articulation of the scope of variables that may influence policy outcomes, emphasis is placed on increasing precision in explaining the relationship between primary causal variables at the structural level and how these may be subsequently altered by feedback loops. Within this framework, more precise definitions of structural variables are offered. The emphasis on threat perception as a structural variable adds to our conceptualization of geopolitical variables that affect state behavior.[107] However, the theory presented herein provides a more complex, nuanced understanding of both power-based and idea-based structural variables. In addition to geopolitical threat, other structural variables—both primary and intervening—play significant roles in policy development. "Societal threat" can be considered a structural variant, based in part on structural patterns of international migration flows and shared ideas about identity and sovereignty. Moreover, the model includes a prominent role for dominant ideas as a significant intervening variable that shapes the *character* (rather than the timing) of state response to a given threat environment. Specifically, the dominance of Ricardian economic principles may be considered "structural" in that it represents a structure of socialized ideas. The articulation and application of both realist and constructivist notions of structure is novel and significant, in that it allows us a means of including power- and idea-based structural variables concurrently and also reveals how the two interact in a given milieu.

Lastly, the strength of the theoretical model presented herein lies in its ability to demonstrate empirical accuracy with regards to state behavior as well as its ability to synthesize and subsume much of the extant theorizing. It does not refute long-standing and widely accepted views of causal relationships, but it is able to encompass them within a larger, though more parsimonious, analytical structure.

Contrary to those who have pointed to global migration patterns and the policy responses of receiving states as evidence of rampant globalization and the declining power of the state to manage flows, there is a political logic at play that underlies state responses to migration and reveals an active state pursuing interests.[108] As argued within the framework of the theory offered here, making sense of this logic requires an understanding of security's three dimensions, the interaction effects among these variables, and the role of central ideas in shaping the type of state response. Moreover, it is important to recognize that among the various facets of security, international migration can be both security *enabling* and security threatening. On the one hand, it can provide the necessary stimuli for economic productivity and can serve an important symbolic function for foreign relations. On the other hand, uncontrolled international migration can provide a direct threat to homeland defense (via the proliferation of global terrorism) and national identity—both civic and ethnic in orientation.

CHAPTER THREE

National Security and Immigration in the United States

We are a nation of immigrants. But we are also a nation of laws. It is wrong and ultimately self-defeating for a nation of immigrants to permit the kind of abuse of our immigration laws we have seen in recent years, and we must do more to stop it.

— BILL CLINTON, Immigration Enforcement Improvements Act of 1995, May 3, 1995

The clash of opinion arises not over the number of immigrants to be admitted, but over the test of admission.

— JOHN F. KENNEDY, *A Nation of Immigrants*

The United States has long espoused the notion that it is a "nation of immigrants," a "melting pot" of courageous individuals from diverse origins who have come together to build a society built on freedom and equality. In addition to Australia, Canada, and New Zealand, its social and political development has been strongly influenced by its status as one of the world's few truly "settler states." From 1820 to 1930, the United States attracted 61 percent of the world's immigrants, more than all other nations of the world combined, and this migration significantly contributed to the economic development of the nation. The national motto, "E Pluribus Unum," expresses a belief in unity through diversity, the sanctity of the individual, and the rejection of special orders in society. Consistent with this liberal take on U.S. state attitudes toward migration, a 1994 report by the Urban Institute argued that U.S. immigration policy is governed by five broad goals, including family reunification, increasing U.S. productivity and standard of living, promoting human rights, stemming illegal immigration, and promoting

41

diversity.[1] This economic and liberal ideology-oriented perspective, however, tells only one half of the story. Desmond King notes that, "Americans' toleration of diversity has always been easier in principle than in practice."[2]

The rising volume of Asian immigration in the late nineteenth century, while crucial to the construction of the Transcontinental Railroad and economic expansion in the West, represented the first dramatic departure from traditional migration streams and created perceptions of threat to American societal security. This perception gave rise to the eugenics movement at the turn of the century, one predicated on defining the national identity strictly in terms of race. This change in the ethnic composition of migration flows initiated a perception of threat and served as the impetus for the first large-scale, comprehensive restrictionist policy enacted in the United States—the Immigration and Nationality Act of 1924. After the passage of the Immigration and Nationality Act of 1924, national origins quotas and a racialized preference system remained the cornerstone of U.S. immigration policy until 1965. Moreover, even after the 1965 amendments to the Immigration and Nationality Act, U.S. migration policy has been shaped by acute sensitivities to domestic ethnic demographic changes as well as qualitative changes in migration flows. These political sensitivities are manifest in racial discrimination that underlies the application process for refugees and those seeking asylum as well as the introduction of "diversity" quotas for "underrepresented" (largely European) immigrant flows. Howard Chang notes, "Nativism . . . is not merely a shameful feature of our past, reflected in a history that includes the Chinese Exclusion Act and the national origins quota system. Nativism afflicts our politics *today*."[3] The societal dimension of U.S. grand strategy is characterized by two divergent, often concurrent, trends that raise one central question: Is the United States a "nation of immigrants," or is it in danger of becoming an "alien nation"?[4]

Rogers Smith has suggested that American national identity is the product of multiple traditions, characterized by both liberal ideology as well as racial exclusion.[5] While these two dimensions are fundamentally incompatible with one another, they coexisted in American political and social life for generations. It was assumed by the founding fathers that the American community of citizens would be primarily constituted by persons of European ancestry (western and northern), and thus did not extend citizenship to blacks or naturalization rights for those who were not "free white persons."[6]

Thus, typifying the United States as a "settler state"—a commonly used classification that may give too much weight to the nation's liberal dimension of community—cannot accurately portray the complexities of American national identity or the politics associated with it.

The Early Cold War Period

Although the United States and the Soviet Union were allies in the war against the Axis powers during World War II, stemming Soviet expansion and containing the spread of Communism dominated the geopolitical security agenda of the United States in the postwar period. The early cold war period was marked by instability, misperceptions, and mistrust between the two global super powers. This affected both the military-economic dimension of grand strategy and the societal dimension. On the one hand, containment emerged as a dominant strategy of geopolitics, characterized by the cultivation of alliances with overseas nations and regional security regimes, such as the North Atlantic Treaty Organization (NATO). On the other hand, foreign-policy objectives began to have direct influence over societal security issues, including migration. It also had a tremendous impact on how the nation defined itself and thus on how societal security was defined and addressed.

As the only state capable of keeping potential Soviet expansionism in check, the United States established policy that was understandably focused on boosting material production and increasing military defense. In terms of migration policy, these goals were manifest in a liberalization of policy for economic migrants, granting access to postwar refugees fleeing the Communists as a symbolic tool of cold war foreign policy and weakening ethno-racial societal security preferences.

LABOR RECRUITMENT AND POSTWAR ECONOMIC GROWTH

Migration policy was an important element of the economic dimension of U.S. grand strategy both during and after WWII. The United States and Mexico signed a bilateral agreement on August 4, 1942, to establish a temporary labor recruitment program in order to fill manpower shortages during World War II. The use of temporary contract labor during the war years not only provided needed manpower in agriculture but also (and perhaps more importantly) enabled domestic workers to shift into industrial production jobs. Initially, these were primarily in war-related production industries. Aided by the influx of foreign labor, employment in shipbuilding rose from 31,000 to 274,000 and employment in the aircraft industry rose from 96,000 to 236,000 from 1941 to 1943.[7] Because of its success in supporting both military and economic dimensions of national security, the agreement was renewed several times during the war until its termination in 1946.

However, even before the original program was officially ended, talks were already underway to extend the program, and on March 10, 1947, the postwar contract labor program, commonly referred to as the Bracero program, was established. Mexican labor served the economic dimension of U.S. grand strategy in two important ways: (1) by providing needed labor during the war; and (2) allowing for a postwar shift in domestic labor from agriculture to jobs in industrial production. As was the case with Germany's initial enthusiasm for a temporary worker regime, U.S. policymakers saw the Bracero program as a way to reap the economic gains of flexible migrant labor while avoiding societal backlash against the permanent immigration of non-Europeans. As domestic labor shifted toward higher paying industrial production jobs after the war, opportunities in agriculture became less appealing both in terms of relative wages, working conditions, and status.[8] The continued use of foreign contract labor after the war ensured that the labor needs of agriculture were met without significantly affecting the domestic labor market or the costs of important commodities.

Participation in the Bracero program increased steadily, from 19,632 in 1947 to 437,643 in 1959 (Figure 3.1).[9] Although initially heralded as a win-win policy solution for U.S. economic needs, unanticipated consequences soon began to prompt public concern. While the number of Braceros continued to rise from 1947 to 1959, this rise was accompanied by rapid growth in the number of illegal aliens apprehended by the Immigration and Naturalization Service (INS) (Table 3.1). In fact, during the life of the Bracero program, the number of illegal aliens apprehended by the INS actually outnumbered the number of legal participants in the temporary labor program.[10] Kitty Calavita notes, "The program precipitated the influx, as returning

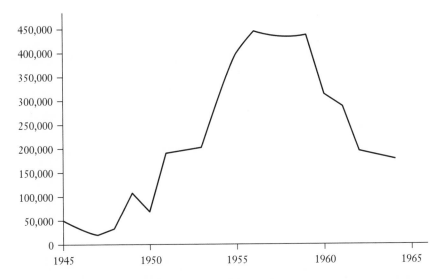

Figure 3.1.   Mexican Foreign Workers Admitted Under the Bracero Program,
1945–1964
 SOURCE: Adapted from Kitty Calavita, *Inside the State* (New York: Routledge, 1992), 218.

braceros spread word of employment opportunities in the United States.
Since there were more bracero candidates than there were official slots for
them, and because it was quicker and cheaper to bypass the contract system,
many Mexican workers took matters into their own hands, crossing the border illegally.[11] The rising number of illegal immigrants led to public alarm
regarding an emerging "wetback invasion." These perceptions of threat were
at least in part a function of how the INS presented the new statistics on apprehensions to the public and to policymakers. INS officials referred to the
growth in apprehensions as characteristic of "the greatest peacetime invasion complacently suffered by a country under open, flagrant, contemptuous
violation of its laws."[12] Media outlets followed suit in magnifying the degree
of the problem: "Illegal immigration from Mexico . . . has reached such
overwhelming proportions that officers of the United States Immigration
Service admit candidly . . . that there is nothing to stop the whole nation of
Mexico moving into the United States, if it wants to."[13] However, it is likely
that apprehensions statistics overstated the degree of the illegal immigrant
population because they included repeat offenders.

TABLE 3.1
Illegal aliens apprehended, 1946–1956

Year	Apprehensions
1946	99,591
1947	193,657
1948	192,779
1949	288,253
1950	468,339
1951	509,040
1952	528,815
1953	885,587
1954	1,089,583
1955	254,096
1956	87,696

SOURCE: INS, *Annual Report* (1959), 54.

In contrast to France, where circumvention of official recruitment channels was, for the most part, politically unproblematic and accepted by policymakers, in the United States public pressure generated by increased publicity pressed Eisenhower to take action.[14] However, rather than abolishing the Bracero program or penalizing U.S. employers that hired illegal workers (which would be contrary to the nation's economic interests), the government instead initiated an apprehensions program dubbed "Operation Wetback." The new program, which began on June 9, 1954, directed the INS to begin apprehending illegal migrants in conjunction with state and local law enforcement agencies. More than one million arrests and deportations resulted, which garnered considerable media coverage. The following year, the commissioner of the INS announced, "The border has been secured."[15] Although short-lived, the highly visible show of force gave the public a strong image of government action to palliate their perception of threat over the specter of uncontrolled migration from the South. This tactic of politically "purchasing" support for generally open migration policies would become more prominent in the politically turbulent 1990s.

The Bracero program was not the only policy established to maximize economic output by facilitating migration. In addition to establishing quotas for Asian nations to forward the U.S. cold war foreign-policy agenda, the McCarran-Walter Act of 1952 also revised the preference system for the assignment of immigrant visas that placed an emphasis on matching migrant skills with national economic needs (Table 3.2). Reflecting growing

TABLE 3.2
Preference system for visa admissions under the McCarran-Walter act

1. Highly skilled immigrants possessing urgently needed services or skills and their spouses and children.
2. Parents of U.S. citizens over age twenty-one and unmarried adult children of U.S. citizens.
3. Spouses and unmarried adult children of permanent resident aliens.
4. Brothers, sisters, and married children of U.S. citizens and accompanying spouses and children.
5. Applicants not entitled to preceding preferences.

awareness of the benefits of skill-based preferences to maximize the economic benefits of immigration, the highest preference was granted to applicants with high skills and professional expertise in areas where policymakers identified acute economic needs. To better attract the best and the brightest in those areas where economic need was acute, immediate family members (spouses and children) of these skilled workers were included in this category.[16]

FOREIGN-POLICY INTERESTS

The foreign-policy interests of the United States in the postwar period were defined by the nature of the emerging cold war conflict as articulated in the Truman Doctrine. The Truman Doctrine, outlined in a speech to the U.S. Congress on March 12, 1947, defined the postwar international order not simply as a clash between rival powers, but rather as a struggle between two distinct worlds, two identities, and two opposing ways of life:

> There is, at the present point in world history, a conflict between two ways of life. One way of life is based upon the will of the majority, free institutions, representative governments, free elections, guarantees of individual liberty, freedom of speech and religion, and freedom from political oppression. The second way of life is based upon the imposition of the will of a minority upon the majority, upon control of the press and other means of information by the minority, upon terror and oppression. . . . It is the policy of the United States to give support to free peoples who are attempting to resist subjugation from armed minorities or from outside forces.[17]

Defining the emergent cold war in such strongly ideational terms had a tremendous affect on U.S. policy toward refugees as well as on how societal security interests were defined. Refugee policy was utilized as a symbolic tool of cold war politics, while the fixation on a global clash of ideology created additional pressures for movement away from an ethno-racial emphasis of societal security.

The Truman Doctrine provided a lens through which migrants were increasingly perceived in a more positive light—a perspective actively cultivated by the American executive. Daniel Tichenor notes, "Since the Second World War, the White House had been the central force behind every successful effort to open the gates—if sometimes only temporarily—for refugees and some immigrant groups."[18] Postwar migrants—in the form of refugees fleeing Communist countries—became a symbolic element of the Truman Doctrine. Their trials and tribulations not only supported the American conception of the Soviet-sphere as oppressive, but by allowing them to enter the country the United States was able to affirm its self-conception as a defender of liberty and personal freedom. In addition, because many of those fleeing Communist countries were highly skilled, their migration represented a net loss to the Soviet economy and military complex, and a gain for the American pursuit of material power.

The Displaced Persons Act of 1948 was the first policy established to respond to the needs of those uprooted by war or fleeing persecution and provided for 205,000 places for refugees that would be "mortgaged" against the sending-nation's future immigration quotas allotments. In 1950, this level was increased to 415,744. The Refugee and Relief Act of 1953 provided non-quota visas for an additional 214,000 refugees to enter the country. Refugee policy quickly became a foreign-policy tool aimed at delegitimizing Communist regimes by demonstrating what people would do if allowed to "vote with their feet."[19] Confirming the link to U.S. foreign policy, a 1953 National Security Council memorandum suggested that the Refugee Relief Act of 1953 served to "encourage the defection of all USSR nations and 'key' personnel from the satellite countries" in order to "inflict a psychological blow on communism."[20] Refugee waves following the Soviet invasion of Hungary in 1956 and the Communist revolution in Cuba in 1959 were admitted to the United States through the authority of the attorney general's parole powers, codified in the McCarran-Walter Act of 1952.[21] Thus, while a comprehensive policy on refugees and asylum was not established for much of the cold war period, the creation and application of ad hoc policies were dominated by cold war foreign-policy considerations. (See Figure 3.2.)

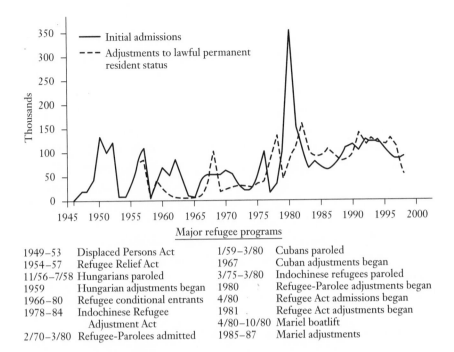

Major refugee programs

1949–53	Displaced Persons Act	1/59–3/80	Cubans paroled
1954–57	Refugee Relief Act	1967	Cuban adjustments began
11/56–7/58	Hungarians paroled	3/75–3/80	Indochinese refugees paroled
1959	Hungarian adjustments began	1980	Refugee-Parolee adjustments began
1966–80	Refugee conditional entrants	4/80	Refugee Act admissions began
1978–84	Indochinese Refugee Adjustment Act	1981	Refugee Act adjustments began
2/70–3/80	Refugee-Parolees admitted	4/80–10/80	Mariel boatlift
		1985–87	Mariel adjustments

Figure 3.2.   Refugee Admissions and Adjustments to Lawful Permanent Resident Status, 1946–1998
SOURCE: INS, *Statistical Yearbook* (1998), 84.

The impact of this positive image of migration—especially refugee flows—created by cold war foreign policy can be reflected in the rapid reduction in nativist sentiment in American public opinion. In 1947, 72 percent of poll respondents did not support the admission of 100,000 new refugees; however, by 1953, 47 percent of respondents supported the admission of 240,000 displaced persons in 1953, more than double the original figure posed in 1947.[22] However, because the United States could not control refugee flows in the same manner that it could manage "economic" migration, policymakers equivocated on setting a "blanket" policy for migration. Instead, until 1980 refugee and asylum policy in the United States was accomplished on an ad hoc basis, creating policy described by some analysts as "confusing and inconsistent."[23] This ad hoc basis allowed the state to manipulate the refugee channel of entry to conform to foreign-policy interests more easily, without becoming encumbered by legal constraints or congressional influence.

In addition to promoting more open policies toward refugees, the Truman Doctrine also had an impact on how internal security was defined. It emphasized the potential threat of internal subversion by Communist groups, and de-emphasized (in a relative sense) ethno-racial societal security interests. American national identity during the early cold war became increasingly defined relative to an external Other. Identity discourse was dominated by an emphasis on one thing: Americans were *not* Communists. Societal insecurities in the late 1940s and 1950s were preoccupied with the "red menace," both in terms of Soviet expansion abroad and, perhaps more importantly, Communist infiltration *within* the United States. While diverting the focus from ethno-cultural dimensions of societal insecurity, this redefinition of American identity certainly did not result in societal openness. In fact, the establishment of the House Un-American Activities Commission (HUAC) ushered in an era of profound internal insecurity that was the direct result of the cold war's ideological struggle. Allowing even a small number of Communist organizers into the country was considered potentially catastrophic. J. Edgar Hoover was fond of pointing out, "It took only twenty-three Commies to overthrow Russia."[24]

In 1949, Representative Edward Gosset of Texas expressed the growing belief that many illegal aliens "come into this country for subversive purposes." He suggested that military intelligence personally be assigned to the INS to protect against Communist infiltration. To deal with this internal threat, Congress established the Internal Security Act on September 22, 1950. Whereas existing migration-related legislation was based on the racial component of migration, the Internal Security Act focused instead on ideology. The Internal Security Act amended various immigration laws in an attempt to strengthen the screening of aliens applying for entry into the United States. The act made present or former membership in the Communist Party, or any other totalitarian party or its affiliates, grounds for inadmissibility. Moreover, the act allowed for the deportation of aliens deemed inadmissible under the provisions of the act, regardless of the length of their residence in the United States. The attorney general was also given the authority to, without a hearing, exclude and deport aliens "whose admission would be prejudicial to the public interest if the Attorney General's finding was based on confidential information the disclosure of which would have been prejudicial to the public interest of the United States."[25]

Although this preoccupation—or perhaps more accurately, paranoia—with cold war political ideology led to a domestic clampdown on both immigrants and citizens, emphasizing nonracialized criteria of national identity may have served to alter public attitudes regarding "cultural proximity." Ethnic discrimination between northern/western European and eastern/southern European migrants remained largely intact throughout the 1950s and early 1960s, cold war ideology served to decrease perceptions of difference (of "otherness") between European immigrants that are today largely seen as a relatively homogeneous group ("Europeans"). This reveals how identity can evolve relative to changing structural conditions. Although race and ethnicity remained significant elements of American identity, we can see evidence of a gradual liberalization of how national identity is construed.

In addition to their emphasis on internal security and symbolic role in cold war foreign policy, migration policies were also used as a tool to forge and strengthen alliances, a strategy already utilized during World War II. In order to bolster relations with key allies, overt discrimination in U.S. immigration policy against nationals of allied nations was deemed counterproductive to the national interest. At that point in time, access to immigration into the United States was largely a function of the racial and ethnic background of potential migrants, reflecting a prior emphasis on societal security interests. This preference system began with the Chinese Exclusion Act of 1882 and eventually led to the comprehensive immigration law passed in 1924. The 1924 Immigration Act established a system of numerical quotas for immigrant-sending nations. According to the preference system stipulated in the act, quota allocations for each migrant-sending state were not to exceed 2 percent of the number of foreign-born of that nationality present in the United States as measured by the census of 1890. Total immigration quotas in any given year were not to exceed 165,000. Moreover, under the national origins scheme, only ethnic groups whose forebears reached the United States *voluntarily* were permitted a quota, a limitation that automatically excluded Africans, Chinese, and Japanese.[26] When this system became active in 1929, nations from northern and western Europe received 83 percent of available visas, southern and eastern European nations received 15 percent, and only 2 percent were allocated for all other nations. In a largely symbolic gesture, Congress repealed the Chinese Exclusion Acts in

1943 in order to improve ties with China, an ally in the war against Japan. Similarly, bills to grant quotas for other Asian allies—specifically India and the Philippines—were introduced into Congress in 1944. Both were granted quotas in 1946.

This connection between the need to foster allied unity and the nation's posture toward immigrants from those nations continued as the cold war began. Cold war alliances required more sensitivity to migrant-sending nations within the Western alliance, such as Italy, Greece, and Turkey. Existing exclusion laws and the national origins quota system suggested that the Americans considered some races or people of some nations undesirable and/or inferior, making the establishment of close political ties more tenuous for foreign policymakers. President Truman was an ardent supporter of restructuring immigration policy in order to forge better foreign relations with key allies. The McCarran-Walter Act of 1952 was passed in large part as a gesture to allied countries that the United States considered them as social and political equals. It did so by stipulating that access to immigration and naturalization in the United States could not be restricted on the basis of race or marital status. It also established nominal visa quotas for Japan, China, and nations of the Asia-Pacific Triangle. Under the terms of the new law, Japan received a quota of 185 annual visas, China received 105, and nations located in the Asia-Pacific Triangle received a quota of 100. Although the political momentum that resulted in the McCarran-Walter Act was initiated by the White House to forward foreign-policy interests, Truman vetoed the bill because he felt that it did not go far enough in establishing equality. Eighty-five percent of available visas were allocated for northern and western European nations, while quotas for Asian nations were numerically insignificant relative to aggregate visa distribution levels. Truman made his objections clear in remarks made upon U.S. inclusion in NATO: "Today, we have entered into an alliance, the North Atlantic Treaty, with Italy, Greece, and Turkey, against one of the most terrible threats mankind has ever faced. . . . But through this bill we say to their people: You are less worthy to come to this country than Englishmen or Irishmen."[27] Congress, however, remained resolute in the terms they were willing to accept and passed the bill over Truman's veto. Given the limited quotas allocated in the act, its passage represents only a nominal move toward a more liberal policy. However, given the extreme exclusionary nature of existing U.S. immigration law, the

TABLE 3.3
Admissions preference system after the 1965 amendments to the INA

Preference	Provisions
First	Unmarried sons and daughters over age 21 of U.S. citizens (20 percent maximum)
Second	Spouse and unmarried children of aliens lawfully admitted for permanent residence (20 percent plus any not required for first preference)
Third	Professionals, scientists, and artists of exceptional abilities (10 percent maximum)
Fourth	Married sons and daughters over age 21 of U.S. citizens (10 percent plus any not required for the first three preferences)
Fifth	Siblings of U.S. citizens (24 percent maximum plus any not required for the first four preferences)
Sixth	Skilled and unskilled workers in occupations for which labor is in short supply (10 percent maximum)
Seventh	Refugees, defined by the 1957 Refugee-Escapee Act as people fleeing persecution from Communism or the Middle East (6 percent maximum)

symbolic significance of this incremental step toward liberalization is nonetheless an important one.

Later administrations would continue to deal with the tension between U.S. immigration and race policies that complicated foreign relations.[28] The Kennedy administration drafted immigration reform legislation in 1963 that would abolish the Asia-Pacific Triangle and phase out the national origins system over a five-year period. However, the assassination of President Kennedy derailed the legislation process, and Lyndon Johnson was initially reluctant to make immigration reform a priority, preferring instead to focus on his social-welfare projects and his idea of the Great Society. It did not take long, however, for LBJ to realize the symbolic importance of immigration reform in the foreign-policy arena. In testimony before Congress, administration officials made this foreign-policy linkage crystal clear: "In the present ideological conflict between freedom and fear, we proclaim to the world that our central precept is that all are born equal. . . . Yet under present law, we choose among immigrants on the basis of where they are."[29] With strong administration support, Congress passed the Immigration Reform Act in October 1965 with large bipartisan majorities in both houses. The new law abolished the national origins quota system and replaced it with a system based on preferences for family reunification and economic skills (Table 3.3). The conventional wisdom on the origins of the Immigration

Reform Act of 1965 suggests that it was primarily a product of the civil rights movement. For example, Desmond King notes, "It is not coincidental that the 1965 Immigration Act was enacted in the wake of the country's civil rights movement: the incongruity between racial exclusion of designated immigrants and the inadequacy of domestic democratization measures was never more graphic."[30] However, ideational effects of the cold war also played a part in the political developments of 1965: "The old system of ethnic and racial discrimination, with its strong preference for northern and western Europeans, had fit a segregated society. But the experience of World War II as well as the end of legal segregation made that vestigial structure an embarrassment to a multiracial nation at the head of the non-Communist world. By eliminating that system, the American government removed a major irritant to nonwhite nations in their dealings with the United States."[31] In a sense, both forces were mutually reinforcing in pushing for change. Cold war foreign-policy considerations pressed for increased openness for ethnic minority immigration to reduce tensions with allied (or potential allied) countries, and conversely, civil rights leaders were able to gain leverage for the Civil Rights Act by exploiting this tension and forcing Americans to practice the liberalism reflected in their founding myths.

SUMMARY OF EARLY COLD WAR PERIOD

In times of high external threat, the Threat and Rally Hypotheses predict migration and border policies that (1) are generally more open, (2) stress economic and foreign-policy interests, and (3) are less focused on societal security interests. In the United States, increased liberalization during the late 1940s, 1950s, and 1960s was manifest in the extension of immigration visa quotas for Asian countries in order to bolster alliance strength among these countries, though quota levels were initially limited in size. In addition, the ad hoc admission of large numbers of postwar refugees represented another avenue of liberalization. The application of the attorney general's parole authority increasingly conformed to U.S. foreign-policy instruments and was used as a tool to combat the Soviet Union, both materially and ideationally. Lastly, the Bracero program of temporary-labor recruitment from Mexico represented another aspect of liberalization also tied to U.S. cold war foreign policy by policymakers. This environment of incremental liberalization and reduced emphasis on racial/ethnic preferences led to the landmark changes evident in 1965.

Toward Détente and the Rise of Societal Insecurity

In terms of external threat perception, several factors suggest a reduction of geopolitical threat during the late 1960s and early 1970s. First, the NATO alliance system coupled with economic growth among members during the 1950s and 1960s increased Western power relative to the Soviet Union. In addition, even though the cold war continued and conflict raged in Vietnam, the bipolar system had stabilized over time. This was in stark contrast to the tension and mistrusts that accompanied the Soviet Union's shift from WWII ally to cold war adversary.[32] Moreover, overcoming near disasters such as the Cuban Missile Crisis increased confidence in policymakers' ability to manage the East-West relationship without a nuclear exchange. Although the trading-state grand strategy that emerged during in the early cold war period resulted in significant economic growth in the United States and Europe, it also served to increase global migration pressures and alter traditional patterns of international migration. The Threat and Rally Hypotheses predict that in an environment of declining geopolitical threat, elements of societal security will gain increasing salience. In response to such changes in threat perception, policy would then become increasingly restrictive and would be focused on those elements of migration that generate perceptions of societal threat.

POLICY LEGACIES AND SOCIETAL INSECURITY

In addition to a structural environment that made sensitivity to societal threats more likely, societal insecurity in the 1970s and 1980s were strongly influenced by the unanticipated effects of prior policy choices. The unanticipated effects of the Bracero program and the 1965 Immigration Act created a feedback loop that contributed significantly to the shift in public attitudes about migration and subsequent policy outcomes.

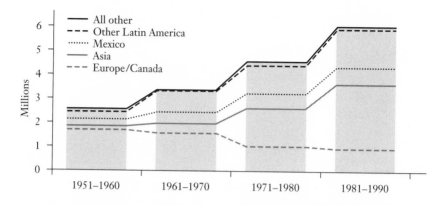

Figure 3.3.   Legal Immigration by Country or Region, 1951–1990
source: Adapted from Michael Fix and Jeffrey S. Passel, *Immigration and Immigrants: Setting the Record Straight* (Washington, DC: Urban Institute, 1994), 26.

Although the national origins quota system was abolished through the 1965 amendments, the creation of family-based preferences was seen by policymakers as a means to promote both liberal principles without applying shocks to societal security. By establishing family preferences, it was believed that future migration flows would likely resemble the existing racial and cultural makeup of the nation. Emanuel Cellar made the connection between preferences for family reunification and efforts to maintain societal stability most explicit: "Since the people of Africa and Asia have very few relatives here, comparatively few could immigrate from those countries because they have no family ties in the U.S."[33] Policymakers believed that this preference system would keep ethno-racial demographics proportional to the existing population. However, Figure 3.3 reveals long-term trends in the composition of immigration flows to the United States. Immigration from Europe and Canada dropped from 46 percent to 22 percent from the 1960s to the 1970s, and fell even further to only 15 percent from 1981 to 1990. Much of the decline in European migration can be attributed to the growing political stability and economic growth in the region after a precarious period of postwar recovery. Conversely, immigration from Asia and Latin America increased markedly.[34] From the 1960s to the 1970s, Asian migration grew from 13 to 35 percent of total immigration. During the 1980s it grew to 45 percent of total immigration, and between 1970 and 1990, the number of Asian Americans in the United States rose from 1.5 to 7.3 million.[35] During this

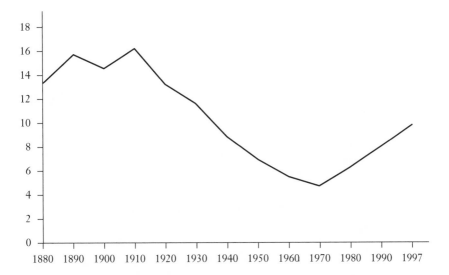

Figure 3.4.   Foreign-Born Population in the United States, 1880–1997

SOURCE: Adapted from Joel S. Fetzer, *Public Attitudes Toward Immigration in the United States, France, and Germany* (Cambridge: Cambridge University Press, 2000), 155.

same period the percentage of foreign-born rose from about 5 to 8.5 percent. Although this level remained far lower than previous highs of approximately 15 percent in the late 1800s (Figure 3.4), it is important to keep in mind that "foreign-born" in the past was largely comprised of European immigrants.

In a country where race has been the determining factor shaping attitudes about immigration, changing ethno-racial demographics is a significant development. After the 1965 Immigration Reform Act, the proportion of the non-Hispanic white population in the United States declined more rapidly (Table 3.4).[36] Moreover, in areas where migration flows have been concentrated, such as in California, this ethnic restructuring of American society has been even more significant. As reflected in 2000 Census Bureau data, the white population in California has decreased from 77 percent in 1970 to 50 percent in 2000.[37] With the level of the black population steady at approximately 7 percent, growth has occurred in the proportion of Latino and Asian populations as a result of migration trends. From 1970 to 2000, the percentage of Latinos in the population grew from 12 to 31 percent, while the percentage of Asians in the population in California grew from 3 to 12 percent. Not surprisingly, given America's history regarding racial preferences,

TABLE 3.4
U.S. population by race-ethnicity, 1900–1990 (in thousands)

Population

Year	Total	Non-Hispanic White	Black	Hispanic	Asian	American Indian
1900	76,195	66,225	8,834	656	243	237
1910	93,879	82,049	10,255	999	299	277
1920	110,747	96,969	11,512	1,632	389	244
1930	127,585	111,543	12,736	2,435	527	343
1940	136,928	119,425	13,767	2,814	577	345
1950	155,156	134,351	15,668	4,039	739	357
1960	182,055	154,969	19,071	6,346	1,146	524
1970	205,567	170,371	23,005	9,616	1,782	793
1980	226,625	180,932	26,482	14,604	3,726	1,420
1990	248,712	187,139	29,986	22,354	7,274	1,959

Percentage

Year	Total	Non-Hispanic White	Black	Hispanic	Asian	American Indian
1900	100	86.9	11.6	0.9	0.3	0.3
1910	100	87.4	10.9	1.1	0.3	0.3
1920	100	87.6	10.4	1.5	0.4	0.2
1930	100	87.4	10.0	1.9	0.4	0.3
1940	100	87.2	10.1	2.1	0.4	0.3
1950	100	86.6	10.1	2.6	0.5	0.2
1960	100	85.1	10.5	3.5	0.6	0.3
1970	100	82.9	11.2	4.7	0.9	0.4
1980	100	79.6	11.7	6.4	1.6	0.6
1990	100	75.2	12.1	9.0	2.9	0.8

SOURCE: Frank D. Bean, Robert Cushing, and Charles W. Haynes, "The Changing Demography of U.S. Immigration Flows," in *Migration Past, Migration Future*, ed. K. Bade and M. Weiner (Providence, RI: Berghahn, 1997), 126.

national public opinion reflected a growing sense of societal insecurity associated with demographic changes.[38] Roper Center and Gallup polls revealed that the percentage of American who favored decreasing existing levels of immigration increased from 33 percent in 1965 to 42 percent by 1977.[39] By 1993, this percentage increased to 65 percent.

Faced with growing numbers of migrants from non-European sources, the first policy adjustment to the 1965 Immigration Act came in the form of new limits. The Immigration and Nationality Act Amendments of 1976 revised the Western Hemisphere ceiling (which only set aggregate, regional levels) by implementing the same 20,000 per-country limits that were estab-

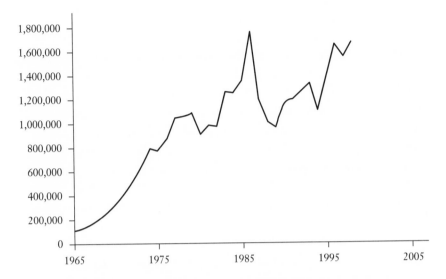

Figure 3.5.   Illegal Aliens Apprehended, 1965–1998
SOURCE: INS, *Statistical Yearbook* (1998), 207.

lished for Eastern Hemisphere countries under the 1965 law. Although these limits were successful in constraining legal flows, the demand for access to the United States remained strong in Latin American countries, especially Mexico. As such, migration from Mexico and Latin America began to move from the front door to the backdoor, documented by a steady rise in the number of illegal aliens apprehended by U.S. law enforcement authorities (Figure 3.5). Coverage of the growth in illegal immigration flows began to manifest itself in major, mass-market publications such as *Time* and *U.S. News and World Report*.[40] Media coverage characterized these trends as evidence of an "invasion" manifest by a "horde of illegal aliens."[41] The government soon sought to quell societal fears with new policy. The Carter administration was the first to set the political agenda. In 1977, it created the Interagency Task Force on Immigration Policy to examine the problem of the rising levels of illegal immigration and to propose policy alternatives. Its findings echoed many of the alarmist concerns regarding the rise in illegal immigration: "Illegal immigration results in massive violation of U.S. immigration law. The INS has in recent years made roughly a million apprehensions annually. There is presently no credible deterrent to illegal migration."[42]

The rise in illegal immigration was not solely the function of new per-country visa allocations that were not proportional to demand in various countries. It was also the product of general historical dynamics of Mexican migration to the United States and to American conceptions of the migration process. A lack of understanding of both of these factors is evidenced by the nature of the Interagency Task Force's analysis of the rising tide of illegal immigration, especially along the U.S.-Mexico border. First, the U.S. preoccupation with *control*, especially after the abolition of the national-origins quota system, presumes that migrants intend to engage in immigration of a permanent nature. Yet, Mexican migration has long been based on a culture of seasonal return migration rather than permanent relocation. Second, with no seasonal, temporary guest-worker program in place since the demise of the Bracero program, Mexican migrants wishing to fill labor demand in U.S. agriculture had no other recourse save illegal immigration. Although rising numbers of illegal aliens accompanied the Bracero program, this was more a function of circumventing the bureaucratic process than an indicator of the desire for permanent migration among Mexican workers. Yet, this would seem to be the "lesson learned" by policymakers seeking to avoid large-scale, permanent immigration from Mexico. The Interagency Task Force report used the European experience with guest workers as evidence that temporary-labor programs invariably lead to permanent migration. The Task Force recommended, "The problems brought upon Western Europe by its experiment with guest workers recommend caution on the part of the United States in any consideration of implementing an expanded temporary worker program as a possible solution to its present illegal immigration problem."[43] Yet, the U.S. case is notably different from the European case in that the Mexican culture is one that has a long history of cyclical migration between the United States and Mexico, a process facilitated by geographic proximity. Conversely, the German guest-worker program was increasingly forced to draw from migrant-sending countries that were neither proximate nor had strong historical traditions of cyclical migration. Thus, while illegal migrants from Mexico indeed were circumventing U.S. immigration law (and its sovereignty), the dramatic rise in illegal immigration (as opposed to the far less socially objectionable legal immigration) is, in part, the result of the policy choices of U.S. lawmakers who sought to "readjust" the (dis)equilibrium established by the 1965 Immigration Act.

Congress followed the Carter administration's lead. In 1978, the Select Commission on Immigration and Refugee Policy (SCIRP) was established to examine U.S. policies and provide recommendations. Like the Interagency Task Force that preceded it, the Select Commission did not propose temporary-worker programs as a means to alleviate the growth in illegal immigration. Rather, the commission recommended (1) sanctions against employers that hire illegal aliens; (2) the development of a secure identification system to document a worker's right to work in the country; (3) enhanced border enforcement; and (4) amnesty for illegal aliens residing in the country prior to some specified date.[44] These recommendations laid the foundation for the political process leading to the most significant immigration legislation during the 1980s—the Immigration Reform and Control Act of 1986.

SCIRP members achieved a wide consensus on the need for increased border enforcement, even though this only responded to one type of migration flow—Mexicans and Latin Americans—while ignoring illegal immigrants from other nations that entered legally and then overstayed the terms of their visa ("out of status" migrants). Members felt that since the 1965 Immigration Reform Act, U.S. immigration policy lacked any semblance of deterrence.[45] It was noted by analysts that both employer sanctions and national identification systems were utilized among European nations to curtail illegal immigration; however, these measures faced considerable opposition among business and civil rights interest groups. What to do about the extant population of illegal aliens also vexed policy analysts: "Members of SCIRP believed that it was neither politically practical nor morally acceptable to engage in the mass deportation of those illegal aliens to their native nations. Rather, many, if not most, of those illegal aliens had demonstrated their capacity to become productive, law-abiding American citizens through their years of residence in the United States."[46] Thus, it was believed that an amnesty program, in conjunction with a new commitment to border enforcement, could ease societal fears of an "illegal alien invasion" by providing a fresh start to immigration control. Opponents, however, saw amnesty as a government sanction of illegal immigration, one that would certainly result in increasing levels of immigration in the future.

The political process leading up to the passage of the Immigration Reform and Control Act of 1986 was indeed contentious, at least in the House,

TABLE 3.5
INS enforcement budget, 1986 and 1990 (in $ millions)

Activities	1986	1990
Border Patrol	150.4	262.6
Inspections	76.1	145.6
Investigations	42.0	95.8
Anti-smuggling	15.0	21.6
Deportation	82.4	164.0
Employer Relations	—	3.9
TOTAL	366.0	694.0

SOURCE: INS.

as prior versions of the bill were presented and rejected in both 1982 and 1984. The 1986 Immigration Reform and Control Act combined border-enforcement provisions with an amnesty program for illegal aliens who could prove residence prior to January 1, 1982. It also provided a special amnesty provision for agricultural workers, called the Special Agricultural Worker program (SAW), which provided permanent resident alien status to workers who had worked in agriculture for at least ninety days in the year preceding May 1, 1986. Its border-enforcement provisions focused on both reducing the availability of employment for illegal aliens and funding for migrant interdiction along the U.S.-Mexican border. IRCA allocated $422 million in additional funding for the INS for fiscal year 1987 and $419 million for fiscal year 1988 to achieve these goals. Moreover, the Moorhead Amendment dictated that the allocation of these funds within the INS effect a 50 percent increase in the Border Patrol. Between 1986 and 1990, the allocated budget for the Border Patrol increased from $154 million to $262.6 million, which constituted the largest portion of the INS's budget for enforcement activities (Table 3.5). While increasing Border Patrol funding was a prominent aspect of IRCA's enforcement provisions—a move that was the harbinger of U.S. policy throughout the 1990s—its most salient illegal immigration program was the establishment of employer sanctions. Many policy analysts suggested that eliminating the "lure" of U.S. jobs was necessary if illegal immigration was to be significantly curtailed, as was stipulated in the SCIRP report. However, implementation of such a program would introduce unwanted externalities on business.

This tension between being responsive to societal demands for closure and economic interests was in some ways "finessed" by policymakers. Even though IRCA placed employer sanctions on the books, safeguards were installed into the provisions to minimize potential government "harassment" of business. These included three provisions that set difficult legal burdens on enforcement agencies. First, IRCA specified that hearings regarding violations of the employer sanctions provisions must be conducted according to the dictates of the Administrative Procedure Act (APA), a stipulation that placed a considerable burden on INS investigators.[47] Second, IRCA required that the INS must produce a warrant or receive consent before conducting a site check, weakening the agency's ability to surprise those circumventing the law. Lastly, IRCA required that employers "knowingly" hire undocumented workers in order for employment to constitute an infraction of the law. This verbiage greatly increased the burden of proof on the INS when prosecuting cases, since proving prior knowledge of employment status often required admission by employers or the testimony of undocumented workers. This element also weakened enforcement due to the lack of secure national identification cards, not implemented as part of IRCA because of vigorous resistance from civil rights organizations.

In addition to legal and procedural safeguards, the economic costs of implementing IRCA's employer sanctions made rigorous enforcement of its provisions a monumental undertaking. Because IRCA required educating all U.S. employers, regardless of size, and monitoring their employment practices, the INS would need a vast amount of additional resources to achieve these goals. Although funding for the INS's enforcement program was greatly increased after IRCA, this funding continued to be spread out among its many enforcement activities. By 1990, budget allocations for inspections and investigations remained only 21 percent and 14 percent of the total budget, respectively. Thus, while IRCA represented a strong de jure stance against both employment of illegal aliens and as a push for border closure, the de facto application of this legislation resulted in a much more lenient position vis-à-vis domestic economic interests. One analyst noted, "There is strong evidence that the employer requirements program is not receiving the mandate or support necessary to allow it to effectively deter undocumented immigration. A number of factors, including easily circumvented documentation requirements, diffused responsibilities, and competing policy objectives, limit the ability of the INS to mount an effective regulatory program."[48] Other analyses point to similar conclusions regarding IRCA's effect on undocumented immigration flows. Although the illegal immigrant stock and the number of illegal immigrants apprehended at the U.S.-Mexico border declined in the years immediately following the passage of IRCA, most analysts attribute this trend to the act's amnesty provisions, which legalized nearly three million undocumented workers, rather than to its enforcement provisions. Frank Bean and Michael Fix suggest that, "The central control mechanism in IRCA, the employer sanctions, appears to be more symbolic than real in its effects [on illegal immigration]."[49]

SOCIETAL INSECURITY AND REFUGEE POLICY

Whereas rising societal insecurities associated with changing migration demographics pushed policy toward closure, refugee policy remained strongly influenced by cold war foreign-policy interests even as societal insecurities pressed for closure. Daniel Tichenor notes, "During the late 1970s, refugee admissions were frequently more generous than most Americans preferred."[50] Through the de facto exploitation of policy loopholes such as the attorney general's parole power (and subsequent legislation of resident aliens admitted through these procedures), 96.8 percent of refugees granted permanent resident status from 1971–80 originated in Communist countries or the Middle East, consistent with U.S. foreign-policy objectives.[51] Even after the passage of the 1980 Refugee Act, which was intended to regularize admissions procedures and conform U.S. law to international conventions, admissions remained dominated by refugees from Communist regimes.[52] Even though the 1980 Refugee Act later repealed the "seventh preference" for those fleeing Communist or Middle Eastern countries, the share of refugees from these sources who were granted permanent resident status from 1981–90 was 94.6 percent.[53]

One of the most conspicuous examples of how foreign-policy interests dominated refugee policy was the favorable treatment afforded to Cuban nationals compared to those fleeing persecution in Haiti and Central America. Soon after the passage of the Refugee Act of 1980, 125,000 Mariel Cubans fleeing the Castro regime arrived in Florida.[54] Most were given permanent resident status under the 1966 Cuban Adjustment Act, save some 2,476 who were excludable by virtue of their criminal status. Although the size of this refugee flow served to alter conceptions of U.S. policy priorities, the preference for refugees from Communist regimes continued to dominate policy. During mass deportation hearings, Haitian refugees were often denied asylum on the grounds that they were simply economic migrants seeking to exploit the asylum policies of the United States. Moreover, in an attempt to thwart the legal protections contained in asylum law (the principle of non-refoulement as stipulated in the Geneva Convention of 1951), the Reagan administration instigated policies to detain asylum applicants pending removal proceedings (if they could not demonstrate a legal right to enter the United States) and to interdict Haitian vessels bound for the United States.

Similar discrimination between Communist and non-Communist sources of refugees is evidenced by U.S. treatment of Central Americans with regard to the granting of extended voluntary departure (EVD) status. Application of EVD provisions and approval of asylum claims from 1984–90 highly favored refugees from Communist-ruled Nicaragua, while those seeking asylum from El Salvador and Guatemala were often characterized by U.S. officials as economic migrants. During this period, 26 percent of adjudicated asylum claims of Nicaraguan nationals were approved, while only 2.6 percent and 1.8 percent of applicants from El Salvador and Guatemala (respectively) were accepted.[55] This politically motivated disparity was challenged in the courts (the so-called ABC case), which later ruled that new asylum hearings must be granted for all Salvadoran and Guatemalan asylum seekers. However, the new hearings produced similar results. Whereas only 1.6 percent of Salvadoran claims and 1.8 of Guatemalan claims were approved, 16.4 percent of Nicaraguan asylum claims were granted.[56]

SUMMARY OF THE DÉTENTE ERA

During the 1970s and 1980s, increasing societal insecurities generated more anti-immigration sentiment and pressed the government for more restrictive policies. Public opinion shows a clear preference for reduced immigration and restrictive policies were established. However, rather than significantly reducing the volume of all migration inflows into the country, the executive branch was instrumental in framing the nature of the debate in terms of the growing problem of illegal immigration. As such, restrictive policies established during the period were focused on this issue. Although the McCarran-Walter Act passed in 1952 might be the first instance of policymakers attempting to "finesse" tensions between conflicting impulses for openness and closure, the practice became more widespread during this period and established a pattern that would guide policy development after the cold war ended.

Migration Control after the Cold War

The end of the cold war represented a further decline in external threat as the United States asserted its position as a global hegemon. Given this decrease in geopolitical threat, the Threat Hypothesis predicts a continued rise in societal insecurities and more restrictive policies. Indeed, several indicators suggest that societal insecurities continued to increase in the 1990s, especially in those areas receiving the highest proportion of migrants. Polls taken in 1993 showed that 65 percent of Americans favored decreased levels of immigration, up from 42 percent in 1977.[57] Moreover, highly publicized images of migrant border dashes through the San Ysidro border checkpoint fueled passionate anti-immigrant rhetoric. In 1994, voters in California overwhelmingly passed Proposition 187, an anti-illegal immigration bill riding the crest of societal insecurities. Organizers and proponents often suggested that the bill was intended to "send a message" to policymakers, even though the law was almost immediately struck down in the courts.[58] If policy developed in the 1980s represented the first steps in "finessing" societal insecurities, policy development in the 1990s reveals an even more focused attempt to direct more restrictive policy on those elements of migration generating societal threat while maintaining policies that forward macroeconomic interests. Specifically, government responses to societal insecurities were focused on adjusting for the unintended effects of the 1965 amendments to the INA with regard to European migration and addressing the issue of illegal immigration by crafting an image of security along the U.S.-Mexico border. In contrast, legal immigration quota levels remained steady, and special provisions were made to recruit highly skilled labor in response to economic interests.

TABLE 3.6
Immigrants admitted by major category, 1987–1993

Category of Admission	Average 1987–1991	1992	1993
Subject to the Numerical Cap	511,427	655,541	719,701
Family-Based Immigrants	439,614	502,995	539,209
Employment-Based Immigrants	58,341	116,198	147,012
Diversity Programs	13,473	36,348	33,480

SOURCE: U.S. Commission on Immigration Reform, *U.S. Immigration Policy: Restoring Credibility* (Washington, DC: U.S. Government Printing Office, 1994), 191.

THE IMMIGRATION ACT OF 1990

The Immigration Act of 1990 represents two key adjustments to U.S. immigration policy, both of which can be seen as adjustments to the 1965 amendments. They include adjusting the visa allocations for employment-based categories and introducing "diversity visas" for immigrants from sending nations deemed to have been "adversely affected" as a result of the 1965 changes in U.S. law. The 1990 Act increased the number of available employment-based visas from 54,000 to 140,000 (not including special immigrants currently admitted under employment-based categories), an increase of 260 percent. As shown in Table 3.6, employment-based immigration rose from its 1987–91 average of roughly 58,000, to 116,198 in 1992 and to 147,012 by 1993.

Although increasing the number of employment-based visas relative to family-based visas would seem to represent a step away from the (de facto) ethno-cultural preference system of 1965, consideration of the ethno-cultural makeup of current flows remained in focus. Family reunification preferences did little to reproduce the ethnic landscape of pre–1965 America nation as intended by lawmakers drafting the 1965 amendments, yet once institutionalized in the system, would prove difficult for lawmakers to dislodge without appearing racist. Again showing the state's proclivity toward "finessing" such contradictions and tensions, the 1990 Immigration Act established an allocation for "diversity immigration" (DV-1). Beginning in October 1994, the program provided for 55,000 visas to be distributed among nationals of nations that had sent fewer than 55,000 legal immigrants to the United States in the previous five years. The act was clearly intended to promote European migration in order to "balance" the dramatic rise in immigration from Asia and Latin America. In the first apportionment of diversity visas, nearly 50 percent (24,550) were allocated to European nations, with the remaining visas divided among the other nations of the world.

The Immigration Act of 1990 represents a political compromise that sought to both correct unanticipated effects of prior changes in U.S. policy and to establish movement toward new preference criteria. On the one hand, some prominent labor economists argued that the 1965 preferences for family-based immigration resulted in immigrants with relatively fewer skills than prior immigrants; thus, they were not adequately forwarding U.S. economic interests.[59] Although not reducing the number of family-based allocations, the number of visas allocated based on skills criteria were raised significantly. On the other hand, family-unification preferences did not result in maintaining the ethnic status quo of 1965 America. Societal insecurities were generated by dramatic increases in Asian and Western Hemisphere migration, as well as the rise in illegal immigration, especially from Mexico. Adding "diversity visas" allowed policymakers to attempt to balance the ethnic makeup of current immigration flows while avoiding racist rhetoric (and policy) and without dismantling the liberal preference system in place for twenty-five years.

REFUGEE POLICY IN THE 1990S

The end of the cold war prompted a significant adjustment to refugee and asylum components of migration policy in the United States. On the one hand, the Mariel boatlift served as a warning to policymakers of the dangers of using refugee policy as a foreign-policy instrument. Establishing a de facto blanket preference based almost solely on foreign-policy considerations leaves the state vulnerable to societal insecurities, as the public becomes wary of large inflows of those who are racially or culturally different, or if the public perceives sending states to be engaged in "migrant dumping." While many current refugee applicants to the United States emanate from former Communist countries, approval rates were not dominated by such considerations as they once were. For example, in 1998, refugee applications from Cuban applicants had only a 14 percent acceptance rate, considerably lower than the 58.7 percent average acceptance rate for all nations. Admitting migrants based solely on foreign-policy criteria often creates dissonance in the national identity of liberal polities. In 1990, Congress ordered that Salvadorans be granted temporary protected status (TPS), later changed to deferred enforced departure (DED) status during the Bush administration. While both TPS and DED essentially provide the same legal protections to those seeking asylum, they reveal an attempt by lawmakers to finesse the tension that exists between liberal and ethno-cultural elements of national identity. Both TPS and DED, while allowing applicants to live and work in the country pending asylum hearings, do not permit family reunification or automatic conversion to permanent resident status.[60] Moreover, while both TPS and DED are essentially other names for EVD, the choice of names also reveals sensitivities to societal insecurities (or potential insecurities). Whereas EVD stresses *voluntary departure*, TPS stresses that protected status is *temporary*, emphasizing state authority to revoke such status and return non–bona fide applicants. DED further emphasizes the language of state control, stressing that protected status is merely *deferred* pending *enforced departure*. As policymakers seek to finesse a compromise between liberal and nativist tendencies in national identity, these semantic details are important in utilizing such symbolic changes to establish compromise.

As policy moved away from its cold war–dominated phase, emphasis was placed on reducing the numbers of refugee and asylum applicants, and on controlling the entry of those whose situation necessitates a humanitarian response. In order to better control such flows, U.S. policy has increasingly circumvented international conventions regarding the handling of refugees. Here, one can witness a divergence between state policy regarding refugees and policy regarding asylum. This was characterized in the handling of Haitian refugee flows in the 1990s. In the aftermath of a coup of president Jean-Bertrand Aristide, thousands of Haitians fled the country in 1991 and sought asylum in the United States. Rather than receiving refugee or asylee status, Haitian refugees were interdicted at sea and diverted to the U.S. naval base at Guantanamo Bay in Cuba to screen their asylum claims. Most were summarily deported. In the period from September 1991 to January 1993, more than thirty thousand refugees were repatriated to Haiti. In May 1992, when migrant flows continued and screening processes became impacted, President Bush announced that all Haitian migrants interdicted at sea would be repatriated without recourse to apply for asylum, a policy that remained intact when Bill Clinton assumed the U.S. presidency.

Alexander Aleinikoff noted, "Overseas admissions programs are likely to continue to bring not insignificant numbers of refugees to the United States each year. This is so because such flows are controlled and controllable."[61] Each year, the president (with the consultation of Congress) determines the number of refugees worldwide that require resettlement, then establishes an admissions ceiling for that year. In addition, the president may also seek to find alternatives to minimize the ceiling required to respond to humanitarian crises. Bilateral agreements have been used to garner sending-country support to deter migration, as was used in Haiti, Cuba, and Iraq. Following the Gulf War, U.N. Security Council Resolution 688 demanded that the Iraqi government establish a "safe area" for refugees in northern Iraq and that international relief agencies be granted safe access to administer aid. By administering aid within the sending country, refugee flows were contained, allowing receiving states to forward their humanitarian commitments without exposing themselves to societal insecurities that may result from large refugee flows. In contrast with refugee policy, because of the non-refoulement provisions in the Refugee Act of 1980 government policy has focused on deterring the arrival of potential asylum application. The United States already utilized a stringent interdiction policy when confronted with large-scale Haitian migration, but is now also considering emulating some European strategies. These include fast-track rejection of applicants arriving from designated "safe countries," detention of asylum seekers pending adjudication of their claims, and granting only temporary protected status.[62]

SECURING THE SOUTHERN BORDER

Other policies developed in response to rising societal insecurities focused on increased control of America's southern border with Mexico. In the president's 1994 report to Congress, the Clinton administration declared, "The Administration inherited serious illegal immigration problems, including 3.5 million illegal aliens residing in the country, uncontrolled movement across the Southwest border, alien smuggling, asylum abuse, and State and local concerns about fiscal impact."[63] Illegal immigration had increasingly raised societal insecurities, especially in states receiving disproportionate numbers of illegal aliens, such as California. Because interior enforcement mechanisms such as employer sanctions were politically problematic for

NATIONAL SECURITY AND IMMIGRATION IN THE U.S. **71**

policymakers hesitant to place the burden of immigration control on domestic employers, policies to combat illegal immigration focused instead on border enforcement. Indeed, the U.S. Commission on Immigration Reform, established through the provisions of the 1990 Immigration Act, suggested that "restoring credibility" to U.S. immigration policy relied largely on border control.[64] What emerged was touted as a policy based on "prevention through deterrence."[65]

The first of a series of border deterrence programs was initiated in September 1993 along the U.S.-Mexico border at El Paso, Texas. Originally titled Operation Blockade, it was later renamed Operation Hold-the-Line in order to stem criticism that the term "blockade" seemed overly harsh and anti-Mexican. The program employed a strong deterrent tactic rather than placing its emphasis on apprehensions. The Border Patrol tripled the number of agents (450) and implemented an around-the-clock watch over a twenty-mile section of the border separating El Paso, Texas, from Ciudad Juarez, Mexico. The program depended on a highly visible line of defense to deter potential border crossers. Operation Hold-the-Line showed initial success in stemming illegal immigration by reducing apprehensions 76 percent in its first year of operation.[66] The program's prominent visibility, coupled with declining numbers of illegal aliens in the El Paso area, served to generate strong public support in the area.[67] Impressed with the initial success of Operation Hold-the-Line, the Commission on Immigration Reform recommended that a similar approach be utilized to establish a comprehensive, borderwide strategy to prevent illegal immigration.

Clearly, the most viable candidate for the new border program was at the San Ysidro port of entry in San Diego, the busiest land border crossing in the world. According to INS statistics, approximately 25 percent of all apprehensions along the two-thousand-mile U.S.-Mexico border occurred in Imperial Beach, a five-mile stretch between the Pacific Ocean and the San Ysidro port of entry.[68] What emerged was Operation Gatekeeper, the most ambitious border control program established to date. Although Operation Gatekeeper employed a similar "visible deterrence" strategy to that utilized by Operation Hold-the-Line, the tactical deployment of resources was noticeably different. Rather than a single line of defense, Gatekeeper employed a multilayered approach dividing resources into several sections. A fourteen-mile stretch of the border was reinforced with a twelve-foot steel fence, followed by a highly lit zone (using stadium lighting) occupied by increased patrols using advanced technology, including night-vision equipment. Rather than deploying agents in a single line, the twenty-four hour watch was divided into three lines, deployed one-half mile apart. This multilayered approach provided both a deterrent dimension (high visibility) and an apprehensions dimension (increasing the likelihood of apprehension should a migrant succeed in circumventing the initial line of defense).

Public officials were quick to laud the success of Operation Gatekeeper. In its first full year of operation, apprehensions in the San Diego sector increased from 450,152 in 1994 to 524,231 in 1995. Moreover, as anticipated by INS strategists, the rise in apprehensions was followed by a steady decline, which they attributed to the deterrent effect of the program. From 1995 to 1998, apprehensions in the San Diego sector dropped continually from 524,231 to 248,092 (Table 3.7). Support for the program increased among policymakers, and subsequent migration legislation allocated additional funding for border-enforcement programs such as Gatekeeper. In addition to establishing strict restriction on public benefits for aliens, the Illegal Immigration Reform and Immigrant Responsibility Act of 1996 (IIRAIRA) provided funding for increased border personnel, equipment, and technology. Between 1993 and 1999, the annual budget allocated to the INS rose from $1.5 to $4.2 billion, with much of the funding directed toward border enforcement. The annual budget for the Border Patrol rose from $354 million in 1993 to $877 million in 1998. IIRAIRA called for one thousand additional Border Patrol agents to be hired annually and anticipated a force of ten thousand agents by 2001. Between 1993 and 1999, the number of agents deployed in the Southwest border sector more than doubled, from 3,389 to approximately 8,200. The political popularity of Gatekeeper-style programs is evidenced by its propagation. In 1995, Operation Safeguard was established in Nogales, Arizona; in 1996, Operation Gatekeeper was expanded to cover the entire San Diego sector, covering some sixty-six miles; in 1997, Operation Hold-the-Line was expanded into New Mexico; and in 1997, Operation Rio Grande was established along thirty-one miles of the Rio Grande in East Texas.[69] Support for these programs among both policymakers and the general public have shown little sign of receding, though immigrant advocacy groups have expressed growing opposition.

TABLE 3.7
Deportable aliens apprehended by border patrol, by sector, 1992–1998

Year	San Diego, CA	El Centro, CA	Yuma, AZ	Tucson, AZ
1992	565,581	29,852	24,892	71,036
1993	531,689	30,058	23,548	92,639
1994	450,152	27,654	21,211	139,473
1995	524,231	37,317	20,894	227,529
1996	483,815	66,873	28,310	305,348
1997	283,889	146,210	30,177	272,397
1998	248,092	226,695	76,195	387,406

SOURCE: INS, *Statistical Yearbook* (1998), 209.

Considerable evidence suggests, however, that these programs have done little to stop illegal immigration. A closer look at examination patterns and immigrant recidivism can be seen to paint a remarkably different picture than that presented by the INS. Although apprehensions in the Gatekeeper zone dropped significantly in FY 1994–95, they immediately rose in the rural areas east of the zone secured by Operation Gatekeeper, suggesting that migrants were simply adjusting their migration strategies. As documented in Table 3.7, apprehensions in zones east of San Diego rose dramatically from 1994–98: In the El Centro sector, apprehensions rose from 27,654 to 226,695; in the Yuma, Arizona, sector, apprehensions rose from 21,211 to 76,195; in the Tucson, Arizona, sector, apprehensions rose from 139,473 to 387,406. The large increase of illegal immigration in these more rural areas resulted in rising threat perceptions in these communities and occasionally has resulted in local police or vigilante responses.

Another element obfuscated by apprehension statistics is the recidivism of those apprehended by the Border Patrol. Because of administrative and detention costs, and the fact that the U.S. court system has proven unable to keep up with the large increase in drug and immigration cases since the inception of the Southwest Border Control program was instigated, the INS and the Border Patrol have made liberal use of voluntary departure procedures when dealing with apprehended migrants.[70] Under the provisions of the INS's voluntary departure procedure, illegal aliens apprehended by the Border Patrol are allowed to return to Mexico without penalty. In 1998, the number of aliens that accepted an offer to voluntarily depart was 1,569,817, while only 172,547 were formally removed with penalties.[71] Although de jure penalties exist for illegal aliens apprehended crossing the border on several

TABLE 3.8
Aggregate border patrol apprehensions, 1992–1998

Year	Border Patrol Apprehensions	Aliens Apprehended Utilizing Smugglers
1992	1,199,560	69,538
1993	1,263,490	80,835
1994	1,031,668	92,934
1995	1,324,202	102,591
1996	1,549,876	122,233
1997	1,412,953	124,605
1998	1,555,776	174,514

SOURCE: INS, *Statistical Yearbook* (1998), 209–10.

occasions, the INS does not currently have an information system that catalogs most of those apprehended. Because there is little cost in being apprehended, little deterrence exists for multiple crossing attempts.[72] The effect this can have on the success rate of border crossers is staggering. Estimates suggest that the probability of apprehension in 1997 ranged from 15 to 30 percent.[73] Given a 30 percent probability of apprehension, 910 out of 1,000 migrants would be able to successfully navigate the border after the second attempt. By the fourth attempt, this number reaches a staggering 992. Even given a 70 percent probability of apprehension, 51 percent will succeed after the second attempt. By the fourth attempt, 76 percent will have succeeded in gaining entry.[74]

The most telling statistics may be overall apprehensions and the estimated annual growth in the number of illegal immigrants. Although concentrated border-enforcement programs have reduced migration in these zones to a trickle, apprehensions in other areas have risen sharply. In aggregate, Border Patrol apprehensions have increased: 1,199,560 in 1992; and 1,555,776 in 1998 (Table 3.8). Moreover, aggregate statistics reveal that the use of smugglers has risen dramatically, making it more likely that migrants will be successful in circumventing the reinforced zones of the border.[75] INS estimates of the size of the illegal immigrant population in the United States suggest that they numbered some 5 million in 1996, with a range from 4.6 to 5.4 million. These same estimates suggest that Mexican migrants represent 54 percent of the total undocumented population. Moreover, the INS estimates that the undocumented population is growing by approximately 275,000 per annum, only 25,000 lower than estimates in 1994. As Wayne Cornelius surmised, "It is clear that concentrating border enforcement resources in [the] most heavily used illegal immigration corridors has failed to stem the tide."[76]

THE POLITICAL APPEAL OF OPERATION GATEKEEPER

At first glance, U.S. border policy in the 1990s may seem nonsensical. It redirects illegal immigration flows rather than stops them and does not enforce the existing employer sanctions laws with sufficient vigor to reduce the "pull" on Mexican migration.[77] Claudia Smith, attorney for California Rural Legal Assistance, cast a critical eye at the much touted success of Operation Gatekeeper: "What has Gatekeeper accomplished other than getting illegal border crossers out of the public eye?"[78] In fact, the current border control strategy has accomplished a great deal, in political terms, on both micro- and macro levels. Peter Andreas writes, "Judged purely on its instrumental deterrent effect . . . the current border control strategy's political popularity seems puzzling. But a failing policy can still success politically."[79] The perception of threat generated by illegal immigration is directly related to its visibility and geographic concentration. The *San Diego Union Tribune* and other media outlets noted that prior to the implementation of Operation Gatekeeper, "illegal immigrants would simply run through the checkpoints in packs."[80] The well-publicized video images of mass "border dashes" through the San Ysidro port of entry provided a vivid image of a complete lack of state control over the border and a complete disregard for American sovereignty over admission to its territory.[81] Meanwhile, visa overstayers, who represent between 40 and 50 percent of the illegal immigrant population in the United States, are essentially "invisible" to the general public and have yet to stir public anxieties in the same manner as mass border rushes or refugee flotillas on the high seas. Moreover, aggressively enforcing employer sanctions would certainly be viewed as government interference in the workings of business; existing safeguards to prevent government "harassment" made such an approach unappealing to both the INS and policymakers.

The border control strategy represents a simple, highly visible program that projects an image of government action and enables officials to substantiate success regardless of changes in apprehension levels. If apprehensions rise, as they did during the first days of Operation Gatekeeper, officials suggested that the increased manpower and multilayered approach was more effective in apprehending those who attempt entry. If apprehensions decline, as they did in the San Diego sector in the years following Gatekeeper's implementation, it was argued that the "deterrent" value of the program was taking hold. News stories that were once replete with images of hordes massing along the fence waiting for nightfall in order to begin attempting to cross, were replaced by stories about the tranquility of the Imperial Beach section of the border. In fact, in 2000, reports began to surface that things had slowed to such a degree in the Gatekeeper zone that Border Patrol morale was declining due to agent boredom and the agency was having difficulty filling employment vacancies for line officers. If the political goal was to respond to cries for control, Operation Gatekeeper and others like it represent a distinct "win-win" situation for policymakers.

On a wider scale, the use of such highly symbolic policy does in fact promote the instrumental objectives of the state. During the 1990s, U.S. emphasis on liberal trade as a fundamental aspect of the economic dimension of grand strategy manifest itself in the process of regional integration, perfected with the creation of NAFTA in 1994. However, while the economic dimension of grand strategy is predicated on a vision of the border as one of connection, the societal dimension emphasizes its role in separating political and social entities. Economists have long maintained that economic integration may begin a process of industrialization that mitigates wage disparities between nations that may quell migration pressures in the long run.[82] This has been consistent with those who suggest that controlling immigration, and illegal immigration in particular, must address the "root causes" of migration, including economic disparity and political conditions in sending nations.[83] However, as noted by economist Philip Martin, trade and industrialization may in fact increase migration pressures in the short- to medium-run time frame.[84] Wayne Cornelius adds:

> In short, the trade-and-investment approach can be considered a realistic option only if U.S. populations and the general public are prepared to accept the lack of short-term payoff—or even a temporary increase in unauthorized emigration, resulting from economic dislocations—in return for a reversal of the trend toward higher illegal immigration at some later point. But there is no evidence that either U.S. political leaders or their constituents are willing to wait that long for effective control of illegal immigration.[85]

Although U.S. border policy has not closed the door on illegal immigration, it has been successful in dispersing these flows along the border—essentially making them "disappear" even as aggregate volume remains relatively constant. Peter Andreas notes that U.S. border policy has been "strikingly successful in terms of constructing the appearance of a more secure and orderly border."[86] By reducing societal insecurities—even if only on a symbolic or superficial level—the Gatekeeper approach serves to buy policymakers time in allowing regional economic restructuring to alter the structural environment that generates migration pressures from Mexico. Moreover, and perhaps more importantly, the construction of an image of control regarding migration can be seen as the "price of the ticket" for U.S. support of NAFTA.[87] Again, constructing the image—if not the reality—of rigid control enabled U.S. policymakers to pursue a grand strategy of economic liberalism and regional economic integration, while concurrently ameliorating societal insecurities stemming from illegal immigration along the southern border.

Lastly, a similar trade-off can be seen when one considers the social price of continued liberal immigration and refugee policy. American identity has two opposing dimensions—one civic, the other ethno-cultural. In much the same way that pursuing the economic dimension of its grand strategy required control over illegal immigration, Peter Schuck argues, "The master theme of immigration politics is the fear that we are losing control of our way of life."[88] From this, he suggests that a primary goal of immigration policy is "to create a symbol and perception of commitment to controlling membership within the society." Thus, the "price" of keeping the front door open to immigration is to close the backdoor, a policy proposal first articulated in the recommendations of the Select Commission for Immigration and Refugee Policy. However, closing the backdoor would require a higher degree of state intrusion into the lives and businesses of its citizenry. Public opinion analysts point out, "Overall, there seems to be a policy tradeoff between measures that are effective and those that will receive broad approval. Many measures that might be expected to cut rather deeply into illegal immigration are seen by the American public as too harsh and are not supported."[89] It would seem that the government's use of symbolic policy serves the function of "finessing" these contradictions, and forwards the grand strategy of the nation, even though it might not maximize its constitutive (and often contradictory) parts.

National Security and Migration After 9/11

If the migration policy during the 1990s represented a delicate balance between economic and societal dimensions of national security, the events of
September 11, 2001, would seem to threaten the existing grand strategy.
Public perceptions of threat that linked the events of September 11 to the issue of migration were manifest rapidly. In a Fox News poll taken in November 2001, 65 percent of respondents supported a complete halt to *all immigration* into the country.[90] The actions of policymakers reflect similar
convictions that immigration had become too risky. Prior to September 2001, Mexico and the United States were engaging in bilateral discussions regarding a new temporary-worker program and a possible amnesty
for undocumented workers. These discussions were tabled immediately
and indefinitely in the aftermath of the terrorist attacks, much to the dismay
of Mexican president Vicente Fox who had invested considerable political
capital in reaching agreements with the U.S. on these issues.

In its most fundamental sense, 9/11 has recast the way we think about
"military" or "geopolitical" aspects of security. Conflict is no longer limited
to engagement between national armies fought along lines of defense.
Rather, global terrorism represents a new type of threat makes it more difficult to separate "external" from "internal" security dimensions. The fact that
the 9/11 terrorists were foreign nationals that exploited existing U.S. immigration policies to infiltrate the country makes the connection between migration and this new security threat abundantly clear. Moreover, the real-
ization that migration is one of the primary means by which "sleeper cells"
are proliferated also makes migration control a security imperative if future
terrorist attacks are to be avoided. Prior to September 2001, security threats
related to migration were generally an issue of societal security that pressed
grand strategy toward more restrictive policy, while the linkage between
military and economic interests pushed policy toward a more open posture
in accordance with Ricardian economic principles. The post–9/11 environment would seem to have changed these relationships. Now, societal interests have converged with military interests, leaving the economic dimension
of the national interests the sole counterbalance to these pressures for closure. The grand strategy crafted during the 1990s was predicated on addressing societal fears of immigration by reducing the visibility of these

flows while allowing a generally liberal regime to continue. The post–9/11 environment would seem to preclude such an approach. In fact, during the 1990s foreign terrorists have exploited all channels of entry to infiltrate the United States. Of the forty-eight known foreign-born militant Islamic terrorists involved in plots within the United States from 1993–2001, 36 percent were naturalized citizens or legal permanent residents, 33 percent used temporary visas, 6 percent used asylum applications, and 25 percent illegally crossed the border in order to gain entry into the country.[91] In contrast to the 1990s, where "out of sight, out of mind" was the rule of the day in terms of addressing societal insecurities, what is threatening about the clandestine entry of alien terrorists and the presence of sleeper cells in the homeland is essentially their *invisibility*. They are a specter lurking in the shadows. Thus, security would seem to require policies that *increase* visibility rather than *decrease* it so that entry of potentially dangerous individuals can be prevented.

The first significant policy developments of the post–9/11 period were indeed more restrictive, including the USA Patriot Act (October 2001) and the Enhanced Border Security and Visa Entry Reform Act (EBSVERA) (May 2002).[92] The USA Patriot Act called for fortifying the country's northern border, increased law enforcement powers for surveillance and detention when dealing with suspected terrorists, and increased grounds for inadmissibility for entry to those involved with terrorist organizations by expanding the legal definition of "terrorist activities." Since the passage of the Patriot Act, Border Patrol deployment along the U.S.-Canada border has increased more than 250 percent. In addition, the act mandated the installation of a comprehensive Integrated Surveillance Intelligence System (ISIS) along U.S. land borders that includes magnetic, seismic, and infrared ground sensors as well as high-resolution infrared video cameras.[93] The Patriot Act also created a larger pool of those who are automatically inadmissible to the country by expanding the legal definition of "terrorist activities" to include material support for terrorists or terrorist organizations. Likewise, EBSVERA increased restrictions by stipulating an increase of three thousand immigration inspectors and investigators, calling for increased scrutiny of visa applications originating in countries suspected of supporting terrorism, and requiring U.S. universities to better account for foreign students attending their institution. Higher levels of security clearance are required for visa applicants who hold passports from countries designated as "state sponsors of terrorism" and/or are employed by those states. These include Cuba, Libya, Iran, Iraq, North Korea, Sudan, and Syria. In order to better monitor the presence and movement of foreign nationals studying at U.S. institutions of higher learning, the Student and Exchange Visitor Information System (SEVIS) was created. Beginning in January 2003, all U.S. universities were required to submit electronic files on the status of foreign students at their institution. EBSVERA also initiated the creation of a new National Security Entry-Exit Registration System (NSEERS) to monitor the entry of foreign nationals. This was initiated exactly one year after the September 11 attacks. Initially, the new program required male foreign visitors from "politically sensitive areas" who were over the age of sixteen to register with the INS. This was done according to a system that officials referred to as "prioritized special registration." Essentially, this meant that the ones who had to register were visitors from mostly Muslim and/or Arab nations.

The new United States Visitor and Immigrant Status Indicator Technology program (US-VISIT) has since replaced NSEERS.[94] Under US-VISIT, nonimmigrant visa-holders must submit a digitally scanned fingerprint and have a digital photo taken when they arrive in the country. Their name and fingerprints are then crosschecked with security databases before they are allowed to proceed. US-VISIT represents a significant expansion of NSEERS, in that it does not limit its scope to travelers from specific places of origin. However, it does have significant limitations—at least at this early stage of deployment. US-VISIT has not been implemented at land-border ports of entry and is limited to use only at major airports and seaports. Moreover, US-VISIT also does not monitor exits as of 2005. It is limited only to entry records, although Department of Homeland Security officials plan on incremental expansion.

Although more restrictive policy is logically expected after 9/11, homeland security interests do not wholly dominate migration policy as much as one might expect given the risks involved. Economic interests continue to serve as a powerful counterweight to the political interests that push for closure, as they did prior to 9/11, though they may have declined in *relative* importance after 9/11. The state remains committed to policies seeking to maximize economic gains through openness to highly skilled migration. Levels of L-1 visas remained unlimited and availability of H-1B remained high, though the sunset of the American Competitiveness for the 21st Century Act of 2000 returned quota levels for H-1Bs back to 65,000 per year beginning in October 2003. Given the slowdown in the IT sector after 2001, there was little incentive to maintain the 195,000 limit on H-1B visas. The unemployment rate in the IT sector increased from 2 to 6 percent from 2000 to 2003, and the size of the workforce declined from 6.5 million to 5.9 million. However, as the economy regained some momentum, policies again sought to maintain the supply of high skilled labor. In 2004 the L-1 Visa and H-1B Visa Reform Act again increased the number of H-1B visas by exempting up to 20,000 foreign workers holding master's degrees (or higher) from U.S. graduate schools from the existing quota limit.[95]

Openness to low-skilled immigration has been far more politically contentious. In 2000, immigrant advocacy groups vigorously lobbied Congress to pass the Latino and Immigrant Responsibility Act, which would have established an extended amnesty program for undocumented workers. However, policymakers were only willing to pass an extension of the H1-B program for highly skilled workers and defeated the proposed legislation. Several bills have been presented to Congress in the meantime, each proposing different ways of dealing with the issue of illegal immigrants and providing access to the U.S. economy for low-skilled workers. Most recently, a bipartisan bill authored by Senators John McCain (R-Arizona) and Ted Kennedy (D-Massachusetts) was presented to Congress in May 2005.[96] The bill proposed the creation of a new temporary guest-worker program and a process by which illegal aliens residing in the United States would be able to regularize their status. Each of the existing bills faces stiff opposition from conservatives who consider such moves a new amnesty program that rewards lawbreakers and would contribute to future undocumented flows. Representative Tom Tancredo (R-Colorado), for example, suggested that the bill is little more than a new amnesty program for illegal immigrants. He remarked, "There is a little more lipstick on this pig than there was before, but it's most certainly the same old pig."[97] Proponents, both domestic and foreign, have sought to shift the terms of the debate to include more security-oriented language. Indeed, the very title of the new McCain-Kennedy bill—the Secure America and Orderly Immigration Act of 2005—stress the proposal's utility to increase the nation's security. In their introduction of the bill, McCain and Kennedy stressed that the bill would contribute to security by providing secure legal channels for needed immigration flows that currently could be exploited by terrorists seeking to infiltrate the country. The bill would also require the use of fraud-proof documents that incorporate biometric identification indicators. McCain and Kennedy also suggested that the bill responded to economic security interests by providing needed manpower for an economy that has grown dependent on foreign labor.

How has 9/11 reshaped U.S. grand strategy in terms of policy? Instead of responding to the post–9/11 security environment by reducing exposure to international migration and dramatically curtailing the volume of immigration, policymakers have put the burden on the bureaucracy of immigration and border control to bridge the tension between economic interests for openness and societal/homeland-security interests pressing for increased closure. The challenge to bureaucratic agencies assigned the task of managing international migration is to create programs and procedures that can identify potentially threatening individuals, interdict and apprehend them prior to entering U.S. territory or airspace, and either deport or incarcerate them before they are able to succeed in inflicting damage to persons or property. This is to be done without unnecessarily interfering with the legitimate movement of persons across borders—a feat that has no historical precedent.

Conclusion

Liberal interest-group models of the politics of migration policy in the United States argue that "migration policies are generally determined bureaucratically by economic interest groups (employers and workers) who interact with public officials outside the public eye, yielding a 'client politics of policy formulation.'"[98] Given that U.S. migration policy has remained largely open toward immigration and immigrant labor greatly benefits U.S. business interests, it is easy to see the appeal of interest-group analyses. However, upon closer inspection (and placed in a wider context), U.S. policy rarely has shown clear and consistent preference for the interests of one group of societal actors over another. Moreover, if a client-politics of business interests do indeed dominate in the United States, then one would expect the following: (1) an even higher degree of openness to immigration, giving business interests a wider pool of labor on which to draw and weakening the bargaining position of workers; (2) policy that does not reflect racial or ethnic biases, since such criteria have no bearing on worker productivity; and (3) a visa preference system based on professional skills that is closely correlated with economic needs. An examination of U.S. migration policy in the twentieth century displays none of these features. Rather, the state can be seen as an active political player that works to balance domestic interests to forward a more expansive national interest through the construction of a grand strategy that maximizes on the whole rather than on constitutive parts.

Aristide Zolberg suggests, "Immigration evokes two very different sets of concerns: one pertaining to national identity and the composition of the political community, the other having to do with economic considerations."[99] How this is played out politically is considerably more complicated than it first appears. As empirical evidence has illustrated, American national identity as manifest in its laws pertaining to immigration and citizenship reveal two countervailing forces—one civic, one ethnic. Given these multiple traditions, we are faced with an important question: How can we explain variability in these national identity impulses? Why did the U.S. implement ethno-nationalist policy in 1924, abolish it for a more civic-oriented policy in 1965, and then adopt policy that reflected a return to concerns about demographic change in the 1990s? The national security paradigm provides an answer. Geopolitical structure not only affects the calculation of state interests but also can affect national identity. The presence of external enemies creates an Other that is conducive to national cohesiveness, whereas the absence of such an Other tends to foster perceptions of difference within societies. Internal "enemies" replace external enemies. Making this more complicated is that fact that social identities do not remain static, though at any given point they are generally treated as such by members of society.

In many ways the story of immigration and border policy development in the United States is about the evolution of American national identity. It is about breaking down the divide between what America aspires to be and what it has been in practice. Immigration policy reflects a continual process toward a true civic identity, one reflecting its aspirations of e pluribus unum. However, this is not necessarily an easily traveled path, as our experience with immigration reveals. Racism and ethnic preferences remain central issues for many in society. Yet, once gains have been made toward more liberal, civic-minded policies, they generally do not revert back to prior policy when sociopolitical conditions change. It is important to note that rising societal insecurities evident since the 1970s have not produced a return to the national origins quota system. Although mainstream citizens may express concerns about migration levels and trends, turning back the clock to an America based on race is simply no longer an option. Instead, pressures for increased restrictions over migration have focused for the most part on retaining sovereignty over the channels of entry and the conditions for inclusion.[100] This is a common thread that unites civic-minded and ethnic-minded members of society.

Illegal immigration threatens a society's sovereignty to control access to the territory and to the polity. Sociologist Douglas Massey notes that "policies in the United States have been largely symbolic, signaling to angry or fearful citizens and workers that their concerns are being addressed while marginalizing immigrants socially and geographically to make them less visible to the public."[101] He adds, "Repressive policies such a vigorous border enforcement, the bureaucratic harassment of aliens, and the restriction of immigrants' access to social services may or may not be effective, but they all serve an important political purpose: they are visible, concrete, and generally popular with citizen voters."[102] From the standpoint of grand strategy, the use of symbolic policies during the 1990s enabled the state to pursue liberal economic integration while keeping domestic anxieties about open borders in check. Border policing has been successful not because it has been able to halt migration flows, but rather because it addressed calls for increased restrictions without significantly curtailing the availability of needed foreign labor.

The events of September 11 have made accomplishing this delicate political balance much more difficult. However, the fundamental political logic of migration and border control is largely unchanged: policy is crafted to *balance* national economic interests with security interests. What *has* changed is the nature of the security interest and the policy options available to policymakers given this change. Prior to 9/11, security interests pertaining to migration were defined in largely social terms—of an "alien invasion" of illegal immigrants flouting U.S. law and significantly altering the ethnic demographics in high-immigration regions. Because this security threat was largely perceptual (and entirely political), policymakers were able to respond to perceptions of public threat through the use of largely symbolic policy, enabling them to maintain a system of both de jure and de facto openness toward migration flows. By focusing on highly symbolic border policies (such as Operation Gatekeeper) while ignoring the large number of "out-of-status" migrants, perceptions of threat were mitigated by creating an environment where "out of sight was out of mind," at least politically. After 9/11, however, security interests primarily are defined in terms of global terrorism. If "out of sight, out of mind" was the rule regarding illegal immigrants prior to 9/11, this is certainly not the case anymore. In fact, the situation is quite the opposite. What this means in terms of policy is that it is not sufficient to simply make illegal immigrants "disappear" through the use of border policies that disperse flows geographically. Instead, policymakers are faced with two options: reduce migration flows altogether, or create improved means of screening and monitoring all those who enter the country. The first option would exact a prohibitive cost to the economy and the American national identity as a country of immigrants. Clearly, policymakers have opted for the latter. This desire for an unprecedented level of intelligence and control mechanisms, however, presents tremendous logistical challenges. The empirical evidence shows a tremendous effort to provide such mechanisms, but we remain far from having effective institutions, policies, procedures, and mechanisms in place that achieve the desired balance between openness and security. If successful—in other words, absent another major terrorist attack on U.S. soil in the short-term time frame—post–9/11 migration and border policies will likely look much like those the preceded them in the 1990s. If the United States is able to avoid another attack, policy restrictivism will likely taper off as perceptions of threat de-escalate in the coming years. In that scenario, the appearance of security may suffice to address fears and allow policy to remain largely open. However, should another major terrorist event occur, the ability of the United States to maintain policies of openness will be jeopardized.

CHAPTER FOUR

National Security and Immigration in Germany

I do not hesitate to assert that, like the reform of nationality legislation, this immigration law constitutes a historic watershed. It marks another step for Germany towards being a modern, democratic state with a tolerant society within a united Europe.

—OTTO SCHILY, Interior Minister, address to the Bundestag, July 1, 2004

Germans have a certain joy about cultural plurality, but then there's this other intriguing thing. . . . To learn tolerance is difficult.

—AXEL HONNETH, Goethe University, quoted in the *Los Angeles Times*, July 13, 2003

In explaining the determinants of immigration and citizenship policies in modern Germany, Rogers Brubaker emphasizes the centrality of social identity, differentiating the policy effects of German ethno-nationalism from the civic nationalism evident in other Western countries, including France.[1] He notes that the "prepolitical German nation, this nation in search of a state, was conceived not as the bearer of universal political values, but as an organic cultural, linguistic, or racial community—as an irreducibly particular *Volksgemeinschaft*."[2] This ethnic conception of the nation delineates "insider" from "outsider" in stark relief based on kinship ties and manifests itself in a citizenship regime based on the principle of jus sanguinis.[3] In social terms, this means that one cannot simply "become German" and that such an identity is immutable and enduring. Ironically, this notion of German nationalism does not have origins in ancient antiquity, as Nazi propaganda professed, but rather, in the nineteenth-century realpolitik of Otto von Bismarck. However, once a part of the social consciousness, such ethno-nationalism has proven to be an enduring legacy. Indeed, Brubaker suggests that even though this racialization of German identity fostered under the Nazis resulted in heinous barbarism levied against social "outsiders" including Jews, homosexuals, and Gypsies, the demise of the regime that "perfected" it did not bring about a concomitant demise in this fundamental basis of German national identity: "The collapse of the Third Reich and the discrediting of *volkisch* ideology might have been expected to discredit German self-understanding as an ethno-cultural nation. . . . Instead, the peculiar circumstances of the immediate postwar period—the total collapse of the state, the massive expulsion of ethnic Germans from eastern Europe and the Soviet Union, and the imposed division of Germany—reinforced and powerfully legitimated that self understanding."[4]

Given the highly exclusionary basis of German identity, one should expect that population transfers would be highly threatening to German perceptions of societal security and that state immigration and border policies would remain highly restrictive. Indeed, the fact that the phrase *Wir sind kein Einwanderungsland* (We are not a country of immigration) has remained a leitmotiv of German conservatism for more than a quarter century provides support for just such a conclusion. In considering the empirical evidence from postwar Germany, numerous questions emerge. Why would Germany maintain an open immigration regime for "ethnic Germans" during the mid- to late-1940s when unemployment and political instability threatened reconstruction, yet restrict such migration in the 1990s? If ethnicity is the sole determinant of policy, why would German policymakers establish the most liberal asylum / refugee policy in all of Europe, even though this could result in a potentially unlimited inflow of people from an array of sources? Why did German policy first aggressively recruit foreign labor only to reverse course beginning in the 1970s, even though it is widely acknowledged that immigration played a key role in German reconstruction and the economic *Wirtschaftswunder* that vaulted Germany to the status of a major economic world power? Lastly, if the immigration of ethnic Germans is not a threat to societal security, why were restrictions established in the 1990s? Such lingering questions suggest that immigration and border policies in Germany cannot be explained solely in terms of national identity or business cycles. Instead, the empirical evidence reveals an evolving security agenda with implications for immigration and border policy.

The German case is instructive for several reasons. First, it supports the notion that when external security is threatened—as it was in Germany during the postwar occupation and the rising threat of Soviet belligerence—societal security interests remain subordinate to geopolitics. However, as geopolitical threats diminish national security interests became increasingly complex, characterized by a rising tension between external and international security priorities. In this process, intervening variables play a large role in shaping the equilibrium between economic and societal security dimensions. Ideas and perceptions have a significant impact on how security is defined and on the resultant political process that culminates in grand strategy. Although the Gastarbeiter program seemed to offer a panacea to Germany's postwar labor needs, hindsight reveals that such notions were based on false presumptions and revealed the sociopolitical problems associated with such "temporary" migration regimes. Lastly, the case of Germany reveals the difficulty of maintaining a stable equilibrium and a grand strategy that maximizes both economic and societal interests, in part because identity is contested and is a dynamic social construction, even in a polity with a strong tradition of ethno-cultural nationalism.

Geopolitics in Postwar Germany

Germany faced one of the most daunting security challenges in Europe following World War II. Its infrastructure endured years of allied bombing, and immense casualties during the war decimated the native population. It was a nation occupied by foreign armies, divided into American, British, French and Soviet zones. Western Allied nations found themselves at odds with the increasingly uncooperative Soviets and were troubled by, among other things, Joseph Stalin's 1946 remarks that "war was inevitable as long as capitalism existed."[5] Winston Churchill succinctly characterized this Western perception of threat in his "Iron Curtain" speech in 1946 at Fulton, Missouri.[6] Germany would find itself on the front line of the emerging cold war. However, in these initial post–WWII years the security threat was centered less on a looming possibility of a Soviet military invasion of Western Europe than on the potential for economic weakness to serve as a fertile breeding ground for domestic discontent and increased the domestic political influence of Communist parties.[7] Widespread poverty and hunger exacerbated by the severe winter of 1946 increased the perception of threat.

Given this security environment, what types of state response should be anticipated? In general, grand strategy should be sharply skewed toward the military and economic dimensions, with lower levels of emphasis on societal security interests. Because of Germany's condition as a defeated power in World War II, militarization was not an option for addressing defense interests—at least in the late 1940s. Instead, policy emphasis forwarding this interest should focus on alliance formation. Economic aspects of grand strategy should also forward the general goal of establishing a system of collective security, in addition to speeding the postwar economic reconstruction and recovery. In terms of societal security, social commonality should receive higher relative emphasis than social difference, as common interest is fostered by common threats. In terms of migration and border policies, these should favor policies of increasing openness and a lower relative preoccupation with societal security.

Forging an alliance structure that promoted both collective security and economic development proceeded along two parallel tracks. The first was directed at the Americans—the emergent postwar hegemon. Amid public sentiments in the United States that favored military demobilization, German policymakers had to convince the Americans that continued military and material support for Germany were vital to U.S. interests. Konrad Adenauer appealed to a sense of common identity—of a common "Western civilization" that linked Europe and the United States—in his efforts to gain needed American support to rebuild Germany and thwart Communism.[8] Although neither France nor the Soviet Union favored rebuilding Germany after WWII, the Americans were keen to avoid the mistakes of Versailles and to contain the spread of Communism in Europe. In his January 1948 testimony before Congress, U.S. Secretary of State George Marshall argued that widespread economic aid to Germany and Europe was imperative not only to avoid economic distress, social discontent, and political suffering, but also to thwart "a new form . . . of tyranny that we fought to destroy in Germany."[9]

Germany succeeded in garnering U.S. support—primarily in the form of direct financial assistance through the Marshall Plan in 1948. Further development of the alliance, as well as a system of collective security, followed the Soviet blockade of Berlin (June 1948) with the creation of the North Atlantic Treaty Organization (NATO) in April 1949. Although Germany was not part of the initial NATO alliance and did not join until 1954 (becoming a full member in May 1955), the North Atlantic Council affirmed a decision in principle to allow German rearmament (and potential inclusion in NATO) as early as 1950. Germany's place on the front line of the cold war ensured its eventual inclusion.[10]

The second facet of Germany's grand strategy of alliance formation took the form of regional integration within Western Europe. Konrad Adenauer and the CDU/CSU coalition government supported free-market economics and considered engagement and integration as the best mechanism to pool scarce resources and facilitate their allocation where they could receive the highest output and return. Moreover, increasing the process of integration beyond the creation of a free-trade zone was seen as a means to alleviate the sociopolitical tensions that had created a long history of intra-European conflict, including World War II. To this end, Germany and France initiated a program of integration that began with the establishment of the European Coal and Steel Community (ECSC) in 1951 that later led to the signing of the more comprehensive Treaty of Rome in 1957. The process of integration was a direct function of the security dilemma faced by European nations, especially those on the continent. Ceding sovereignty enabled insecure Western European states to pool their economic resources—both capital and labor—in order to maximize the reconstruction effort and reduce internal weaknesses that may lead to Communist uprisings. Initially, openness was focused on the movement of goods, as the ECSC contributed to a 23 percent increase in coal production and a 150 percent increase in the production of iron and steel.[11]

If alliance formation along these lines was a priority for postwar German grand strategy, then the question facing policymakers was, what was necessary to establish and strengthen such essential relationships? As it turns out, migration policies played an important role in forwarding such a grand strategy, as well as in the reconstruction of the German economy.

MIGRATION AND GERMAN GRAND STRATEGY

The key in establishing new alliances for Germany centered on distancing itself from its identity as World War II adversary and refashioning itself as a western ally. Politically, this involved reconstituting social identities that stressed commonality with desired allies, and conversely, differentiating the "new Germany" from Nazi Germany. Ulrich Herbert remarked, "People in the Federal Republic were interested in dissociating and distancing themselves from the past—yet without making mention of those years openly or even trying to deal with the Nazi era in critical terms. The fiction of a new beginning unencumbered by any past conditions—a kind of *tabula rasa* in policy toward foreigners as well—made it possible to evoke such friendship between nations, quite ingenuously and untroubled by inhibitions."[12] The question facing policymakers at the time was how exactly to do this beyond simple political rhetoric. As was the case in the United States, policy regarding the treatment of refugees and asylum seekers would prove instrumental in forwarding important normative aspects of early cold war foreign policy.

To do this, augmenting German national identity became a key component of foreign policy. In order to establish itself as an "enlightened" liberal nation of civil rights and social tolerance (intended to both address internal insecurities about its own past, and to forge bonds with other Western nations who were now important cold war allies), policymakers engaged in an active program of "reimagining" the political community to distance itself from its virulent ethno-nationalist past. A more civic German nationalism was codified in German law, as were liberal principles of rights and governance. These included an extremely liberal asylum regime included in the *Grundgesetz*. Article 16 of the post–WWII German Constitution clearly stated that all politically persecuted people have a right to asylum in Germany. The constitutional proviso protecting all potential asylum seekers is unique in international law and can be seen as a postwar reaction to Nazi-era persecution and nationalism.[13] Desires to incorporate liberal norms into German identity also drove policy regarding family reunification provisions afforded to immigrants, as policymakers considered the promotion of family reunification as a humanitarian gesture.[14] However, the extension of family reunification rights was not solely a humanitarian consideration; it was also motivated by the competition for foreign workers with other European nations.[15] While extension of rights of family reunification made the German employment offer increasingly attractive to potential migrants, in the long run this policy served to generate much of the social tension that would drive migration policy in the 1970s and beyond, as these provisions ultimately contributed to a considerable increase in the Turkish migrant population.[16]

Another concrete gesture that Germany was charting a new, liberal course in terms of national identity involved reestablishing German citizenship for Jews and others stripped of their citizenship during the Nazi era through the Nuremberg Laws. Article 116 (2) states, "Former German citizens who between January 30, 1933, and May 8, 1945, were deprived of their citizenship on political, racial, or religious grounds, and their descendants, shall on application have their citizenship restored. They shall be deemed never to have been deprived of their citizenship if they have established their domicile in Germany after May 8, 1945 and have not expressed a contrary intention."[17] The article represents a direct rejection of Nazi intolerance and persecution that is both functional, in terms of policy, and highly symbolic as a defining element of the "new Germany."

These elements of the postwar *Grundgesetz* had other security implications in addition to their symbolic use for "reimagining" a postwar Germany that stressed cultural commonality with its fledgling Western allies. Germany also faced a threat to internal stability from the wave of postwar refugees streaming into the country from the East. By 1950, some twelve million refugees and expellees (*Vertriebene*) had entered Germany.[18] Two-thirds of these refugees settled in West Germany, where they constituted one-sixth of the population.[19] These continued throughout the 1950s, where migration from the DDR to the Bundesrepublik continued at a rate of roughly 210,000 per year until the creation of the Berlin Wall (Figure 4.1). During these early postwar years the German economy was plagued by massive unemployment, and wartime bombing of residential areas in many cities made living conditions difficult. Conditions were so challenging that public opinion polls showed that up to half of the population in postwar Germany desired to emigrate in search of economic opportunity and better living conditions.[20] Given the structural conditions in Germany at the time, one might expect heightened competition between natives and migrants over scarce jobs and resources. In other words, tremendous pressures existed for Germans to make sharper differentiations between "domestic" Germans and "foreign" Germans. Failure of societal insecurities to materialize and generate pressures for restrictive policies has generally been explained by noting that much of this migration stream consisted of ethnic Germans (*Volksdeutsche*).[21] However, such an explanation encounters difficulty in explaining restrictions placed on ethnic German migration in the early 1990s.

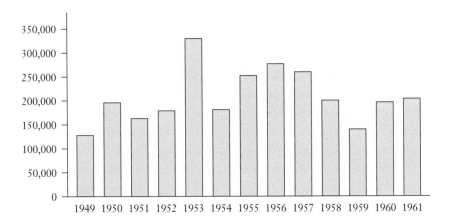

Figure 4.1. Migration from the DDR to the Federal Republic of Germany, 1949–1961
SOURCE: Adapted from Albert O. Hirschman, "Exit, Voice, and the Fate of the German Democratic Republic," *World Politics* 45, no. 2 (1993): 179.

The Threat Hypothesis and Rally Hypothesis provide an answer that accounts for such variation. External threats and the need to strengthen alliances with the U.S. and Western Europe shaped the direction of grand strategy (and resultant policies), while the rally-effect created conditions where internal differences were mitigated rather than accentuated.

First of all, restricting the entry of refugees and expellees would run counter to the "liberalization" of postwar German identity necessary to strengthen emergent alliances. Moreover, because refugee flows emanating from the Soviet bloc emerged as an important symbolic element of Truman Doctrine cold war politics, attempts to refuse or repatriate these people was politically unacceptable. Given these foreign-policy constraints, the only option was to facilitate their entry and to mitigate obstacles to integration. The *Grundgesetz* achieved this by affirming jus sanguinis German citizenship and by granting a right of return for German nationals living abroad. Article 116 (1) states, "Unless otherwise provided by a law, a German within the meaning of this Basic Law is a person who possesses German citizenship or who has been admitted to the territory of the German Reich within the boundaries of December 31, 1937 as a refugee or expellee of German ethnic origin or as the spouse or descendant of such person."[22] Defining German citizenry in the more inclusive sense also was part of a desire among German policymakers to affirm a commitment to reunification in the future. The by-product of this was that the *Völkisch* ideology of German national identity was reinforced, even while Adenauer and German policymakers attempted to reshape Germany toward a more liberal identity.[23]

If the political tension of grand strategy relevant to migration policies in the late 1940s was to find a balance between foreign-policy interests (open, expressing tolerance) and economic/domestic stability interests (closure), this changed dramatically in the 1950s and 1960s. The German recovery, and hence its national security, was increasingly a function of its ability to maintain an abundant supply of labor to stock its quickly growing industrial sector. Abundant labor enabled industry to expand economic output without raising wages. This kept inflation down while making German exports competitive in the world marketplace.[24] Although Germany incurred considerable wartime damage, its production potential was not completely obliterated by the war. Wartime destruction resulted in a 17 percent loss of productive capacity, but this must be taken in the context of the 75 percent increase in investment in industrial plants from 1936 to 1945.[25] Wartime economic expansion improved the quality of German industry in addition to its volume. Ulrich Herbert notes, "Perhaps even more important [than the number of plants] was the quality of these industrial plants. A large segment of the machinery was new; in 1945, 55 percent of total industrial plant capacity was no older than ten years. German industrial plant capacity had been not only appreciably expanded during the war but significantly improved in qualitative terms."[26] In fact, this wartime economic growth and the conscription of German manpower into the military effort made labor a scarce commodity for industry. In the first eight months of the war, some four million workers left the economy to serve in the military, and seven million more were drafted from May 31, 1940, to September 30, 1944.[27] Nazi policymakers addressed these manpower shortages by coercing foreign workers, prison camp inmates, and prisoners of war to fill production needs. By May 1944, the number of these workers in Germany was more than seven million and constituted more than 21 percent of the work force.[28] For German industry, the challenge in the postwar period was replacing this labor supply that was returning en masse to their home countries. It is not surprising that for German policymakers, migrants seemed ideal for meeting the manpower requirements of a rapidly growing economy. The skill levels of the initial refugee flows were generally high, so much so that Charles Kindleberger suggests, "The expellees and refugees constituted one of the finest sources of additional labor in all of Europe. They were skilled in much higher proportions than the unemployed, peasants, and foreign workers."[29]

With the help of Marshall Plan aid, West German economic productivity rose by an average of 6.7 percent annually from 1950 to 1960.[30] Although aggregate unemployment averaged 5.1 percent nationally in 1955, key industrial areas such as Baden-Württemberg and North Rhein-Westphalia enjoyed significantly lower levels of unemployment (2.2 and 2.9 percent, respectively).[31] In economically strong and healthy regions there was virtually full employment among most German workers, and unemployment among males in the Federal Republic averaged only 1.8 percent.[32] Stocks of Vertriebene immigrants served to fill much of the increasing demand for labor in the economy, but it soon became clear that consistent levels of high growth would generate labor shortages in the near future. Beginning in late 1952, the idea of foreign-labor recruitment entered German economic discourse, spurred in part by Italian requests to German policymakers to admit seasonal workers.[33] Germany's practice of forced labor and utilization of POWs in its factories during the war provided German managers with confidence in their ability to deal with a foreign workforce.[34] The German-Italian Agreement on Worker Recruitment was subsequently signed in Rome on December 22, 1955, and established Germany as an active importer of foreign labor.[35]

The Italian agreement was highly successful, in that the labor supply was well received by German employers. In fact, two-thirds of the Italian workers hired by German employers through the guest-worker program were asked to return.[36] However, at no point did Germany consider its bilateral arrangement as a means to facilitate permanent immigration; rather, it was seen as a tool for managing a highly elastic source of labor—one based on an assumption of temporariness and circularity (rotation): government officials suggested, both publicly and privately, that the recruitment of foreign labor was intended as a temporary measure to address an acute economic need at a time when few alternatives were available.[37] Under the terms of the agreement, Germany would select workers for recruitment based on manpower needs of German industry, to be facilitated by the Bundesanstalt für Arbeit (Federal Institute of Labor) in Nuremberg. When the foreign workers were no longer needed by the German economy, policymakers argued that they could simply be returned home. John Bendix points out, "Permanent jobs were meant for natives, seasonal and temporary jobs were where foreigners could boost the native economy. In the event of a recession, foreigners could be sacrificed to save German jobs."[38]

Labor Supply and Economic Growth

During the late 1950s, unemployment dropped sharply, as did labor flows into West Germany, causing spiked demands from German industry for additional government action in meeting the manpower requirements necessary to continue the rapid pace of economic growth (Table 4.1). As unemployment levels in Germany dropped from 539,000 in 1959 to 180,000 in 1961, the gross national product increased by 21.7 percent, from DM 283.8 billion in 1959 to DM 346.2 billion in 1961. The German need for labor, coupled with widespread beliefs in the success of the bilateral agreement with Italy, prompted policymakers to expand the existing Gastarbeiter program.[39] Bilateral agreements for labor recruitment were reached with Spain and Greece in 1960. These agreements represent a considerable turning point because, unlike Italy, Spain and Greece were not EC member nations at the time and thus were not part of the "frontier free" European space. The cessation of East-West migration from the German Democratic Republic (DDR) resulting from the construction of the Berlin Wall in 1961 placed further strains on the labor market and prompted business leaders to call for further extension of the guest worker program. Considering that *Ostvertriebene* migration from the DDR averaged some 210,000 per annum in the period from 1949 to 1961, the stoppage of this labor pool was a significant shock to Germany's already thin labor market after 1961.[40]

The Gastarbeiter program continued to expand with subsequent labor agreements with Turkey (October 30, 1961), Portugal (March 17, 1964), and Yugoslavia (October 12, 1968), all patterned on the original bilateral arrangement made with Italy.[41] After signing the series of bilateral agreements, some four hundred employment recruitment offices were established in participating countries in order to process German requests for foreign labor.[42] High levels of unemployment and low relative wages in migrant-sending countries

TABLE 4.1

Economy and labor market in the Federal Republic of Germany, 1959—1967

	1959	1961	1963	1965	1967
GNP (billions DM)	283.8	346.2	372.5	419.5	430.8
Total employed (in millions)	26.4	26.8	27.0	27.1	26.6
Germans employed (in thousands)	26,253	+61	−71	−269	−588
Foreign employed (in thousands)	166	507	822	1,164	1,023
Foreign employed as % of total employed	0.8	2.3	3.6	5.5	4.9
Unemployed (in thousands)	539	180	185	147	459

SOURCE: Ulrich Herbert, A *History of Foreign Labor in Germany, 1880–1980* (Ann Arbor: University of Michigan Press, 1990), 291. © 1990 Verlag, J.H.W. Dietz Nachf. GmbH. Reprinted by permission.

created interest among workers to participate in the guest-worker program and also allowed the Bundesanstalt für Arbeit to be selective in its choice of recruits. Thirty to forty percent of Turkish workers participating in the Gastarbeiter program were classified as "skilled" labor in their home country, and it was estimated that 40 percent of Turkey's stonemasons and carpenters found employment in Germany in 1970.[43] The influx of foreign labor accompanied significant economic growth during the 1960s (Table 4.2). From 1959 to 1967, the German GNP increased 150 percent, from DM 283.8 billion to DM 430.8 billion. Although the percent of the German work force that was of foreign origin increased from 0.8 percent in 1959 to 4.9 percent in 1967 (with a high of 5.5 percent in 1965), it does not appear to have had a negative effect on the native labor market. During the period, the number of employed remained steady, while unemployment plummeted. By 1966 the number of foreign workers reached 1.3 million and increased to 2.6 million by 1972, constituting 12 percent of the German workforce.[44]

The Wirtschaftswunder of the 1950s and 1960s was certainly aided by the availability of labor (both in terms of Vertriebene immigrants and those recruited through the Gastarbeiter program); however, given Germany's strong sense of ethno-nationalist identity, how did Germany avoid the sociopolitical problems (*Volkstumspolitik*) often associated with large population transfers? First, and perhaps foremost, German security was defined almost entirely in terms of reconstruction and economic development

TABLE 4.2
Foreign workers in West Germany by sending country, 1955–1975

Origin	1955	1960	1965	1967	1970	1973	1975
Italy	7,500	121,700	372,300	266,800	381,000	450,000	297,100
Spain	500	9,500	182,800	118,000	171,700	190,000	129,800
Greece	600	13,000	187,200	140,300	242,200	250,000	203,600
Turkey	—	2,500	132,800	131,300	353,900	605,000	553,200
Portugal	—	—	14,000	17,800	44,800	85,000	70,500
Yugoslavia	2,100	8,800	64,000	95,700	423,300	535,000	418,700
Morocco	—	200	9,000	5,800	9,200	—	16,300
Tunisia	—	150	500	800	6,200	—	—
Other	68,900	125,550	254,200	214,800	315,900	480,000	381,500
Total	79,600	279,400	1.22mil	991,300	1.95mil	2.6mil	2.07mil

SOURCE: Klaus Bade, *Vom Auswanderungsland zum Einwanderungsland: Deutschland 1880 bis 1980* (Berlin: Colloquium, 1983), 70. Reprinted by permission of the author.

(consistent with the Threat and Rally Hypotheses). The Bundesanstalt für Arbeit (and other institutions charged with guiding postwar economic recovery) continually asserted that growth could only be attained through the importation of foreign labor, at least in the short run. This linkage was certainly evident in the industrial sector. From 1961 to 1970 the percentage of foreign workers (among all foreign workers in the Federal Republic) employed in industrial production increased from 54.6 to 64.5 percent. Expansion of industrial production was based largely on the availability of foreign workers.[45] Because of the strong link between economic development and labor market dynamics, coupled with the reluctance of policymakers to hinder the pace of Germany's strong economic recovery, guest-worker policies were seen as a pivotal element of German security.[46] There was little public debate in the early 1960s regarding the extension of the Gastarbeiter program because policymakers were confident in the state's ability to manage flows effectively to continue trends in economic growth.

The widespread belief among German policymakers that the government could strictly manipulate labor inflows on a temporary, rotating basis contributed to the expansion of foreign-labor recruitment. Indeed, the term Gastarbeiter not only conveys the inherent transience of employment contracts but also emphasizes the sovereignty of the German state in dictating the terms regulating labor inflows and the duration of employment contracts. The term Gastarbeiter implies that participation is for a *limited stay* for *invited* working guests.[47] Policymakers had reason to believe that such a program could be effectively implemented, since it responded to the wants and needs of both German business and foreign migrant labor. While business sought a highly elastic source of labor, foreign workers sought higher relative wages and the opportunity to accumulate savings in order to better their family's economic situation upon their eventual return to their homeland. Early migrants participating in the Gastarbeiter program were predominantly male (84.5 percent male to 15.5 percent female in 1960), 20–40 years of age, and tended to travel alone, leaving their family behind.[48] Interviews of migrants tended to support the notion that they were primarily interested in short-term economic gain, not permanent immigration.[49] In 1963, 40 percent of all foreign workers returned within one year, and these figures rose as high as 68 percent for Portuguese guest workers in 1965.[50] Moreover, the government had additional reasons to believe that it could successfully control labor flows to coincide with domestic economic demand.

The April 1965 Law on Foreigners granted German authorities discretionary powers in dealing with foreign migrants. These powers were designed to adjust the process of importation of foreign labor (from non-EC countries) to match the needs the domestic economic environment.[51] The application of such discretionary powers was implemented during the economic downturn in the following two years. During the recession of 1966–67, the government sought to limit migrant inflows by reducing the number of work permits issued to foreigners. Moreover, about 320,000 foreign workers returned home, convinced that their German workplaces were no longer secure.[52] Figure 4.2 shows how foreign-labor inflows decreased as domestic demand decreased during the economic downturn. Indeed, it appeared clear to policymakers that reducing work permits resulted in decreasing flows, and that economic conditions also contributed to return migration. Rogers Brubaker points out, "The recession of 1966–67, during which the number for foreign workers declined by 25 percent, seemed to confirm that the foreign workers were temporary labor migrants, *Gastarbeiter*, whose presence in Germany was governed by the rhythms of the business cycle."[53] However, such figures were misleading, at least in terms of the ethnic demographics of such flows. By disaggregating return statistics, one study found that rates of return varied by sending state, ranging from a high of 90 percent for Italians to a low of 30 percent for Turks.[54] The

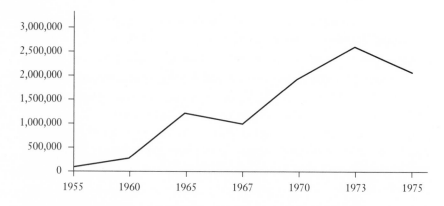

Figure 4.2. Foreign Guest Workers Employed in the Federal Republic of Germany, 1955–1975

SOURCE: Adapted from Klaus Bade, *Vom Auswanderungsland zum Einwanderungsland: Deutschland 1880 bis 1980* (Berlin: Colloquium, 1983), 70.

demographic effects of such disparities would become apparent in subsequent political discourse regarding guest workers and immigrants in general.

One factor that made the importation of foreign labor palatable from a sociopolitical standpoint was the perception that not only was such migration managed to conform directly to German economic needs, but also that mechanisms were in place to ensure German sovereignty. Control policies established in the 1930s, including the Foreigner Policy Ordinance (Ausländerpolizeiverordnung) of 1938 and the Ordinance on Foreign Workers (Verordnung über ausländische Arbeitnehmer) of 1933, bolstered perceptions that migration could be strictly managed to conform to economic demands.[55] However, government control mechanisms, initially established to better provide for the labor requirements of German business and industry, began to be considered a negative externality by businesses that required foreign labor, especially in terms of the administrative costs of recruitment. In many ways, this follows the distinct pattern that accompanied government labor-recruitment programs in the United States and in France. These "unnecessary" costs prompted many businesses to recruit needed labor independent from the government bureaucracy established to process labor inflows. By 1960, 50 percent more workers were in the country than had been recruited through official channels and in 1961, 32 percent of the Italians and 57 percent of the Greeks and Spaniards were entering in ways other than through officially sanctioned recruitment offices.[56] Migrant smuggling emerged as a profitable black market enterprise for unscrupulous opportunists. After 1965, 90 percent of the Italians entering Germany for employment purposes did so without contacting the Bundesanstalt für Arbeit due to European Community provisions that sanctioned freedom of movement for workers among member states of the EC.[57] Without reliable intelligence regarding the timing and magnitude of intra-European labor migration, manipulating the labor supply with precision was becoming increasingly difficult for the Bundesanstalt für Arbeit.

As foreign labor became ever more embedded in the postwar German economy, it was increasingly associated with certain occupational niches, and there was little direct economic competition between native German workers and the Gastarbeiter. Foreigners began occupying certain jobs in disproportionate numbers. Over time those jobs were no longer acceptable to most German workers, even in periods of high unemployment. Similar patterns of immigrant niches are evident in other countries with high proportions of immigrant workers.[58] By shifting immigrant labor to undesirable, though extremely necessary, job categories, the use of foreign labor has also enabled native workers to shift into higher employment strata, including management and other highly skilled labor categories. The availability of foreign workers filled a gap in the German labor supply, creating opportunities for German workers to transfer into service employment without causing disruptions in the production of investment goods.[59] By filling labor needs in the unskilled and blue-collar sector of the economy, foreign labor increasingly enabled German workers to shift into white-collar positions, though this process also created an institutionalized underclass of foreign workers (increasing social marginalization). Some analysts have suggested that such labor transfers, while beneficial in the short run, incur economic costs in the long run, as the exploitation of inexpensive and highly elastic foreign labor reduces pressures for technological development: "Instead of capital-deepening—the work-saving rationalization of investment—we have capital-widening—that is, expanded investment. There is less substitution of capital for labor that would lead to an increase in work productivity. Old jobs with low work productivity continue to be maintained."[60] In 1972, German Labor Minister Arendt echoed similar concerns, suggesting that the continued influx of foreign labor may result in businesses not engaging certain labor saving investments because utilizing foreign workers was less costly to business in the short run.[61] Although there may be diffuse, long-term economic costs to the economic strategy employed by Germany, these did not foster economic competition between natives and guest workers. Rather, the speed and magnitude of the Wirtschaftswunder and the positive role foreign labor played in achieving such development, at least in the short run, enabled policymakers to extol the benefits of foreign labor to the German public and maintain a grand strategy skewed toward security's economic pole.

MIGRATION AND EARLY COLD WAR GRAND STRATEGY

The empirical evidence supports both the Threat and Rally Hypotheses. The Threat Hypothesis predicts that in an environment of external threat, policies should emphasize foreign-policy interests and material production, while societal difference it mitigated. Although formal labor recruitment was not established until 1955 and did not bring in large numbers of migrants until 1961, the fact that Germany was largely open to a tremendous wave of postwar refugee flows must be considered as an important dimension of liberalization. This liberalization was largely a function of a combination of both foreign-policy interests and internal-stability interests. Moreover, the evidence suggests that even in the face of tremendous potential conflict over scarce jobs and resources in the early postwar period, societal security interests stressed commonality within a broadly conceived German "nation" rather than conceiving identity in more limited, parochial terms. Economic development was a central element of grand strategy throughout the early cold war era, initially to facilitate reconstruction and later to maintain growth and development. Given labor's role in this process, German liberalization of migration policy during this period is consistent with its national security interests.

Crafting migration policy to conform to foreign policy and economic interests enabled German policymakers to effectively counter the Communist threat during the early cold war period. Not only did rapid reconstruction and development bolster Allied material power to counter potential Soviet expansionism in Western Europe, but these same factors also kept the specter of Communist insurgency at bay. However, as the structural environment evolved, it would become evident that the Gastarbeiter approach was not a panacea, and that labor mobility inevitably leads to societal tensions in nations undergoing significant demographic transformation.

Societal Insecurity and Migration Control

After the tremendous economic growth of the 1950s and 1960s, sociopolitical problems associated with Germany's guest-worker program began to materialize. As postwar security threats waned with the rise of economic prosperity, regional integration, and collective security through the establishment of NATO (1949), the German security agenda began to shift its orientation from one stressing external threats to one increasingly concerned with internal, societal threats. Decreasing perception of military threat led to increasing social introspection and a recognition of the changing demographics brought about by the Gastarbeiter program. In addition to conforming to the predictions of the Threat and Rally Hypotheses, policy outcomes in the 1970s and 1980s also provide support for hypotheses that link societal insecurity to migrant visibility. The evidence also suggests that feedback loops, which were the product of changing patterns of migration, informed subsequent policy decisions.

LEGACY OF THE "MIGRATION STATE"

Although using a trading-state logic to migration policy in the 1950s and 1960s resulted in profound economic output and was instrumental in early cold war security in Germany, the unintended consequences of Gastarbeiter policies established a challenge to policymakers as the structural environment changed. In the period from 1968–72, the foreign workforce in Germany rose from 1 to 2.6 million, which amounted to an increase from 5 to 12 percent of the total German workforce.[62] More importantly, it was the number of Turkish workers in Germany that grew most dramatically, from approximately 130,000 in 1967 to more than 600,000 by 1973.[63] It soon became apparent to German policymakers and the general public that the "temporary" guest workers were becoming less interested in returning to their home countries and that patterns of return migration were increasingly a function of migrant perceptions of conditions in the home country.[64] Survey evidence suggested that migrants were staying longer than they had originally planned because employment opportunities at home remained unchanged, it took the migrants longer than they had anticipated to reach certain savings targets, and their tastes and expectations also changed.[65] From 1963 to 1965, there was an 11–14 percent reduction of those Greeks and Turks who stayed for less than a year, while between 1963 and 1967 the percentage of all foreign workers who had been in Germany for more than three years jumped from 22 to 45 percent.[66] The increasing permanence of foreigners in Germany was also signaled by the changing housing patterns of guest workers. The communal housing the German government offered to its guest workers was initially appealing (in that workers were able to accumulate savings more quickly), but by the end of the 1970s more than 80 percent of the foreign workers chose to live in individual apartments and rooms secured on the open market.[67] This change brought the resident foreign population into closer contact with German society—in other words, it became increasingly visible.

The 1973 OPEC oil embargo and the recession it initiated are often given as a rationale for the abatement of the Gastarbeiter program; however, growing public concern over the increasing presence of foreigners in major cities was the more likely cause. Policymakers beginning in the late 1960s raised questions regarding the continued need for large numbers of foreign laborers, though no legislation was enacted to halt existing recruitment programs. Rather than creating anti-immigrant sentiment, the recession of the early 1970s served to focus existing anxieties and prompted a reexamination of the social changes cultivated by the Gastarbeiter program. Ulrich Herbert argues, "The oil embargo had been little more than a supplementary factor; it had provided a useful occasion to check the influx of foreign workers and reduce their numbers—without any great resistance from the worker-exporting countries and without wearying public discussion on the social consequences of this measure."[68]

As the German economy slowed in 1972–73, similar measures to those instigated during the 1966–67 recession were taken. In November 1972, visas were no longer issued to non-EC nationals wishing to work in the Federal Republic, and in February 1973 the fees levied on employers seeking foreign workers was tripled in an effort to discourage recruitment requests.[69]

The labor recruitment program was halted altogether (*Anwerbestop*) in November 1973. However, migrant flows did not stop with the discontinuation of the guest-worker program. In fact, migrants fearing that they would be unable to return to Germany if they went home decided instead to bring their families into Germany, resulting in *increasing* demographic change and an increase in the number of births in young migrant families. Moreover, the immigrant community was no longer dominated by young males; rather, it was characterized by increasing proportions of women. From 1974–84 the number of women over sixteen years of age per 1,000 men increased from 585 to 715.[70] Moreover, in 1974, 17 percent of children born in the Federal Republic had foreign parents.[71]

Additional measures were soon taken to gain control over foreign labor. The government established new regulations regarding the distribution of *Kindergeld* (allowances for children) in 1975, stipulating that these were available only for children living in Germany. However, rather than motivating migrants to move back to their home country, the new Kindergeld rules prompted many migrants to bring their children into Germany.[72] In 1978, additional restrictive measures were taken that limited residency permits for particular metropolitan areas that were considered "saturated" by foreigners.[73] Neither policy had the desired effect in reducing the volume and concentration of the immigrant population. After the cessation of labor importation programs the foreign population in Germany actually rose from 4 million in 1973 to 4.5 million in 1980, and the migrant community was restructuring into a more settled, permanent foreign population.[74] More rigorous means of reducing the foreign population, that is, abolition of family reunification provisions or forced deportation, were judged to be too politically volatile, especially considering Germany's totalitarian past and its contemporary desire to be perceived as a liberal state. Because of legal protections articulated in the German Basic Law, mass expulsion was both politically and legally impractical, not to mention distasteful to most Germans.[75]

The fundamental demographic changes taking place prompted the government to appoint Heintz Kuhn, former prime minister of North Rhine Westphalia, as ombudsman for foreigners and to provide an assessment of Germany's new "immigrant problem." Kuhn's report, commissioned in 1977 and published in 1979, surmised that the illusion of rotation had to be dispelled and the German government would have to recognize that it had become a de facto, if not de jure, site of permanent settlement for millions of immigrants.[76] He writes, "Future policy towards foreign employees and their families living in the Federal Republic must be based on the assumption that a development has taken place which can no longer be reversed and that the majority of those concerned are no longer guest workers but immigrants, for whom return to their countries of origin is for various reasons no longer a viable option."[77] Although the Kuhn report was a significant indicator that the illusion of nonpermanence had slipped away, its calls for increased rights for foreign residents and its focus on integration provided for a significant threat to the traditional ethnic conception of identity that lies at the core of German nationalism. Efforts were made to finesse this tension by suggesting a "right to settlement" (*Niederlassungsrecht*) be extended to the foreign population as a substitute for extending formal citizenship rights.[78] The report served to change the nature of immigration discourse; however, by and large the liberal SPD-FDP coalition government in power at the time did not implement its policy prescriptions. In March 1980, the government maintained that "permanent settlement was seen as the exception rather than the rule."[79]

After Germany's foreign population reached a peak of 4.7 million in 1982, the Kohl government established a "foreigners policy" based on three elements: (1) encouraging repatriation of foreign workers; (2) restricting further inflows of migrants; and (3) integration of the existing foreign population. Chancellor Kohl declared openly that he sought to reduce the number of foreigners in Germany by one million. In 1983, the government passed the Gesetz zur Förderung der Rückkehrbereitschaft von Ausländer (Return Migration Assistance Act), which attempted to generate return migration through financial incentives similar to the approach attempted in France.[80] These incentives provided premiums of DM 10,500 to foreign workers from former countries of recruitment that chose to return to their home country. An additional DM 1,500 per dependent child was also available through the program.[81] Although the program managed to nominally reduce the foreign population in Germany, these reductions were at levels that represented the normal rate of return migration.[82] Sarah Collinson points out, "No return policies introduced during the late 1970s and early 1980s had any significant impact on migration trends."[83] This is not to say that such programs did not have symbolic, political value to policymakers: "The real impact of the law was probably ideological: it made people think that the government was doing something about the 'foreigners problem,' and that migrants were not just being pushed out, but being offered a humane alternative."[84] Peter O'Brien adds, "The change in language alone suffices to appease critics by giving the impression that something is being done to alleviate a certain political problem."[85]

The other two facets of Kohl's migration policy—increased control and integration of existing foreigners—proved equally, if not more, challenging, especially as Germany was confronted with a "third wave" of migrants in the late 1980s—asylum seekers.

THE RIGHT OF ASYLUM

Not only did the return migration incentive program prove unsuccessful in reducing the foreign population in Germany, but also soon after the labor recruitment stoppage the number of asylum applications to Germany began to rise. In the year following the Anwerbestop, the number of new asylum claims jumped from 5,595 (in 1973) to 9,424 (in 1974).[86] The number of new claimants rose steadily in the following years, and by 1980 the number of new asylum seekers surpassed one hundred thousand.[87] Suspicions that many—if not most—of these new asylum seekers were actually economic-migrants rose as it became apparent that more than half of these new asylum claimants were Turks. Turkish newspapers published the German form used to apply for asylum and tour operators began offering one-way air tickets to Germany replete with legal instructions on claiming asylum once on German soil.[88] By the early 1980s it was apparent that migrant flows had simply adjusted to the change in government policies regarding guest workers, moving from labor-recruitment channels (through the *BfA*) to asylum channels, taking advantage of Germany's uncommonly liberal stance on providing refuge to persecuted persons.

Once again, Germany's Nazi past was significant in the formation of its policies regarding asylum (as well as family reunification), making them the most liberal in Europe.[89] Christian Joppke points out, "The fathers of the Basic Law, many of them exiled during the Nazi regime, conceived of an asylum law that went far beyond existing international law as a conscious act of redemption and atonement."[90] Article 16 of the Basic Law guarantees the

Figure 4.3. Asylum Applications in Germany, 1980–1994

SOURCE: Adapted from Philip L. Martin, "Germany: Reluctant Land of Immigration," in *Controlling Immigration: A Global Perspective*, ed. W. Cornelius, P. Martin, and J. Hollifield (Stanford, CA: Stanford University Press, 1994), 212.

right of asylum to persecuted peoples and places the locus of such rights on the individual to claim such rights, not the state's right to grant them. When the front door to immigration closed (with the cessation of the guest-worker program), the "side door" mechanism that Germany's liberal asylum policy provided soon became exploited by would-be migrants. For many migrants, applying for political asylum became the only way to enter one of the richest counties in the world.[91] During the 1980s, asylum claims in West Germany rose dramatically (Figure 4.3), and by 1992 German authorities were receiving more than twelve hundred applications for asylum each day.[92] Because other West European states were able to enact more stringent asylum policies, Germany began to receive a disproportionate share of asylum applications in the region. Throughout the late 1980s, Germany received 60 to 70 percent of Western Europe's refugees, and by 1992 this proportion reached 80 percent.[93] The massive influx of asylum claims created a significant backlog in the processing of such claims, while constitutional provisions demanded that the German government provide for housing and expenses of asylum claimants while their applications were pending review. This process sometimes lasted more than five years, and the housing and living expenses per applicant averaged $10,000 per year. Public concern regarding this new influx was strong and swift.

Initial responses centered on administrative and procedural changes. In 1982, the Asylum Procedures Law sought to enact fast-track procedures to dismiss "patently unfounded" asylum claims.[94] Such procedures kept acceptance rates extremely low; by 1992 more than 90 percent of asylum applications were denied.[95] However, the effectiveness of such policies was mitigated by the fact that more than 75 percent of refused asylum seekers remained in the country illegally, and only 1 to 2 percent of those denied asylum were eventually deported.[96] Although deportation was the de jure remedy for those denied asylum, such policies encountered significant obstacles.[97] Even though international law requires that a state admit its own nationals, these nations may be disinclined to receive them and may challenge their nationality. Conversely, applicants denied asylum might conceal his or her nationality by destroying identification materials and passports. In this way, nations may be discouraged from receiving such deportees where nationality has not been established.

RISING SOCIETAL INSECURITY AND POLICY DEVELOPMENT

The 1970s and 1980s marked a significant shift in the mix of security interests that comprised grand strategy in Germany. The changing structural environment, combined with the unintended effects of the liberal policies of the 1950s and 1960s, augmented the pattern of migration to Germany and the way that the general public perceived migration. Consistent with the Threat Hypothesis, declining perceptions of geopolitical threat resulted in a relative increase in sensitivity to societal security interests and a shift toward policies of closure. These changes were most conspicuous in the sudden halt to labor importation through the Gastarbeiter program and through subsequent policies to stem chain migration initiated by past flows. Moreover, the fact that restrictionist sentiment was directed at Turkish migrants lends support that visibility of migration flows is an important facet of societal insecurities. "Visibility" factors include a combination of perceptions of social proximity, spatial concentration of flows and settlement patterns, and concentration of flows in time. The fact that Turkish migrants were considered less "socially proximate" than earlier waves of ethnic-German refugees and other Europeans was a major element that shaped attitudes about immigration and hence migration policy. So, too, was the fact that Turkish migrants were concentrated geographically—both in the country and within sections of these cities that received most immigrants—a phenomenon that not only made them more visible to the general public, but also exaggerated perceptions of the magnitude of Turkish migration more generally.

Migration Policy After the Cold War

The fall of the Berlin Wall in 1989 and the subsequent end of the cold war mark the end of a geopolitical threat that dominated world politics for half a century. The Threat Hypothesis and Rally Hypothesis would predict that the decrease in geopolitical threat should increase the relative salience of societal security interests. Moreover, societal security would be the product of increasing degrees of differentiation within society—in other words, increased particularism in defining "us" and "them." Several indicators support these predicted outcomes. Negative public reactions to immigration ranged from benign discontent to violence. At the extreme, violent attacks against foreigners rose sharply, from 103 reported instances in 1989 to 2,584 in 1992. Violent outbreaks occurred in cities such as Hoyerswerda, Rostock, Mölln, and Solingen.[98] Among moderates, polls taken in the early 1990s suggested that societal security issues had emerged as a dominant concern. One poll conducted in November 1991 showed that 71 percent of respondents regarded the issue of immigration and asylum as "very important."[99] Another poll conducted in September 1992 showed that 78 percent of West Germans believed that reforming immigration was their top priority.[100] This was supported by another poll taken in October 1992 that suggested that the "problem of foreigners" was the most important policy issue facing the country.[101] Yet another 1992 poll showed that 75 percent of Germans supported drastic action to control immigration—primarily by restricting access to the asylum channel of entry.[102]

In an environment where societal security interests became increasingly salient, how did the German state respond? On the one hand, societal insecurities pressed for increased closure and restrictionism, as well as dealing with the lingering "foreigner problem." On the other, the German economy in the 1990s was experiencing the same knowledge-based transformation evident in other advanced industrial countries as the IT and service sectors emerged as the engine of economic production. As in the U.S. case, policymakers showed an increased desire to respond to societal fears while still utilizing foreign labor to full economic advantage. As with other European countries, this was largely accomplished by establishing at least the appearance of a hard-shell boundary around the European Union while maintaining soft-shell borders internally in order to take advantage of labor mobility. An effort to integrate the existing foreign population through access to naturalization as accompanied by increased restrictionism emerged in the areas of asylum policy, efforts to curb clandestine migration, and new limits placed on ethnic German migration.

NATURALIZATION AND INTEGRATION

By definition, integration and assimilation of nonethnic Germans is impossible under a purely ethnic conception of the national community. However, beginning with the Kuhn Memorandum, it became increasingly clear to German policymakers that social cohesion within Germany depended on avoiding a completely bifurcated, balkanized society. Naturalization of the existing foreign population, together with efforts to curb future flows, became reluctantly recognized as a necessity to foster societal security. In 1991, the Aliens Act was passed; the act provided access to naturalization if foreigners had lived in Germany for more than fifteen years, had no felony criminal convictions, could support themselves financially, and were willing to renounce other citizenship ties. Although this access was a significant departure from traditional German policies, local government officials retained the right to determine if access to naturalization of a given applicant was in the best interests of the nation.[103] However, few migrants were applying for naturalization even as the opportunity to do so was more accessible. In fact, the number of foreigners born in or immigrating into Germany has risen much faster than the number of foreigners that become naturalized German citizens.[104] Few foreigners were willing to relinquish prior citizenship, as it is linked closely with cultural identity and with hopes of return.[105]

One way to bridge this impasse would be to permit dual citizenship. In 1998, about two million Germans possessed a second passport according to figures released by the Association of Binational Families (Verband binationaler Familien).[106] However, state policy regarding dual citizenship is largely a function of national identity. Most of those holding dual citizenship in Germany were ethnic Germans naturalized under *Anspruch* (naturalization by right) provisions that did not require them to give up their previous citizenship. In contrast, naturalization procedures required Turkish applicants to give up their passport. While these naturalization rules limit the ability of existing nonethnic Germans to assimilate into the *Leitkultur* through the process of naturalization, the aim of the CDU-CSU coalition is predicated on the desire to stem future flows from Turkey. During the debates leading to the rejection of dual-nationality provisions in German immigration law in 1997–98, Helmut Kohl warned that approving dual nationality might encourage more Turks to migrate to Germany: "If we today give in to demands for dual citizenship, we would soon have four, five, or six million Turks in Germany instead of three million."[107]

Because the 1991 law was largely unsuccessful in facilitating the integration of the foreign population in Germany through naturalization, the new SPD-Green government succeeded in passing a new *Staatsangehörigkeitsgesetz* (Citizenship Law) in May 1999 that went into effect January 1, 2000.[108] The new law reduced the existing residency requirement for naturalization from fifteen to eight years, and although it maintained the requirement to relinquish other citizenship, it allowed dual citizenship if the home country does not permit the loss of citizenship or if release is unusually difficult. The law also included the first jus soli feature in German citizenship law. The law grants citizenship at birth to children born in Germany of foreign parents provided that a parent has lived in Germany legally for at least eight years and has held either an unlimited residence permit for at least three years or possesses a residence entitlement (*Aufenthaltsberechtigung*).[109] These children are then required to select a single citizenship within a five-year period beginning at the age of majority. Amid these changes, conservative CDU policymakers maintained their emphasis that foreigners must "show a credible integration into our social and state order."[110] Accordingly, access to naturalization under the new law required that language and cultural knowledge be displayed by passing state mandated exams.

THE ASYLUM COMPROMISE

In addition to dealing with the domestic "foreigner problem" by opening access to naturalization and pressing for integration, societal insecurities were responded to with increased restrictionism in the area of asylum policy. Like some other advanced industrial democracies, there exists a tension between two opposing ideational facets of German identity: on the one hand, postwar Germany sought to distance itself from its totalitarian and intolerant past by incorporating liberal principles into its conception of nationhood; on the other hand, when such liberal notions are institutionalized in policies such as those dealing with asylum, they come into direct conflict with Germany's enduring conception of itself as a primarily ethnic community based on jus sanguinis citizenship. Abolishing Article 16 of the German Basic Law that provides for humanitarian policies regarding refugees and those seeking asylum is anathema to this postwar emphasis on social toleration. However, leaving it intact was proving to be socially destabilizing and producing unwanted social demographic changes and widespread perceptions that Germany's societal sovereignty was in jeopardy. What emerged from this tension was a political compromise—an attempt to finesse seemingly irreconcilable differences in the evolving German identity.

The "asylum compromise" of July 1993 modified Article 16 by introducing the concept of the "safe third country" and also implemented new asylum procedures and administrative practices. Under the provisions of the constitutional amendment, nations could be designated as "safe countries of origin" if political persecution or inhumane punishment would be unlikely to occur. Asylum seekers arriving from either EU member states or from such designated "safe third countries" were not eligible for asylum in Germany, but had to apply for asylum there. Because such "safe countries" geographically surround Germany, these changes served to reduce applications for asylum by approximately 75 percent.[111] Some, however, question whether such reductions were due to the constitutional or the procedural changes made to asylum policy.[112] Moreover, fast-track provisions enabled the Federal Office for the Recognition of Foreign Refugees to reject manifestly unfounded applications for asylum, while Section 18a of the Asylum Procedure Law provided that asylum proceedings were to be carried out before the applicant enters the country, if doing so via a safe third country.[113]

Even though some critics have asserted that such changes effectively thwart the liberal humanitarian spirit of Article 16, the asylum compromise seemed highly effective.[114] By 1995, asylum applications numbered some 125,000 — roughly 70 percent less than 1992 levels, while recognition rates rose from 10 to 25 percent during the same period.[115] Moreover, of those whose asylum applications were rejected because they originated in "safe countries" such as Poland or the Czech Republic, few applied for asylum once returned to these countries and many simply "disappeared," presumably to find other means of gaining entry.[116] Germany's ability to square the circle between the liberal / humanitarian and ethno-cultural aspects of its identity was also greatly aided by the continuing process of European integration. Because other EU member states had more restrictive asylum regimes and desired to maintain higher levels of control, harmonization served as an effective pretense for German policymakers to deflect criticism regarding constitutional changes made to Article 16 of the Basic Law.[117]

CLANDESTINE IMMIGRATION

Another area that saw increased restrictionism was in dealing with clandestine immigration flows. Whereas EU integration initially sought to facilitate migration flows in order to take advantage of the economic gains to be had through factor mobility, it has since evolved to (1) establish cooperation and harmonization with regard to refugee and asylum policies of member states, and (2) represent a quasi-collective-security arrangement to seal the border against illegal immigration. Although EU member states continue to pursue asylum policy harmonization pursuant to the Dublin Convention, closing the asylum door has served to shift flows to the "backdoor": illegal or clandestine immigration. The dismantling of internal border controls as articulated in the Maastricht and Amsterdam Treaties, as well as in the Schengen Agreement, has served to increase fears and sensitivities among member states regarding increases in clandestine migration.[118] During the 1990s, illegal immigration has joined asylum policy on the front line of societal insecurity and concerns over state sovereignty.

At the turn of the millennium, Germany was estimated to have anywhere from 150,000 to 1.5 million unauthorized foreign residents, depending on how one defines the illegal population.[119] Concern over border control has resulted in dramatic changes in the border patrol (*Bundesgrenzschutz*), signaling the increasing security function of such forces. Border patrol budgets increased dramatically during the late 1980s and early 1990s and the border police tripled in size in the period from 1995–2000.[120] Along one section of the German-Polish border, thirty-three hundred border guards were deployed in 1996 where five years earlier only four hundred were stationed. In 1997, the Ministry of the Interior added an additional fifteen hundred border police to patrol the borders with Poland and the Czech Republic, bringing the total to seventy-three hundred agents.[121] Increasing latitude in apprehension procedures was granted to the border patrol as well. A 1994 law extended the intensive search jurisdiction for the border patrol from 2 km to 30 km from the border.[122] Increased patrols gradually resulted in a decline in apprehensions along the border. From a high of fifty-two thousand in 1993, border apprehensions declined to forty thousand in 1998 and thirty-eight thousand in 1999.[123] As was the case with asylum policy, Germany's totalitarian past served to constrain policy choices by dictating that border patrol action should avoid becoming too heavy-handed. Rather, they should depend on the vigilance of the public to help generate apprehensions. During the 1990s the Bundesgrenzschutz successfully used posters and newspaper ads to appeal to the public to report "suspicious people" that may be illegal aliens, a move that allows the police to maintain a relatively low profile and to avoid being seen as authoritarian. Government records indicate that some 70 percent of apprehensions along the border corridor are due to public informants.[124] Similar tactics of utilizing public help in identifying illegal immigrants are used to make Germany's employer sanctions rules work more effectively. Workplace citations and fines against employers harboring undocumented workers rose from twenty to thirty thousand in the early 1990s to approximately forty-three thousand in 1999.[125] Some analysts are skeptical of the success of such limited enforcement mechanisms and suggest that only a more active and assertive police presence can effectively stem clandestine immigration: Thomas Faist remarked, "It is hard to see how, short of rigorous border control through police-state methods, Germany can substantially decrease the total number of immigrants, especially with respect to clandestine population movements."[126] The challenge of securing the borders is particularly acute given the fact that migrant smugglers have made the migration process increasingly well organized. Interior Minister Manfred

Kanther reported that in 1996 some 7,400 foreigners were apprehended trying to enter Germany with the help of migrant smugglers.[127] During the first three months of 1997, 1,058 foreigners and 277 migrant smugglers were apprehended along the Czech border, and 656 foreigners and 145 smugglers were detained along the Polish border, up sharply from 1996 levels in these areas.[128] In defending the national identity, German policymakers once again walk that fine line between its core ethnic component and its newer liberal dimension. As is the case in the United States, often establishing the appearance of a secure border will suffice in order to quell social fears and reaffirm societal sovereignty.[129]

In a reversal of the worker recruitment regime of the 1950s and 1960s, cooperation with migrant-sending states is increasingly sought to curb migrant flows rather than facilitate them. With the numbers of border crossers escalating at key points, such as the German-Polish border, assistance of sending states is sought to help manage border flows into Germany. In order to secure cooperation, Germany has linked economic incentives to sending state cooperation in controlling flows. Such linkages take two forms: (1) direct foreign aid; and (2) making migration control cooperation a prerequisite to be considered for admission into the EU. In 1997, Germany provided Poland with $66 million worth of border control equipment in order to help secure the border and stop clandestine immigration into Germany.[130] In addition, Italy has faced increasing pressure from Germany to secure their border.[131] In 1997 Germany's foreign minister threatened to impose economic sanctions, including cuts in development aid, on countries that refused to accept the return of criminal immigrants.[132] Acceptance into the EU is also used to gain political leverage. Peter Andreas notes, "The carrot of future entry into the EU and visa-free access to the west helped assure Polish and Czech cooperation in stemming the smuggling of migrants into Germany from the east."[133] Because admission to the EU includes freedom of movement, current members actively seek cooperation from applicant states to help reduce the possibility of large migrant flows once membership has been bestowed.

LIMITS ON ETHNIC GERMAN IMMIGRATION

Maybe the most significant evidence supporting the Threat and Rally Hypotheses was the change in attitudes about ethnic German migration and the consequent shift in policy. Since the end of WWII, ethnic Germans had

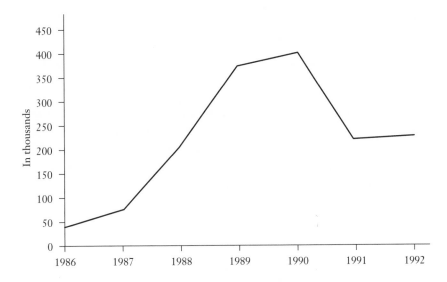

Figure 4.4. Immigration of Ethnic Germans, 1986–1992
SOURCE: *Bundesverwaltungsamt, Europäisches Forum für Migrationsstudien*

open access to immigration into Germany. As the Berlin Wall came down and the cold war ended, Germany faced a tremendous surge of ethnic German migration from Eastern Europe, similar to the late 1940s. Between 1989 and 1993, some 1.3 million East Germans moved west (Figure 4.4).[134] However, public reaction and the policy response to this movement were markedly different in the 1990s than they were in the 1940s. Most of the focus concerning societal security had centered on the "problem" of Turkish migration, but now Germany's uncompromising acceptance of "ethnic Germans" from East Germany had become increasingly problematic. Growing feelings among many West Germans that they shared few cultural norms and values with East Germans complicated the sudden integration of its ethnic brethren. Dominique Schnapper writes, "West Germans have suddenly become aware that foreign workers—the great number of which have been settled in Germany for more than 15 years—had become more integrated into their society than their 'compatriots' from the east. Contrary to what many imagined before reunification, Turks have created fewer political and identity problems for West Germans than have the East Germans."[135] East Germans were seen lacking in both the spirit of enterprise and experience with democracy, both of which are considered fundamental to German prosperity in the postwar period. They were also increasingly seen as a burden on Germany's welfare system. This new ambivalence regarding ethnocultural unity among Germans has had a tremendous affect on how ethnic German migrants from other sending states (such as the former Soviet Union) are perceived.

Whereas prior to German reunification foreign governments were urged to permit Aussiedler to emigrate, the 1990s were marked by government efforts to provide assistance to the Aussiedler so that they could remain where they were.[136] Moreover, a series of incremental restrictions on ethnic German migration represented a significant shift in attitudes about German nationhood, societal security, and immigration in general.[137] The first measure was a legal restriction (*Aussiedleraufnahmegesetz*) implemented in July 1990 that required ethnic German immigrants to apply in their country of origin. This enabled German policymakers to better regulate the flow of ethnic Germans into the country.[138] In 1993, quotas were introduced limiting the number of Aussiedler allowed to immigrate to approximately 220,000 annually (*Kriegsfolgenbereinigungsgesetz*). Moreover, the law restricted future ethnic German migration by stipulating that ethnic Germans born in the Soviet Union and Eastern Europe after December 1992 were no longer entitled to apply for admission to Germany based on the right of return. Perhaps the most direct evidence that such restrictionism was based on societal insecurities and new emphases on more restrictive definitions of social identity was the establishment of language proficiency examinations required for naturalization. This new requirement, established in July 1996, was intended to confirm the *Volkszugehörigkeit* (condition of belonging to the German people) of potential immigrants and to facilitate integration. During the first three years of conducting such exams, almost half of the 150,000 applicants who took the test failed, and none were allowed to retake it.[139]

Openness toward ethnic German immigrants since 1945 was a function of three factors: (1) the need to stress postwar German liberalism toward refugees and migrants from the Soviet bloc; (2) to maintain the goal of reunification as a foreign-policy objective; and (3) to reduce domestic instability from the massive postwar influx of refugees and expellees. As external threats declined, however, societal insecurities cultivated a narrower definition of national identity that not only increased anxieties about the nonethnic

German foreign population and increased opposition to the entry of third-country nationals, but also prompted a wholesale reevaluation of who is a German and who is not.

ECONOMIC PRESSURES FOR OPENNESS

Although the demise of the Soviet Union left all NATO countries without a geopolitical adversary that resulted in increased societal insecurities and increased closure of migration policy, changing circumstances generated contrasting pressures for policy openness. Currently, fertility rates in Germany range from 1.4 in the West to 1.2 in the East, and figures released by the federal government suggest that the country would have to admit a net 310,000 immigrants per year to maintain its current population of 82.2 million (in 2000).[140] Migration currently accounts for 100 percent of Germany's population growth.[141] Moreover, Germany's expansive welfare and social security system requires stability, if not growth, in order to maintain solvency in the future.[142] In a June 1996 speech to the German Federation of Industry, German President Roman Herzog suggested that "an active immigration policy" was essential to preserving Germany's social welfare state.[143] If current immigration levels and naturalization policies are maintained, experts forecast that the German population could shrink to 77 million by the year 2030.[144]

In addition to an aging population that put strains on social welfare systems, the changing structure of Germany's economy was creating increasing demands for highly skilled labor. In a study conducted for Microsoft, the research firm Datamonitor suggested that without the influx of 1.7 million foreign professionals over the period 2000–2003, the GDP of the EU would be $375 billion smaller.[145] Chancellor Gerhard Schroeder made job creation and increased labor-market flexibility the foundation of his "new center" platform when he defeated Helmut Kohl in 1998. These economic pressures also affected the perspective of the conservative CDU. On November 6, 2000, the CDU, always a stringent defender in the notion that Germany is not a country of immigration, released a position paper that called for more immigration, so long as it was limited, controlled, and based on assimilation into a German Leitkultur.[146] Given the pressures for increased restrictionism evident during the 1990s, lawmakers sought to "finesse" contrasting pressures for openness and closure by utilizing temporary migration programs.

In May 2000, Germany established a "green-card" program to facilitate the importation of foreign (non-EU) computer professionals on five-year work visas to begin August 1, 2000. Schroeder extolled the economic virtues of the program, stating, "There is a huge amount of international competition for the best people and Germany would be making a big mistake if it didn't take part."[147] Many of these workers would most certainly come from India and Asia. India has some 4.1 million scientific and technical workers, and the number of computer programmers has been increasing by approximately 70,000 per year.[148] By mid-May 2000, fifty-seven hundred foreign workers submitted green-card applications, including twelve hundred Indians, five hundred Algerians, and four hundred Pakistanis, while about one hundred non-EU foreign professionals were contacting the Zentralstelle für Arbeitsvermittlung (ZAV) expressing interest in the program. Moreover, German employers posted roughly eleven thousand job vacancies with the agency, signaling the demand for such skilled labor in high-growth sectors of the IT economy.

Although the government seeks to maximize its economic growth by adopting flexible labor programs (for the highly skilled), domestic resistance must be taken into account. Most opinion polls taken during the debates regarding the need for a new labor recruitment program showed that 55 to 65 percent of Germans opposed introducing the green-card program.[149] While most Germans recognize the economic need for high-skilled labor, the societal costs of the Gastarbeiter program remain conspicuous in German society. Opponents, some adopting the slogan *"Kinder statt Inder"* (Children instead of Indians), argue that "temporary" migrants become permanent settlers and that priority should be placed on training native Germans to fill labor demand in high-tech growth sectors. Others suggest that the ad hoc basis of the green-card program will establish a slippery slope that will result in a new wave of foreign immigration to Germany. The argument was that once one sector of the economy gained clearance to bring in foreign nationals, other sectors would soon follow. Angela Merkel, at this time serving as CDU Secretary General, argued, "First we'll let 20,000 Indians in for the electronics industry, then 20,000 nurses, then whatever comes next. That's not good policy."[150]

This conflict between economic development, social integration, and national identity remains highly contested between the political Right and

Left. Clearly, the economic incentives of aggressive labor importation programs are strong. But as experience in Germany has shown, societal backlash against large-scale immigration, especially non-European migration, can be acute. A poll released by the Emnid Institute in October 2000 found that 66 percent of the respondents found current immigration levels "too high and exceeded the limits of what is bearable."[151] Earlier that year, Interior Minister Otto Schily reflected this attitude, remarking, "There is no need for an immigration law, because, if we had one, the quotas would be zero."[152] As in France, the United States, and Great Britain, German policymakers face conflicting interests and increasingly have tried to establish a politically stable balance between strategic and symbolic interests. In Germany, this involved a protracted and incremental move toward its first comprehensive immigration policy.

Toward an Immigration Policy

In April 2002, a new immigration bill was signed into law that reflects state efforts to balance economic and societal interests. The new immigration laws were intended to allocate visas in accordance with economic need, as determined by the government. The laws established provisions though which foreign entrepreneurs who could provide an initial investment of one million Euros and whose business would create at least ten jobs would be afforded with a temporary-residence permit. Unlimited residence permits would be available for highly skilled applicants whose services were considered essential to economic growth. The Interior Ministry anticipated initial admission of approximately five thousand highly skilled workers and five hundred entrepreneurs, though no specific quota levels were included in the legislation. The new laws also allowed foreign students who studied at Germany universities to remain in the country and work, providing yet another source of highly educated and skilled labor.

Societal security interests also figured prominently in the 2002 legislation, both ethno-nationalist and civic-nationalist in orientation. For those who have maintained that post war German identity must break with its ethno-nationalist past and embrace liberal ideology, these new laws represented the manifestation of such ideals. After its passage in the Bundestag on

March 1, 2002, Otto Schily announced, "With this law Germany shows itself to be an open country."[153] However, the legislation also reflected an interest in mollifying ethno-nationalist societal insecurities initiated by the immigration of third-country nationals and the presence of a large, unnaturalized foreign population living in Germany, many for more than a quarter century. The new laws contained provisions to promote the integration of existing foreigners by requiring them to take courses on the German language, social institutions, and governance / legal structure. Failure to attend such courses could result in being denied an unlimited residence status. Although accepting the presence of the existing foreign population can be interpreted as a remarkable transformation toward openness for a country reluctant to accept its position as a "country of immigration," the inclusion of integration requirements provides some measure of symbolic weight for conservatives concerned with what they perceived as a threat to the German Leitkultur.

As in other Western nations, the events of 9/11 had a restrictive effect on the political climate and on policy outcomes. The most conspicuous example of government responsiveness to the new security challenge posed by 9/11 was the legal challenge levied against the newly passed immigration law by CDU policymakers. This resulted in the new immigration laws being declared unconstitutional by the German Federal Constitutional Court in Karlsruhe in December 2002. Moreover, in the emergent homeland-security-centered environment, new laws and policies were passed to increase internal security. These gave additional powers to intelligence agencies to pursue German-based members of extremist organizations abroad, increased surveillance authority for policy, and deployed armed police on airplanes. Although such measures were not directed solely at immigrants, they have had an increasingly restrictive effect on migrants living in Germany—especially Muslim migrants. German authorities have also been working with representatives of other EU countries to increase cooperation and coordination of border policing.

After the initial shock of 9/11 subsided, policymakers returned to the negotiating table regarding the immigration law. Deliberations were based largely around the previously agreed terms, though conservatives pushed for increased security measures. These deliberations resulted in the Gesetz zur Steuerung und Begrenzung der Zuwanderung und zur Regelung des

Aufetnhalts und der Integration von Unionsbürgern und Ausländer (Act to Control and Limit Immigration and to Regulate the Residence and Integration of EU Citizens and Foreigners), passed into law on July 9, 2004, and put into effect January 1, 2005. The new Zuwanderungsgesetz forwards a preference for attracting highly skilled and educated labor by offering permanent-residence permits to those with such skills and their family members. Like the 2002 version, residence permits are available to foreign entrepreneurs. Moreover, foreign students graduating from German universities are allowed to remain in the country for one year after completion of their studies to find employment. In response to conservative societal security interests, integration measures are included. The law mandates that permanent-residence permits are conditional on demonstrating adequate command of German language, culture, and institutions. Integration measures are processed through the newly established Federal Office for Migration and Refugees, which is also responsible for maintaining the central register of aliens. Homeland-security measures represent the most significant departure from the 2002 version of the immigration legislation. First, the 2004 law provides stronger authority for deportation.[154] Under the law, a person may be deported if there is reasonable suspicion that he belongs to, supports, or previously belonged to a terrorist organization. Moreover, those who are members of organizations considered violent, as determined by the Federal Office for the Protection of the Constitution in an annual report, are subject to deportation. The law also facilitates the deportation of "preachers of hate"—defined as those who incite others to violence, make threat of violence, or endanger public security. Lastly, the law stipulates that all foreigners who do not have legal residency in the country are illegally present and must leave the country.

Conclusion

The power of economic dimensions in the construction of grand strategy is strong, especially when territorial security or relative power in the international system is acutely threatened. In the German case, this is clearly evidenced by Germany's grand strategy in the unstable period following World War II. German policymakers willingly ceded degrees of sovereignty in order to partake in a program of economic integration with its European neighbors to maximize economic recovery and thwart Communist insurgency. The emphasis on economic openness even applied to labor mobility, as immigration was encouraged—at least initially—in order to facilitate economic growth. After initial flows of Vertriebene from Eastern Europe stopped as demand for labor in the quickly expanding West German economy continued to grow, policymakers responded to the economic needs of reconstruction by implementing a policy that facilitated labor importation. Although the labor-recruitment programs of the 1960s served Germany's economic needs extremely well, the belief that temporary recruitment could be effectively managed without creating societal insecurities was a fiction based on false and overly optimistic presumptions. As Germany's territorial security increased through the economic prowess cultivated during the Wirtschaftswunder, the implications of immigration on German societal security became more acute, creating pressure to shift Germany's grand strategy toward its societal pole. After 1973, "foreigners were no longer seen primarily as useful labor, but as a problem of social order."[155] The Gastarbeiter were arriving from sending countries that were ethnically and culturally distant, and these workers (and their families) were becoming permanent settlers in Germany rather than temporary sojourners.

Dominique Schnapper writes, "In different ways, all European nations are experiencing a crisis created by the impact of modernisation on national integration and by the need to rethink the relationship between the market, society and the State."[156] If neoliberal policies shape the scale and scope of the economic aspects of European grand strategy, conceptions of identity drive its societal dimensions. Although imperial legacies strongly impact the equilibrium between economics and identity in Britain and France, Germany's societal dimension of grand strategy is strongly influenced by its ethno-cultural (primordial) conception of *das Volk*. The strength of this societal dimension of grand strategy is evident by the politics of immigration and identity during the 1970s and 1980s. Thomas Faist notes, "In Germany, as in all other West European countries, immigration has moved from 'low politics' to 'high politics,' as immigration came to be a highly politicized issue during the 1980s."[157]

Even though German postwar liberalism was at least in part a function of national security interests, postwar policies set in motion a process of "reimagining" German society and national identity. This liberal, civic-oriented idiom of identity has grown over time, and with it, the societal security dynamic has become more contested and fluid. Policy development since the 1990s has revealed not only the tensions evident between political impulses for openness and closure but also an ongoing debate in which the very nature of German identity is the focus. In this period of ideational turbulence regarding the national identity, policy outcomes have shown the state to be an active player in brokering a stable equilibrium between these conflicting impulses. Although neither side finds its position fully articulated in policy, the grand strategy equilibrium forwards a national security logic that favors stability as it navigates these potentially treacherous waters.

CHAPTER FIVE

National Security and Immigration in France

National identity is a bit of a myth, but in politics, myths count, they count a lot, more than reality.

— MARCEAU LONG, 1988, quoted in Feldblum, *Reconstructing Citizenship*

As was the case in Germany following World War II, France faced an acute security dilemma. It had been an occupied nation during the war, endured considerable damage to its infrastructure and capacity for economic production, and wartime casualties were significant, numbering some six hundred thousand.[1] Exacerbating France's postwar population problem was the fact that it had the lowest fertility rate in Europe during the interwar period (less than 2). It should come as no surprise that French grand strategy following the war was focused on the idea of "populate or perish." Repopulation was seen by French analysts and policymakers as both a military and an economic imperative, made all the more pressing given the quickly changing balance of world power and rising tensions between the Western bloc and the Soviet Union. The unusually harsh winter of 1946 made things even worse, deepening France's postwar economic woes. At that time Winston Churchill described Europe as "a rubble heap, a charnel house, a breeding ground of pestilence and hate," a situation that heightened insecurity both externally and internally.[2] There was growing concern among Allied leaders that domestic economic instability would encourage the rise of Communist parties internally and perhaps encourage Soviet designs on Western Europe. Both the tripartite government of Charles de Gaulle and the prominent French demographers explicitly made the connection between France's population problems and its security agenda. Alfred Sauvy, of the Institut National d'Etudes Demographiques (INED), recommended that France immediately utilize immigration to bolster manpower resources needed for reconstruction, estimating that the nation required a minimum of 5,290,000 immigrants to achieve this purpose.[3] French policymakers were confident in their ability to utilize immigration to promote economic interests. One reason for this confidence was that France already had experience with immigration since the late nineteenth century, utilizing foreign workers in its factories during the process of industrialization.[4] Moreover, and perhaps more importantly, elites strongly believed that French republicanism made the country amenable to liberal immigration, so long as immigrants were willing to assimilate into France's civic national culture.[5]

Although it is not a traditional "country of immigration" in the American sense, Rogers Brubaker has suggested that France is "a classical country, perhaps *the* classical country, of assimilation."[6] French revolutionary ideals are characterized by the notions *Liberté, Egalité, Fraternité*, emphasizing the idea that the French nation was imagined not so much by the traditional markers of nationhood, but rather by a shared belief in the fundamental liberal principles of the revolution. Brubaker suggests that the rhetoric of inclusion that permeates these revolutionary notions are "grounded in a distinctive national self-understanding, in a sense of the grandeur of France, the assimilatory virtues of French territory and institutions, and the universal appeal and validity of French language and culture."[7] Because French nationhood is defined by ideological foundations rather than blood descent, there is no reason why anyone, regardless of their race or background, could not become French, so long as there is a firm commitment to the ideals of the French state. Given of its assimilationist tradition, one might expect little in the way of societal threat in the face of immigration flows, regardless of origin.

The early postwar period would seem to support this notion, as the French government embarked on a labor-recruitment program that sought to utilize immigrant labor to spur its postwar recovery and economic expansion. Indeed, during much of the *trente glorieuses*—the thirty-year period of profound economic growth from 1945–74—the economic benefits of migration were garnered with few repercussions in the area of societal security. However, as the structural environment evolved over the course of the cold war, reactions to international migration changed as well. Whereas the early cold war period was characterized by liberal migration policies, these were followed by rising Right-wing xenophobia and increasing anti-immigrant discourse among the mainstream that prompted more restrictive policies. In 1991, François Mitterand suggested that France was as susceptible to societal insecurities as any other migrant-receiving country when he suggested that France had a "threshold of tolerance" (*seuil de tolerance*) regarding immigration from culturally distant sending nations.[8] Thus, while intellectuals have argued that French nationhood transcends ethnic particularism, it is clear that French national identity is more complex, and less accommodating, than is often argued by those who focus solely on the liberal republican dimension.[9]

In some important ways, French identity is similar to American identity; it is characterized by a binary opposition between liberal (civic republican) and ethno-cultural dimensions. Brubaker notes, "French nationalism and xenophobia have had a peculiarly double character, engendering two distinct responses toward immigrants—one assimilationist, the other exclusionist."[10] Here I aim to explicate not only how migration fit into the economic dimension of postwar grand strategy in France, but also how a changing structural environment and the unintended effects of the government's open policies toward foreign labor cultivated societal insecurities and led to more restrictive policies. Given that some "populationists" expressed reservations about utilizing a highly open system of migration to foster economic development, how was the government able to implement such a liberal regime for nearly thirty years with generally little societal insecurity?[11] Three primary elements address the question: (1) the structural security environment in postwar Europe; (2) the role of republican ideals; and (3) France's imperial grand strategy. I also seek to explicate why government policy toward migration reversed itself since the mid–1970s. How has France's experience with migration affected its perceptions of societal threat and conception of national identity, and how was the equilibrium between economic and societal dimensions of grand strategy manifest during the 1990s? Lastly, how have the events of September 11 affected migration policy in France and grand strategy more generally?

Reconstruction and Security in the Early Cold War Period

As in other West European nations, devastation left by WWII and the emergent Soviet threat initiated a period of acute external security threat. There was widespread agreement among French policymakers, economists, and demographers that immigration would be necessary to address France's desire for economic modernization and expansion as well as to address manpower shortages resulting from wartime casualties and the nation's declining fertility rate during the interwar period.[12] Given the acute security dilemma facing France after the end of World War II, there is little wonder the government assumed an active stance in establishing a postwar plan to realize these goals deemed necessary to maintain the security of the nation in an unstable postwar milieu. Not only was population seen as the "number one problem in the whole of French economic policy," but it was also closely associated with military preparedness.[13] Traditional notions of "populate or perish" developed during the mercantilist era made large populations both a military and economic asset.[14] Although France was part of the victorious alliance during World War II, regional instability and the devastation wrought by the war left France weak and vulnerable.

MIGRATION AND FOREIGN POLICY

The Threat and Rally Hypotheses predict a liberalization of migration policy in the early cold war period focused on forwarding the macroeconomic and foreign-policy interests of the state. Although not as central to postwar French grand strategy, as was the case with Britain, maintaining colonial ties remained an important part of French foreign policy after WWII, and migration policy played an important role in grand strategy. Like the British, French policymakers sought to promote colonial ties by stressing equality with colonies and departments. Extending French citizenship to colonials was intended to facilitate this sense of connection. An essential component of the rights afforded to citizens included the right of movement between colonies and the French metropole. The law of September 20, 1947, conferred French citizenship on all Arabs in Algeria and established a regime of open migration between Algeria and the metropole independent of the Office National d'Immigration (ONI) restrictions.[15] This policy had an immediate impact on immigration to France. From 1946–55, Algerian immigration outstripped the total number of immigrants recruited through the ONI.[16] As a result, the Algerian population in France increased from 20,000 to 210,000 during this period. An even larger flow of Algerian immigrants was generated in the early 1960s as a result of the war for independence. In 1962 alone, nearly one million *pieds noir* (French colonists) took advantage of their rights to immigrate and returned to France.[17] After the Evian accords (March 1962), Algerian workers maintained unrestrained access to the French metropole, though they were supposed to facilitate migration through a special government office in Algeria established by the French government (ONAMO). Many, however, simply bypassed this system and entered the country as tourists and then sought work on their own.[18]

A relatively open migration policy was also pivotal as French grand strategy was increasingly based on the notion of European integration. Integration began on May 9, 1950, with French foreign minister Robert Schuman proposing the integration of the coal and steel industries in France and Germany. The idea was that by integrating the key sectors necessary for a country to wage war, France would be able to keep German power in check. However, the notion of European integration was far larger in scope for both Schuman and Jean Monnet, who would serve as the first president of the newly created European Coal and Steel Community (ECSC). The ECSC was simply "a first step in the federation of Europe."[19] When European integration was expanded through the Rome Treaties of 1957, the design was not simply one of establishing a free-trade zone to forward Ricardian comparative advantage among member states, but to achieve a deeper level of integration. Schuman believed that in order to fully integrate as an economic and political entity, it must also become a social community. The key starting point that began the process of a deeper integration of Europe was the signing of the Rome Treaties in March 1957, creating the European Economic Community (EEC) and the European Atomic Energy Community (Euratom).[20] As noted in the preamble of the Treaty establishing the

EEC, nation-states signing the treaty were "determined to lay the foundations of an ever closer union among the peoples of Europe."[21] What sets the European common market established in 1957 apart was that it afforded the rights for the free movement of labor among member countries. This was not only to serve economic interests to maintain supplies of needed labor, which were becoming increasingly scarce for rapidly developing France and Germany, but also to signify equality for citizens of member states, in much the same way such rights were used relative to colonial citizens in the 1940s and early 1950s.

MIGRATION, RECONSTRUCTION, AND ECONOMIC SECURITY

The first five-year plan (the Monnet Plan) adopted by the newly created Conseil General du Plan (National Planning Commission, or CGP) made immigration an important and necessary element of French grand strategy for both military manpower requirements as well as economic growth.[22] The Monnet Plan (1946–51) projected a need of 1.3 million foreign workers, and suggested that France would require approximately 430,000 new immigrants in 1946–47 alone.[23] The Office National d'Immigration (ONI) was established through the ordinance of November 2, 1945, in order to facilitate the inflow of foreign labor as stipulated in the general plan. In contrast to the laissez-faire manner in which labor was recruited during the 1920s and 1930s (usually done directly by businesses), the state now sought to serve as an active participant in its efforts to recruit the labor necessary to modernize and expand the economy. As noted by James Hollifield, "From the beginning of the postwar period, immigration policy was controlled by policymakers with specific objectives."[24] Through the ONI, employers facing labor shortages could request foreign workers who would then recruit workers in their country of origin, evaluate their skills, and obtain work (*carte de travail*) and residence (*carte de séjour*) permits from the Ministry of Social Affairs and the Ministry of the Interior.[25]

In the early phase of its labor importation program, France utilized foreign labor to forward the economic dimensions of its postwar grand strategy without much regard for issues of societal security. Because the importation of foreign labor was not accompanied by perceptions of societal threat, France was able to maintain liberal policies and obtain significant economic

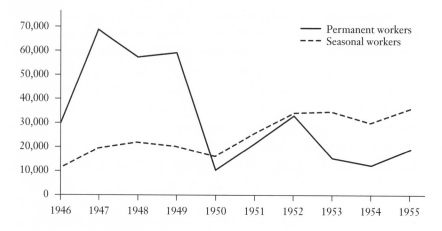

Figure 5.1. Foreign Labor Inflows to France, 1945–1955
SOURCE: *Office des Migrations Internationales* (OMI).

benefits. The availability of foreign labor served to create an environment that was conducive for investment, increased productivity, helped to keep inflation low, and increased consumer consumption.[26] However, as was the case in Germany, early success in utilizing foreign labor to promote postwar recovery and economic growth gave policymakers a false sense of confidence that labor could be managed as a factor of production, without much concern for societal security. Several factors led to this sense of optimism regarding the state's capacity to manage migration in the national interest.

The level of immigration seemed responsive to the dynamics of the business cycle and to the changing requirements for labor inputs. From 1945–55 the total number of immigrants entering France was relatively low.[27] Figure 5.1 shows that permanent immigration ranged from a low of 10,525 in 1950 to a high of 68,223 in 1947. Total immigration during this period, including both permanent and seasonal immigrants, ranged from 35,222 in 1950 to 105,426 in 1948. This low level of immigration can be attributed, in part, to the fact that the "pull" forces of the French economy remained relatively low during the early period of reconstruction. Although Marshall Plan aid infused the necessary capital to speed up economic growth and increase the economic "pull" to potential migrants, France had to deal with competition for immigrants by other European states. East-West migration following the war flowed primarily into Germany, whose cultural ties made immigration appealing to ethnic Germans fleeing the Soviet Union and emerging Soviet-bloc nations. Moreover, while ONI-sponsored recruitment brought in thousands of new immigrants into France from 1946–55, the number of foreigners living in France actually declined from 1,743,000 in 1946 to 1,553,000 in 1954 as a result of emigration.[28] This represented a drop in the percentage of foreigners living in France from 4.2 percent in 1946 to 3.6 percent in 1954.

In addition to promoting permanent immigration after World War II, policymakers also sought to establish programs to recruit temporary workers as well. The CGP's first plan recognized that the economic conditions of the country would certainly change, and with it, its manpower requirements. As such, the plan also included openness for temporary foreign labor, a policy that would enable policymakers to supplement permanent immigrants if levels dropped and also to send foreign workers home should domestic economic conditions worsen in the future.[29] Indeed, permanent immigration levels were increasingly supplemented by more temporary immigration. Figure 5.1 shows that after an initial spike in 1945, levels of permanent immigration generally declined in the following years. In contrast, the levels of temporary migration generally increased from 1946 to 1955, increasing from 11,542 to 35,276.

The fact that most initial migration flows were European in origin increased confidence in the state's ability to maintain liberal policies, since there were few public expressions of concern during the early years of labor importation. The "cultural proximity" of postwar immigration flows also served to minimize perceptions of societal threat in France. During the construction of the first plan, there was widespread agreement among policymakers and analysts that European immigrants were favorable to those from more distant regions, and there was considerable debate concerning whether France should adopt a national-origins quota regime similar to that in place in the United States.[30] Specifically, Italians were preferred because of geographical proximity, cultural similarity, absence of political obstacles, and their long-standing presence in France.[31] The ONI established recruiting offices in Italy in 1945, and in 1947 the Ministry of Labor negotiated a bilateral agreement with Italy governing the conditions for Italian immigration into France.[32] In 1946, Europeans represented 88.7 percent of the foreign population in France, and 27,831 of the 30,171 foreign workers who entered France that year came from Italy.[33] As the pool of Italian labor decreased, recruitment efforts were expanded. Subsequent bilateral agreements for the recruitment of foreign labor were established with West Germany (1950), Greece (1954), and Spain (1961).

The importance of migration to French postwar grand strategy is evident in the government's desire to facilitate immigration flows to best meet France's economic needs. The success of this trading-state approach to migration gradually led to a reduction of strict government control over migration processes in favor of one that was primarily market-driven. Gary Freeman notes, "France slipped into a long period of haphazard and lackadaisical control of immigration that amounted to a *laissez-faire* approach. While the forms of control (ONI, bilateral accords) were maintained, in reality immigration was largely spontaneous, often clandestine, and usually carried out with the government's open collusion, or under its swiftly averted eye."[34] While Freeman's characterization of the later phase of postwar labor recruitment as laissez-faire is accurate, this does not necessarily mean that it was either "haphazard" or "lackadaisical." Laissez-faire does not necessarily suggest government ineffectiveness or lack of appropriate priorities; rather, it suggests that policymakers adopted a free-market attitude regarding foreign labor.

As economic reconstruction progressed, the manpower requirements of the economy grew, placing increasing pressure on employers to secure an adequate supply of workers. Many employers soon found the ONI system of recruitment to be inefficient, time-consuming, and more costly than if they proceeded on their own. They soon began to engage in direct labor recruitment with workers abroad, who then entered France without appropriate documents. This practice led to a rise in the number of illegal foreign workers (*clandestins*) residing in France, as well as the creation of migrant-smuggling networks that often charged potential migrants exorbitant fees to transport them to France. Rather than initiating deportation proceedings against undocumented workers, the government established a process of ex post facto "regularization" to provide employed foreign workers with the necessary permits. As shown in Figure 5.2, the use of this de facto application of recruitment procedures increased in frequency throughout the late 1950s and 1960s. Whereas 72 percent of foreign workers were recruited and processed through official channels in 1956, by 1968 the proportion of

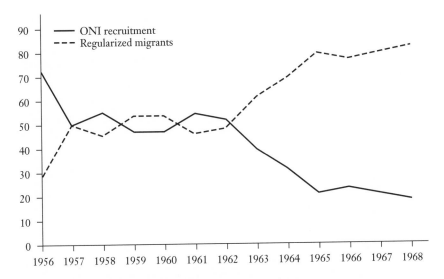

Figure 5.2. Percentage of Foreign Workers Regularized Compared to Admission Through Official Channels (ONI), 1956–1968
SOURCE: Adapted from Gary P. Freeman, *Immigrant Labor and Racial Conflict in Industrial Societies* (Princeton, NJ: Princeton University Press, 1979), 78.

workers entering through these channels fell to only 18 percent. In contrast, while only 28 percent of foreign workers were regularized ex post facto in 1956, by 1968 this proportion skyrocketed to 82 percent of immigrant workers. Because regularization remained the prerogative of the ONI, it would be remiss to conclude that the laissez-faire approach to migration in the late 1950s and 1960s represents the withdrawal of the state from immigration processes.

The Interministerial Committee on Immigration commissioned to study the issue of private recruitment suggested a more active role for the government in setting immigration levels in 1965. It emphasized the importance of a readily available pool of labor to continue France's rapid economic growth. The economic importance of immigration led policymakers to accept the rising number of illegal aliens that were recruited directly by employers without going through official government processing channels. Reflecting concerns that reducing the supply of immigrant labor would be detrimental to economic growth, the minister of social affairs noted that "clandestine immigration itself is not useless, because if we stick to a strict application of

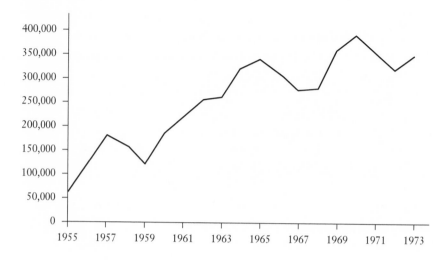

Figure 5.3. Annual Immigration into France, 1955–1973
SOURCE: OMISTATS.

international regulations and agreements, we will perhaps be short of labor."[35] Even though economic planning remained a prominent feature of French grand strategy, the Gaullist regime seemed willing to allow business considerable latitude in securing needed resources, including labor.[36] As noted by Gary Freeman, "Relatively uncontrolled immigration was beneficial economically . . . , and those benefits would be reduced if one moved to a more rigidly controlled system."[37]

The laissez-faire application of immigration laws during the latter phase of postwar reconstruction led to a sizable increase in the volume of immigration into France. Figure 5.3 traces the rapid rise in immigration during the late 1950s and early 1960s. From 1955 to 1973, the total inflow of foreigners rose from 58,952 to 347,160. The availability of foreign labor was crucial in promoting growth in key sectors of the French economy, including steel, mining, and electric power production. In addition, rebuilding the infrastructure of France certainly established construction as another key sector of postwar reconstruction. All of these sectors utilized large portions of foreign labor (Table 5.1). During the early phase of postwar reconstruction (1946–55), the mining and construction sectors accounted for more than one-third of all immigrants in the French labor force. From 1956–67,

TABLE 5.1.
Foreign workers in selected economic sectors in France, 1950–1973

Sector	1946—55	1956—67	1968—73
Mining	56,614	41,823	9,906
(% of total)	(17.4)	(3.5)	(2.4)
Manufacturing	31,236	198,596	116,505
(% of total)	(9.6)	(16.5)	(14.5)
Construction	56,880	452,391	269,818
(% of total)	(17.5)	(37.5)	(33.7)
Services	—	169,736	152,846
(% of total)	—	(14.1)	(19.1)

SOURCE: OMI.

service industries employed 169,736 foreign workers, while use of foreign labor in the construction and manufacturing sectors rose to 452,391 and 198,596, respectively. As economic growth progressed during the 1960s, the manufacturing and service sectors began increasing their use of foreign labor to assist productivity. Significant users of foreign labor in the late 1960s included the steel industry, whose 1967 workforce consisted of 32,600 workers (15.6 percent of the total), and the auto industry, whose 1967 workforce consisted of 28,300 workers (8.4 percent of the total). By 1973, the percentage of foreign workers in the steel industry rose to 16.5 percent, while the percent of foreign workers in the auto industry rose to 24.8 percent.[38] The advantages of foreign labor—including flexibility, willingness to do work the native workforce finds unappealing, low wages—were significant to the economic growth during France's trente glorieuses, especially in key sectors of the economy.

The growing importance of foreign labor during France's period of rapid economic growth during the late 1950s and 1960s resulted in increasing competition with other European countries to attract an adequate supply of immigrants. With rapid economic growth, the demand for labor remained high, a phenomenon acutely felt in Germany as well as in France. Although economic growth in France made it appealing to potential migrants, reconstruction and economic growth throughout much of Europe also served to reduce emigration pressures, since domestic economic conditions were improving. French economic growth did, however, increase economic disparities between it and developing, non-European countries, a process that increased migration pressures from those areas. Both government and

TABLE 5.2.
Immigration of workers and family to France by nationality, 1946–1973

Nationality	1946–55	1956–67	1968–73
Italians	27,838	36,813	9,359
Spaniards	1,490	49,785	24,240
Portuguese	424	26,359	91,413
Moroccans	600	7,994	27,383
Tunisians	—	2,418	15,852
Turks	—	279	8,505
Yugoslavs	29	3,152	11,208
Others	11,302	7,407	16,131
Total	41,683	134,179	204,090

SOURCE: James Hollifield, "Immigration and Republicanism in France," in *Controlling Immigration: A Global Perspective*, ed. W. Cornelius, P. Martin, and J. Hollifield (Stanford: CA, Stanford University Press, 1994), 153.

business recruitment channels had to look beyond the initial selection of "preferred" sources if labor requirements were to be met. Early preferences sought the immigration of Italian immigrants; bilateral agreements were later reached with Spain (1961), Portugal (1963), Morocco (1963), and Tunisia (1963) to increase immigration from these sources. In 1965, additional bilateral migration accords were reached with Yugoslavia and Turkey. The pattern of extending bilateral agreements toward increasingly remote sources of foreign labor is consistent with the German experience, as competition over labor forced governments seeking additional inflows to look further abroad. Table 5.2 documents the shifts in immigration flows during the period of rapid economic expansion and increasing European competition for immigrant labor. As shown, Italy accounted for 66.8 percent of immigration into France between 1946–55, but then dropped to 27.4 percent between 1956–67. By 1968–73, Italian immigration represented only 4.6 percent of immigration to France. From 1956 to 1967, flows from Spain and Portugal increased dramatically, representing 37.1 and 19.6 percent of immigration flows, respectively.

The acute security threat perceived by French policymakers in the wake of the war placed material interests at the forefront of postwar grand strategy. The role migration was to play in this strategy was clearly articulated in the first Conseil General du Plan (1946) and resulted in policy liberalization similar to that initiated in Germany during the early cold war period. Labor-recruitment programs were initiated by the government and managed through the ONI to help the reconstruction effort and spur economic growth. Also consistent with the Threat Hypothesis, migration policy conformed to foreign-policy interests. Similar to the approach taken in Great Britain, where imperial legacies continued to influence grand strategy in the early cold war period, migration policy was used as an instrument to bolster ties with colonial holdings. Such policies were symbolic of political and social equality between the French metropole and its colonies. It was also a function of European integration. National unity in the face of external threats kept issues of societal security largely at bay even as migration from less proximate migrant sending countries increased, consistent with the Rally Hypothesis. However, in addition to structural security factors, the combination of French confidence in its ability to assimilate foreign immigrants, dominance of immigration from culturally proximate European sending countries, the moderate levels of overall migration, and the migration patterns of colonial migration all served to mitigate the visibility of migration and domestic demographic change and gave policymakers confidence in their ability to effectively manage foreign labor strictly as a factor of production. As was the case with the German use of guest-worker programs, this confidence would lead to an economically dominated approach to migration that led to unprecedented economic growth, yet also established processes that sharply increased societal insecurities and demands for social closure over time as the structural environment changed.

The Rise of Societal Insecurity

The conventional wisdom attributes French restrictionism during the 1970s to the OPEC oil crisis in 1973 and the recession that followed. However, a closer look at the historical evidence suggests that the evolution of French grand strategy toward a new emphasis on its societal dimension actually preceded the economic recession of the early 1970s. Similar to the German case, "It was not economic slow-down and manpower surplus which provided the initial justification for immigration controls in the modern period ... ; it was more a question of 'ethnic balance' and fears of the social tensions which would ensue if this balance was not maintained."[39] As a consequence of the economics-oriented (and largely laissez-faire) approach to migration during

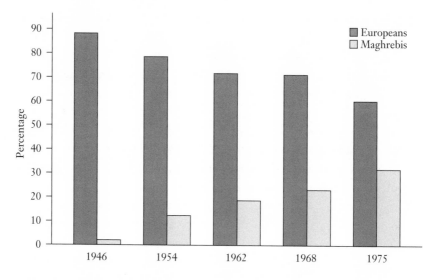

Figure 5.4. Nationality of the Foreign Population in France, 1946–1975
SOURCE: INSEE.

the late 1950s and 1960s, the level of immigration continued to rise and was becoming more ethnically diverse.

Because business was given a freer hand at labor recruitment during this period, and because labor recruitment was seen as largely unproblematic during its early phase, the increasing diversity of inflows was allowed to proceed without much scrutiny by the government throughout the 1960s. Increases in Spanish or Portuguese immigrants posed little problem for societal security, but the steady rise in immigration from the Maghreb region in northern Africa soon led to increasing perceptions of societal threat. Figure 5.4 shows a relative decline in the proportion of European immigration and a concomitant rise in immigration from the Maghreb. Moreover, migration and settlement patterns were concentrated, magnifying the perceptions of the magnitude of immigration flows. In contrast with prior immigration streams, migrants coming to France during the 1960s were concentrating in the industrial Paris (Ile-de-France) and Lyon (Rhone-Alpes) regions, where the industries that utilized foreign labor were likewise concentrated, including manufacturing, construction, and services.[40] The lack of suitable housing and the propensity for migrants to settle in concentrated

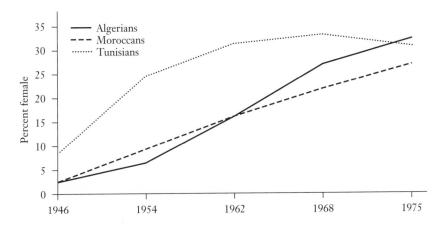

Figure 5.5. Females as Percentage of Selected Nationalities in France, 1946–1975
SOURCE: INSEE.

ethnic enclaves created urban ghettos and shantytowns (referred to as *bidonvilles, caves, hotels de fortune,* or *baraques de chantier*) in many of these French industrial centers. Where immigrants were previously associated with economic growth and postwar reconstruction, they increasingly became associated with urban plight and ethnic segregation.

Not only was the relative proportion of European immigration declining relative to that from the Muslim Maghreb, but the characteristics of these migrants were also changing during this period. Migration during the early phase of postwar immigration was largely composed of single males in search of economic opportunity on a temporary basis. Figure 5.5 documents the rising proportion of females among immigrants from the Maghreb that suggests a dramatic rise in family immigration—an immigration stream generally indicative of permanent rather than temporary migration. Among Algerians in France, the proportion that was female increased from 2.3 percent in 1946 to 26.7 percent in 1968; for Moroccans, the percentage of females increased from 1.7 to 21.8 during the same period, while Tunisians saw an increase from 8.5 percent to 33.3 percent. Increased family migration served to heighten the visibility of the changing immigration streams because new migrants interacted with French society on a greater number of levels. Where immigrant workers were previously housed in hostels, the rise in family immigration led to deeper societal penetration into the mainstream housing market; moreover, immigrant children enrolled in French schools, providing additional opportunities for interaction with mainstream French society. Alec Hargreaves notes, however, that the "increased visibility would not . . . have been so marked had it not been for one other crucial point: far more than earlier generations of immigrations, those originating in Third World countries were instantly recognizable because of their skin colour and other somatic features."[41] In addition to race, religion played a key role in distinguishing the new migrants from earlier, European-dominated flows, as the Islamic presence in France became increasingly pronounced.[42] The changing nature of immigration flows prompted the French government to begin to take action to control immigration from Algeria beginning in 1964. The Franco-Algerian Accord of April 10, 1964, created a framework to limit Algerian immigration and set an immigrant quota of twelve thousand per annum.[43]

In 1969, reports published by prominent analysts, including Corentin Calvez, Michel Massenet, and Maurice Schumann, recommended that France reexamine its immigration policies. All three suggested that France could no longer maintain an open-door (or a laissez-faire) policy with regard to migration, even if the economic gains were considerable.[44] The linkage between uncontrolled migration and societal insecurity was perhaps best articulated by Massenet, who writes, "The problems that immigration poses to our society put at risk society's future cohesion."[45] As such, Calvez suggested that immigration must be considered an issue of the highest importance and cannot be relegated to the vagaries of the market and private sector. Although immigration forwarded the economic interests of the nation, it also had the potential to cause social problems and create domestic instability.[46] Calvez suggested that the combination of a largely uncontrolled, free-market approach to immigration was leading to drastic demographic changes in France that would lead to an "unassimilable island" of foreigners, a trend that would be magnified due to the generally higher fertility rates among Algerian families.[47] Both Calvez and Massenet forwarded the notion that French society, while based on liberal principles founded during the French Revolution, had a "threshold of tolerance" (seuil de tolerance) for assimilating immigrants, and that neglecting this dynamic could have significant negative political and social effects. Even though it was a sentiment not often articulated openly, all of the reports generally suggest that it was North

African migration that challenged France's seuil de toleration, as opposed to migration in general.[48] What Calvez proposed was to encourage permanent immigration from other European countries whose citizens would more easily assimilate into French society while non-European migration would be utilized primarily on a temporary basis.[49] In October 1968, the 1960 agreement to permit the free circulation of member nationals within the EEC was implemented. European integration provided the means to encourage intra-European migration and also would be increasingly used as a multilateral approach to securing the external borders of the EU from the inflow of "third-country nationals." In contrast, subsequent agreements to the 1964 Franco-Algerian Accord were signed in 1968 and 1971 that added additional restrictions on Algerian immigration. For example, the 1968 agreement established residency permit requirements and placed time limits on Algerian immigrants to find work. Failure to secure work within the allotted time-frame could result in deportation. Moreover, new sanctions were implemented in 1968 against employers of illegal aliens in an attempt to regain control of the labor-recruitment process and end the overuse of regularization practices. However, even though the legalization rate declined in 1968 with the implementation of employer sanctions, overall levels of immigration nonetheless continued to increase. In 1972, the Marcellin (January 24) and Fontanet (February 24) *circulaires* established procedures to coordinate the issuance of residence and work permits under the authority of the Prefecture of Police (under the Ministry of the Interior). The circulaires sought to address the problem of the growing bidonvilles by predicating worker regularization on an immigrant's ability to secure decent housing.[50] The state also began to seek sending-state assistance in controlling immigration flows. From 1968–70, agreements were reached with Algeria that required immigrants to obtain a single work/residency permit, a process that served to slow the rate of increase in Algerian immigration.[51] Similar attempts were made in 1970–71 to extend control over West African countries of the franc zone, though migration continued in the form of false tourism.[52] As noted by James Hollifield, the new government of Valery Giscard d'Estaing "was willing to sacrifice the special relationship between France and its former colonies if this could help put an end to further immigration."[53] Where colonial relations were formerly seen as a fundamental component of French grand strategy, these new developments signaled a significant change in grand strategy, one that increasingly took into account societal as well as economic security dimensions.

On July 3, 1974, a ministerial circular "temporarily" halted worker immigration into France (*l'arête de l'immigration*), officially ending the nation's long-standing policy of openness to migration and also marked the end of the trente glorieuses. The temporary suspension of worker immigration in 1974 was later extended to family immigration (on October 9, 1974), and the government began to seek increased cooperation between national and local agencies to address immigration problems. Although the economic downturn of 1973–74 may have prompted the severity of France's statist response, the recession was certainly not the sole—nor even the most salient—factor in France's turn toward restriction. Maxim Silverman argues, "Immigration controls in contemporary France were not at first the result of the economic crisis of the 1970s; instead they were influenced largely by concerns about assimilation, ethnic balance, and social cohesion."[54] Public sentiment against the new immigration had been increasingly negative in the years preceding the *arête*.[55] Although the arête de l'immigration represented a significant and highly symbolic sea change in French policy regarding migration, the cessation of worker recruitment did not have the instrumental effects desired by policymakers. The arête was effective in reducing immigration levels of permanent workers; however, considerable levels of immigration continued due to family reunification provisions in French immigration law (Figure 5.6). From 1974–75, immigration of permanent workers dropped sharply, from 64,461 to 25,591. By 1980, the level had dropped down to 17,380. However, while the state sought to halt all forms of migration (both worker and family), the Conseil d'Etat decreed that the government could not deny the right of family reunification (1978) and also struck down restrictive elements of the Marcellin, Fontanet, and Gorse circulaires. As shown in Figure 5.6, levels of family-based migration remained relatively stable in the period between 1965 and 1980. Because immigration of families leads to deeper penetration of immigrants into mainstream society, "the presence of Third World immigrants and their descendants has become ever more visible in virtually every sphere of French society."[56] Societal insecurities thus remained politically salient even after the arête.

The institutionalization of the liberal dimension of French national identity not only precluded extending the arête de l'immigration to family-based

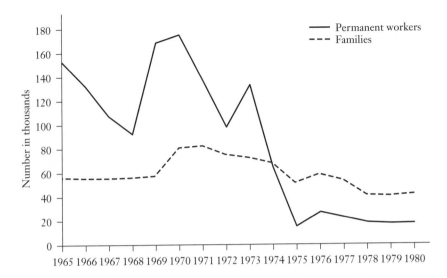

Figure 5.6. Permanent and Family Immigration into France, 1965–1980
SOURCE: OMISTATS.

migration but also made mass deportation politically untenable, as was the case in Germany. Yet policymakers remained eager to reduce the number of foreigners currently in the country in order to address the societal problems that their presence presented. In 1977, the government established a new policy that offered financial incentives to foreign residents to voluntarily return to their home country (*l'aide au retour*), a program similar to one launched in Germany. Lionel Stoleru, minister of state for immigrant workers, encouraged the voluntary repatriation of immigrants by offering monetary compensation from the state to those willing to voluntarily leave France.[57] Under the program, immigrant workers with at least five years of residence in France were eligible to receive ten thousand francs in exchange for their voluntary return to their home country.[58] However, as was the case in Germany, the voluntary repatriation program met with little success. Although Stoleru had hoped to process hundreds of thousands of foreigners, only about eighty thousand immigrants participated—far short of the program's goals.[59] Moreover, those who participated the most—generally Spaniards and Portuguese—were not the intended targets of the new policy. Few North African migrants participated in France's voluntary repatriation scheme.[60]

SHIFTING CHANNELS OF ENTRY

France soon became aware that migration flows were capable of responding to governmental action and circumventing the front door when it closes. Because certain sectors of the economy preferred foreign labor and had grown to depend on its availability, employment opportunities provided a continuing pull for migrants, whether they entered the country through legal or alternative channels.[61] Illegal immigration and the presence of a large marginalized immigration population in France continued to fester as a challenge to policymakers. Because mass deportation ran counter to France's liberal republican dimension of identity, policymakers instead adopted a dual strategy that consisted of promoting the social integration of existing migrants while attempting to thwart future flows. This would be achieved by regularizing the existing illegal immigrant population to promote assimilation while concurrently stepping up controls to stem future clandestine migration.[62] The circulaire of August 11, 1981, granted amnesty to illegal aliens who entered France before January 1, 1981, and were employed. Immigrants who met these criteria would be granted a temporary three-month residence permit in order to complete the process of adjusting their immigration status (*regularisation exceptionnelle*). Although the level of illegal immigrant participation was not on par with the amnesty program implemented in the United States (wherein some three million undocumented workers were legalized), the fact that the French government received 145,000 applications for regularisation confirmed suspicions that migrant flows had moved increasingly from front-door channels to the backdoor.[63]

Another channel of entry that began to exhibit an increasing volume of inflow was through France's refugee and asylum provisions. While total immigration flows remained steady between one hundred and two hundred thousand annually from 1975 through the 1980s, increases in migrant flows were manifest primarily in the number of people seeking asylum (Figure 5.7). Like Germany, France's commitment to liberal asylum policies was codified in its constitution as well as its acceptance of the 1951 Geneva Convention and the subsequent 1967 protocol adopted in New York. Early cold war refugee movements were a function of France's colonial legacy, as many of the applicants desiring asylum in France originated in what was once French Indochina (Vietnam, Cambodia, Laos). Even though the one hundred thou-

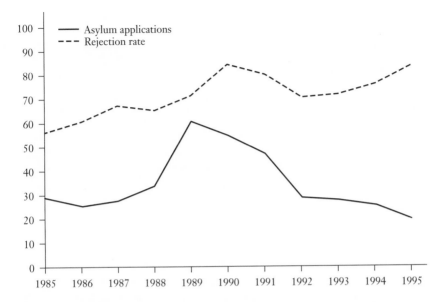

Figure 5.7.   Asylum Applications (in thousands) and Rate of Rejection (percent) in France, 1985–1995
SOURCE: OFPRA.

sand or so refugees admitted from Southeast Asia were assimilated into France without much problem, the 1980s saw a distinct rise in asylum seek-ers from other third world nations, especially from Africa.[64] As was the case in both Germany and Britain, there was increasing concern that many of those applying for asylum were in fact economic migrants seeking to cir-cumvent the arête de l'immigration established in 1974.[65] In response, while levels of asylum seekers grew throughout the 1980s, the rejection level of ap-plications increased as well, rising from 56.8 percent in 1985 to nearly 85 per-cent in 1990 (Figure 5.7).[66] The high rejection rate and limited possibility of appeal served to keep the numbers of those admitted relatively low, but a number of those refused asylum simply remained in the country illegally.[67] Estimates of the numbers of illegal immigrants who remained in France af-ter being denied asylum numbered some one hundred thousand in 1990.[68]

As is the case with other liberal European nations, asylum and refugee policy represents a significant political challenge for policymakers. Defense of refugees fleeing political persecution became a central feature of a liberal identity in many Western European nations, including France. Yet, the fact that refugee flows can be large and highly visible (both in terms of space and time) make them politically difficult to manage without either abandoning commitments to liberal norms (codified in the Geneva Convention) or increasing the probability of societal insecurity and domestic disturbances, as was evident when worker migration occurred outside of strict government control. Moreover, because many of these liberal norms protecting refugees and asylum applicants have been subsumed in domestic legal institutions, protecting against possible nativist backlashes against such flows becomes even more precarious for policymakers.[69] Policymakers are frequently caught in crossfire between "alarmed restrictionists" and "vocal refugee advocates."[70] The rise of societal concerns in France served to transform asylum policy from one primarily focused on human rights, to one increasingly associated with the general "problem" of immigration.[71] The technique increasingly used in Europe to square the circle between the desires to maintain a commitment to human rights while concurrently increasing the ability to control such flows has been to adopt a multilateral approach to management.[72]

Eleven member states of the European Community, including France, signed the Dublin Convention on May 27, 1990, in order to better manage asylum applications. The convention is an intergovernmental approach intended not only to harmonize asylum policies in Europe but also to thwart the exploitation of those policies by economic migrants seeking to circumvent state controls. Under the terms of the Dublin Convention, the first country that an asylum seeker enters is responsible for handling his or her claim, a policy intended to insure that claimants receive only one review of their application among member states. If unsuccessful in one state, the applicant cannot reapply with another member state. In 1992, EC ministers created further control policies at the meeting of the Ad Hoc Group on Immigration in London. In order to facilitate rejection of "manifestly unfounded" asylum applications, the concept of the "safe country" was introduced, wherein entry is rejected if transit occurs through countries in which there is generally no serious risk of persecution.[73] This principle of the "safe third country" has been applied in national policies of several EU member states, including France. In a similar fashion, France's participation in the Schengen Agreement promotes a cooperative approach to controlling migration from outside of the European Community. Yet, even with Schengen's emphasis on controlling illegal immigration and the movement of third-country nationals (TCNs) within the European Union, French authorities remained skeptical of relinquishing sovereignty over controls.[74] Ultimately, France's participation in the Schengen and Dublin Agreements enable it to promote internal mobility within Europe, while utilizing collective action to curb unwanted migration from outside of the union, creating what many have described as the "fortress Europe." The European approach to migration in the context of societal security is a grand strategy that promotes internal openness and external closure.

ETRE FRANÇAIS, AUJOURD'HUI ET DEMAIN?

Perhaps more important than the policy adjustments made by the French government after the immigration stoppage of 1974 was the fact that the new trends in migration underscored fundamental contradictions and tensions present in modern French national identity. Although French national identity is not based on a dominant myth of immigration, as is the case with the United States, the two nations are remarkably similar in that a fundamental tension exists between liberal republican and ethno-cultural elements of the collective identity of the nation. Many scholars have pointed out that the rise of Jean-Marie Le Pen's National Front Party in the 1980s ushered in divisive debates regarding French culture and identity.[75] These domestic political forces, however, were simply exploiting an existing (though long latent) condition in French society. In a 1985 opinion poll taken by BVA, two-thirds of respondents believed that French national identity was in jeopardy if steps were not taken to limit the size and inflow of the foreign population.[76] In 1989, a poll taken by the same organization found that the proportion of respondents holding this belief had increased to three-quarters.[77] Rather than instigating societal insecurities, the rise of the National Front simply tapped into a latent tension already existent in the French mainstream population. The political turbulence that has accompanied French debates regarding immigration and national identity and the difficulty policymakers face in crafting a stable political equilibrium between impulses for openness and closure results from the fact that, in the French case, what constitutes "societal security" is manifestly ambiguous and contested. What dimension of French societal security must be defended by the state—its liberal republican aspect, or its ethno-cultural aspect? Although the liberal republican tradition appeals to intellectual ideologies and has been vigorously espoused by the French intelligentsia, the latent ethno-cultural dimension that rose during the 1970s and 1980s (and, in fact, continued to be active in the 1990s) appeals to the more visceral terms of romanticism and found considerable public support with the mainstream during this period.[78]

The combination of increasing (primarily Muslim) proportions of Maghrebi migrants and acts of Islamic terrorism in 1986 served to exacerbate already existing societal insecurities. Terrorist bombings in Paris linked to Iranian Islamic groups heightened the sense of crisis for several reasons. First, and most obviously, the linkage between Islamic fundamentalism and terrorism within France increased sensitivities to the presence of Muslims in France, mostly immigrants and foreign workers and their families. Second, North African immigrants in France represented a threatening political force in the domestic politics of France because of their growing numbers and closely held notions of Islam as a collective identity.[79] Lastly, the French mainstream believed that Muslim immigrants' ability to assimilate was compromised by the presence of Islam in the construction of their personal and social identity. This was directly at odds with the French emphasis on the notion of *laïcité*, or liberal secularism. In a SOFRES poll taken 1984, 70 percent of respondents answered that Algerians integrated "badly" in society, followed by Gypsies (64 percent), Moroccans (48 percent), black Africans (48 percent), Turks (43 percent), and Tunisians (42 percent).[80]

In response to the terrorist bombings and increasing public concern about the foreign presence in France, Charles Pasqua, minister of the interior under the coalition government of Jacques Chirac, initiated a series of "get tough" policies that restricted the civil liberties of foreigners, including granting new deportation powers to the Police de l'Air et des Frontieres (PAF) when encountering individuals who did not possess proper documentation (commonly referred to as the first Pasqua Law). Even though the Pasqua Law did not result in a significant decrease in the number of foreigners present in France, it symbolically represented a government committed to regaining a sense of societal control.[81] More significant, however, was the attempt by Pasqua and the Chirac government to weaken France's adherence to jus soli citizenship criteria by amending the Nationality Code of 1945, a political agenda that was a cornerstone of Chirac's election platform.[82] The focal points of reform were Article 23, which attributed French citizenship at birth to third-generation immigrants, and Article 44, which attributed citizenship at majority to most second-generation immigrants.[83] When these articles were reviewed more carefully for revision, the complications of revoking Article 23 became readily apparent. "If the Article we revised were to be declared inoperative only with reference to Algeria and other former colonies [as would be necessary to curb the specific *type* of foreign population of concern to the increasingly nativist French public], this would be tantamount to denying the historical legitimacy of French colonization; it would also raise difficulties for the *rapatries*."[84] Because of these complications, the emphasis of reformers was placed on Article 44, which automatically granted citizenship to those born on French soil when they reached the age of majority.[85] The proposed reform of Article 44 sought to replace the automatic granting of citizenship upon majority age with an active declaration of citizenship by applicants combined with a loyalty oath. While these proposed changes did not abandon the adherence to jus soli, it was intended to send a strong symbolic message. James Hollifield notes, "The message was quite clear: the acquisition of French citizenship is a privilege, not a right, and it should be withheld from those who have not made a clear commitment to the French nation and society."[86] Questions regarding the loyalties and assimilative capacity of Muslim immigrants reflected in public opinion polls make the objects of this symbolic policy clear and unmistakable. Immigrant's rights groups and civil liberties organizations levied strong political opposition to the proposed changes, prompting Chirac to table the reform bill in Parliament in November 1986.[87] However, this was by no means the end of the debate, nor did it constitute the ultimate triumph of the liberal Left on the immigration question. Maxim Silverman notes, "Although there was much opposition to the proposal by the Chirac government to modify the Code, there was a far wider consensus on the need to change the Code in some way."[88] However, it was clear to policymakers that the new discourse was proving to be politically volatile and required a more nuanced approach to dealing with the question of societal security.

In an attempt to garner consensus and to craft new policy that responds to mainstream concerns rather than the demands of the political fringe (on both the Left and the Right), Chirac decided in January 1987 that a special commission would be created to examine the question of immigration and French national identity (Commission des Sages). In order to depoliticize what could create rancorous debate on the issues at hand, the commission, established on June 22, 1987, was composed of experts from various disciplines and included a wide spectrum of political orientations, though emphasis was placed on the need for political independence. The commission was given free reign with regard to the scope of issues considered, the testimony of those asked to address the commission (which numbered more than fifty), and the nature of the discourse among the members of the commission. Garnering the lion's share of the commission's attention was the issue of Muslims in France and the question of the Nationality Code.[89] This preoccupation with the Muslim question prompted the need to add an additional session so that testimony from those representing the Portuguese and Asian point of view could be heard.[90] Although the commission was designed as a committee of experts, the process of deliberation was not insulated from the public. Rather, hearings were broadcast live on French television, a procedure designed not only to ensure a sense of participation among the general public but also to increase the possibility of achieving some kind of general consensus upon its conclusion.[91]

The findings of the Commission des Sages, including a full transcript of commission hearings, were published in January 1988 in two volumes entitled, *Etre Français, Aujourd'hui et Demain* (What it means to be French, now and in the future).[92] The volumes stressed two dominant themes—a communitarian perspective of French nationhood and the voluntaristic tradition of French citizenship—and set out recommendations for reform of the Nationality Code. As it had been designed to do, the recommendations of the commission sought to define a political middle ground between the competing conceptions of nationhood. The commission agreed that Article 44 of the Nationality Code should be amended to include a positive declaration of citizenship and to limit the benefits of new procedures to those between the ages of sixteen and twenty-one (who had resided in France in the five years preceding the application); however, the commission recommended that a liberal approach be maintained with regard to the application of such requirements. Rather than requiring both a stated declaration of citizenship and an oath of allegiance upon reaching majority, assent to acquisition of citizenship would require only the ticking of a box and the applicant's signature on the form. With regard to amending Article 23, the recommendation of the commission again sought middle ground. It suggested that a distinction be made between French *departements* and colonies, and that Article 23 should apply only to former departements and not former colonies.[93]

Because the commission sought to achieve a broader sense of public consensus on the issue of national identity by holding to the middle ground, some critics dismissed the significance of the Nationality Commission, stating that the "changes" proposed amounted to little more than continuation of current policies. Although a radical change of policy did not occur as a result of the commission's findings and recommendations, this does not necessarily imply that the commission had little real use. Miriam Feldblum argues:

> The National Commission on Nationality [Commission des Sages] constituted a critical phase in the new citizenship politics. . . . The Commission gradually provided the keys for a specifically nationalist reconstruction of citizenship. Their understanding of citizenship incorporated four kinds of claims: the fusion of national and pluralist identity, the necessity of a national integration of immigrants, the appropriateness of a voluntarist citizenship, and finally, the reaffirmation of a statist perspective on citizenship. Via this reconstruction of citizenship, an effective consensus formed across the political spectrum. The consensus rejected pluralist arguments for a "right to difference" and defined the Maghrebi, Muslim immigration as a challenge to be managed through national statist integration.[94]

Gerard Noiriel has suggested that "a 'collective memory' of immigration had not yet been forged in interwar France because two alternative expressions of collective identity held the stage."[95] As is the case with U.S. identity, this bifurcation of the dominant mode of French identity is configured in oppositional and seemingly incompatible terms (liberal-civic versus ethnocultural identity). The work of the commission highlights how difficult it is for liberal, democratic states to square this circle. In such societies, the choice is not simply between economic rationalism (promoting openness and flexibility) and societal nationalism (stressing closure), but that responding to societal interests is often conflicting in and of itself. The Commission des Sages represents a unique attempt to respond directly to these issues through the use of public debate held in an open forum.

The empirical evidence drawn from the 1970s and 1980s lends strong support for the Threat Hypothesis, as well as others dealing with societal variables. As relative external threats declined with the rise in French material power, European integration, the NATO alliance, and emerging détente between the Soviets and the West, sensitivities to societal insecurities gained salience in the security agenda. Moreover, these societal insecurities were magnified by the changing characteristics of migration flows. Societal insecurities were definitely exacerbated by a rise in migration from North Africa. In addition, the concentration of Maghrebi migrants in certain geographic locales and their increased association with urban ghettoization contributed to negative perceptions of migration among the French public and also to societal insecurities. Ironically, many of these societal insecurities were the function of trading-state grand strategy in the early cold war period. Not only did imperial legacies prompt French policymakers to sign agreements with colonial governments regarding migration to the French metropole, but labor recruitment policies driven by macroeconomic dimensions of grand strategy shaped many of the changes that prompted societal insecurities in the 1970s and later. Government response to increased societal insecurities resulted in a sharp turn toward restrictionism throughout the 1970s and into the 1980s. However, the severity of this restrictionism was tempered by liberal principles codified in French legal institutions and in the French national consciousness. What is unique in the French case was the attempt to address societal insecurities not only through more restrictive policy but also through public discourse and compromise in the 1980s.

Migration Policy after the Cold War

If détente represented a relative decline in external threat compared to the immediate post–WWII period, the end of the cold war certainly represented a further reduction in geopolitical security pressures. The Threat Hypothesis predicts that in an environment characterized by diverse migration flows, societal insecurities should grow in strength and government policies should become increasingly responsive to such interests. As in the

1980s, Muslim migration remained a central issue of societal insecurity, and the 1990s saw movement in the French Right that capitalized on such growing sentiments. In a 1991 poll, 49 percent of respondents felt that Islam was "sufficiently alien" to French societal norms to make their assimilation impossible.[96]

Although public and policymakers alike largely praised the work of the Commission des Sages, no changes to the *Code d'Nationalité* occurred during the 1980s.[97] However, in 1993, the rise of a Center-Right alliance marked the beginning of the effort to implement the changes stipulated by the Commission des Sages. Boldly stating that the goal of French migration policy would be "zero immigration," Interior Minister Charles Pasqua set out to stem non-EU migration, curtail abuse of French asylum policies, and reform the Nationality Code according to the recommendations of the Commission des Sages. Reaction from the Left protested the new directions set by Pasqua, but public opinion strongly supported the new initiatives, including increased identity checks of foreigners (and those who "looked foreign") and granting police authority to "control" those suspected of being foreigners. Fifty-seven percent of respondents in a 1994 public opinion poll said that they supported the new identity checks.[98] Most prominent of the legislative developments in 1993, however, was the establishment of the Pasqua Law that amended the Nationality Code. While the Pasqua Law did not abolish the jus soli basis of Article 44, it did mandate an active declaration of intent to naturalize in addition to meeting the requirements that applicants be able to demonstrate consecutive residence in France for the five-year period preceding naturalization. Application for citizenship was to occur between the ages of sixteen and twenty-one. Failure to do so during this time period would result in the loss of eligibility to gain French citizenship via Article 44, though other avenues for naturalization remained available. The law also restricted the ability of parents to obtain French nationality for minor children born in France, an additional modification to Article 44. However, the Conseil d'Etat would later overturn several of the more restrictive elements of the Pasqua Law, namely the one-year ban on reentry for those deported from the country, longer waiting periods required for foreign students and workers seeking to be joined by immediate family members, and restrictions placed on marriages of foreigners with French citizens.[99]

Events in the early 1990s kept the societal dimensions of migration in the political spotlight. The number of illegal immigrants residing in France was increasing, in part due to a provision of the Pasqua Law that forbade the regularization of French-born children of illegal immigrants and foreign spouses of French citizens yet did not allow them to be summarily deported by the government. This group of undocumented (*sans papiers*) foreigners received considerable public exposure in the summer of 1996 when a group of Africans challenged the government's position regarding those sans papiers by occupying a church in Paris. Moreover, the volatility of the Algerian political situation in the mid–1990s spilled over into France, as Islamic terrorists initiated attacks throughout France. In 1996, Minister of the Interior Jean-Louis Debre proposed steps to crackdown on illegal immigration and thwart fundamentalist violence. Debre proposed that all private citizens be required by law to notify the government if they receive any non-EU foreigners in their homes. The infringement on the civil liberties of French citizens and the obvious bias against African immigrants caused a political uproar on the Left.[100] Even though the version of the Debre Law finally passed through the French Parliament (March 1996) did not include the most draconian of its original provisions, it again brought the national identity question to the forefront and guided the political developments of the new Socialist government elected in 1997.[101]

Mimicking the pattern set earlier, newly elected Prime Minister Lionel Jospin sought a reevaluation of migration policy and commissioned political scientist Patrick Weil to prepare an analysis to guide possible revisions.[102] Like the Commission des Sages that preceded him, Weil sought to avoid the "restrictionism" of the Right and the "blind egalitarianism" of the Left, seeking instead to promote consensus-building middle ground.[103] As James Hollifield notes, "The report was designed to placate the right, while trying to meet the pro-immigrant left 'half-way.'"[104] As such, Weil's recommendations were largely consistent with the previous findings of the Nationality Commission, though he suggested that voluntarism was not an integral part of the tradition of French nationality. The report recommended that the government remain vigilant in combating illegal immigration while concurrently promoting the integration of those already in the country.[105] Based on the recommendations contained in the Weil report, the government began the political process that resulted in the Guigou Law (December 1997), which proposed adjustments to the 1993 changes in the Nationality Code, and the Chevenement Law (May 1998), which eliminated the "legal entry requirement" of the Pasqua Law and enabled the government to reevaluate the claims of the large population of sans papiers living in France. Although the Guigou Law established *automatic* citizenship for children born in France of non-French parents when they reach majority (if they have resided in France at least five years since the age of eleven), it did not rescind all of the changes enacted in 1993. The prior requirement of positive affirmation of the desire for French citizenship was replaced with a provision that would allow applicants to decline French nationality within six months preceding their eighteenth birthday and for one year following that date. Even though the 1997 changes to the Nationality Code did not return French policy to its pre–1993 status, its emphasis on the automatic granting of citizenship represents a turn to the political Left of the original compromise articulated by the Commission des Sages. The bill narrowly passed in the National Assembly (267–246), and public opinion does not suggest widespread support for its move away from voluntarism in the naturalization process. A 1997 IFOP poll found that 76 percent of respondents believed that citizenship should be granted to French-born children of foreign parents only if specifically requested.[106] The incongruity between public opinion and the beliefs of France's liberal political elite suggest that the Guigou Law does not represent a stable equilibrium and will likely not serve as the last word with regard to France's evolving conception of national identity.

As has generally been the case among other European nations facing the same societal security dilemma, French grand strategy can be characterized by internal openness and external closure. The process of European integration that began with the Rome Statue in 1957 served not only as a collective action to bolster European security and promote economic development but also to create a migration regime that forwards the economic and political preferences of member states. Societal security was generally not threatened by intra-European migration, but rather by the rise in migration of "third-country nationals." The free mobility clauses in the Rome Statute and later the Maastricht Treaty on European Union (1993) established a regime that promotes both culturally proximate and elastic labor flows that respond to labor requirements without unduly exacerbating societal tensions. Whereas the free-mobility provisions of European integration maximize economic gains while minimizing societal insecurities, the process of integration has also led to cooperative multilateralism to stem the flow of "less desirable" migrant flows. Policy harmonization both of immigration policy (Schengen Agreement) and refugee/asylum policy (Dublin Convention) reflect a willingness to cede a degree of Westphalian sovereignty in exchange for increasing the ability to control flows. In addition to multilateral control mechanisms, France, like Germany, has sought to shape its foreign policy to promote its societal security needs. Linking foreign aid with securing sending-state cooperation in controlling flows partly accomplishes this goal. Not only do such measures help control existing flows, but also linking aid with migration policy serves to reduce economic disparities that initiate migration pressures. During a 1996 Franco-African summit in Ouagadougou, Burkina Faso, Jacques Chirac announced that France was reorienting its development aid to Africa to areas that generate migration flows to France. He suggested that accelerated economic development represented the only way to stop "the problem of excessive immigration" to France.[107] Lionel Jospin articulated the same position in December 1997 during a tour of Africa.[108] This connection between development and migration has also figured prominently in U.S. discourse and policy regarding NAFTA and migration from Mexico.

During the 1990s, societal security remained a volatile issue in French society and French politics. A 1998 public opinion poll showed that 75 percent of the French population believed that French national identity was in jeopardy if measures were not taken to limit the size and inflow of the foreign population.[109] The percentage of French citizens expressing such sentiments increased 10 percent over similar polls taken a decade earlier, and they reached their highest numbers in 1999.[110] However, the increasing importance of migration to the French economy and welfare state, as well as to the liberal dimension of French national identity, pressed policymakers to craft migration policy that represented a compromise between competing interests. Similar to the approach taken in Germany, French policymakers have sought to shore up border control to restrict entry of third-country nationals, while maintaining a commitment to intra-EU openness and policy harmonization with other member states. In terms of the "control and integration" strategy for dealing with societal insecurities resulting from migration, policy has been focused sharply on those elements of migration that spur societal insecurities while maintaining a liberal posture vis-à-vis migration in general. Consistent with an emerging consensus among advanced industrial liberal democracies, the focus of grand strategy has been on dealing with *fears* while facilitating *flows*.

Migration and Security After 9/11

One might expect that the new linkage made between global terrorism — the emergent "military" threat of the new millennium — and international migration would result in a significant redistribution of security interests reflected in state grand strategy. Whereas prior to 9/11 states sought to craft a political equilibrium between the economic interests that favored openness and the societal interests that favored closure, states now found another compelling reason that migration control was a central state imperative. Moreover, given the fact that Muslim migrants were already the source of much societal insecurity in the country, the widespread association of Muslims with the events of 9/11 and the al Qaeda network would seem to make France the most likely case for a migration clampdown. However, although new security measures have been established since the fall of 2001, migration policy in France remains marked by a similar attempt to address fears while still maximizing the economic gains available through migration.

An initial government response to the new security environment involved increasing authority for law enforcement personnel in dealing with suspected terrorists operating in the country and in increasing cooperation with other countries to control clandestine migration flows. Interior Minister Nicolas Sarkozy obtained funding for 6,500 new police positions, and quickly deployed an additional 750 officers to patrol France's borders. In addition, Sarkozy received government commitments for increased jail capacity to be created and announced that police will be given added power to search houses and vehicles to increase security. A new restrictionist climate in migration policies in France was also marked by increased ID checks and forcible deportations. Initially, policies toward Afghan and other refugees were consistent with prior policies. Sarkozy established a new program in September 2002 offering two thousand euros to Afghan refugees who willingly return home. A year later, however, this carrot was replaced with a stick. The immigration law passed on November 26, 2003, reversed a prior reluctance in France to aggressively pursue the deportation of illegal aliens. This practice had already begun in March 2003, prior to the passing of the new law, when some 270 illegal immigrants were deported to Romania and Afghanistan on government-chartered planes.[111] The new law sought to begin forcibly repatriating from twenty to thirty thousand illegal aliens each year. Moreover, the law permits law enforcement to hold illegal aliens in custody for one month before being deported and also provides additional judicial power to speed up the deportation process. The law sought to address loopholes often exploited by illegal immigrants to circumvent government control. Migrants have often utilized the practice of destroying visas and identification documents to avoid deportation. Under the 2003 law, immigration officials began collecting biometric identification data from foreign visitors who were issued three-month tourist visas in order to confirm the identities of those who might claim to have lost their documentation.

In addition to pursuing new policies internally, Sarkozy has also increased cooperation with Britain in managing migrant flows across the Channel Tunnel in an effort to increase control. Under pressure from the British government, who had suggested that a Red Cross center in Sangatte was being exploited as a staging point for illegal immigration from France into the United Kingdom, the French government closed the center in December 2002. Sarkozy also deployed one thousand gendarmes in the area who apprehended hundreds of illegal immigrants and arrested some 250 migrant smugglers.

Even though homeland security interests have become more pronounced in the formation of immigration and border policies, societal aspects of security remain prominent in French policymaking. Indeed, 9/11 may have in fact increased the level of debate, given that the al Qaeda terrorists were from Muslim countries—the source of much of France's ethno-nationalist societal insecurities. The unprecedented support garnered by Jean-Marie Le Pen in the April 2002 elections is evidence of a continued sense of ethno-cultural societal threat. Such sentiments appeared especially strong in areas with high concentrations of immigrants where Le Pen's National Front Party received many of its votes. New policies aimed to reduce societal insecurity have taken the form of the Sarkozy law, an anticrime bill approved by the French cabinet in October 2002 which criminalizes begging and vagabondage, "passive soliciting" by prostitutes, and squatters who occupy private property. Migrant advocacy groups see such policies as evidence of government scapegoating and harassment. Moreover, the 2003 immigration law includes additional measures to address societal insecurity. It increased the minimum wait time for migrants to be granted residency permits from three to five years. More important, perhaps, is the requirement that applicants would have to prove their integration into French society.[112] Consistent with the approach taken during the late 1980s and 1990s, President Jacques Chirac has proposed integration contracts to be initiated between migrants and the government. These contracts would provide migrants with French-language instruction and job training in order to bolster integration into French society.

The post–9/11 environment most certainly has seen an increase in restrictionism. However, the overlap between military and societal security interests make it difficult to isolate causal variables at play. In both respects, Muslim immigrants are the focus of restrictionist policies. Although there has been an increase in restrictionist policies, the environment in France does not necessarily suggest that grand strategy has undergone a fundamental transformation. In many respects, the policy equilibrium resembles that which was built during the 1990s. However, the new security environment has reduced liberal constraints regarding civil liberties, as well as with the issue of deportation of illegal aliens and refugees deemed non-bona fide. At the same time, however, policymakers remain cognizant of demographic factors that put stress on the viability and solvency of the welfare state, as well as on the need for skilled and unskilled immigrant labor to drive economic production. As was the case prior to 9/11, the search for a viable equilibrium continues.

Conclusion

What factors account for French state behavior with regards to migration in the post–World War II period? Scholars who focus on interest-group and / or collective-action dynamics in the domestic political sphere argue that a statist perspective is inadequate to explain general changes in French policy. Jeannette Money dismisses analyses that focus on ethno-cultural or identity factors because, according to her, they "provide no explanation of why these concerns elicited a reaction at one time whereas in an earlier period the same concerns were ignored."[113] Moreover, she questions, "Why would the government initially promote non-European immigration only to decide later that these groups were unacceptable?"[114] Domestic politics models profess to elucidate the "black box" of state decision making by tracing political interests from the bottom up. However, during the postwar period, policy in France has consistently been driven from the top down, in the form of a series of general plans developed by the Conseil General du Plan (CGP) and by executive order and decrees in the early period, and by consensus-seeking policies after the arête de l'immigration in 1974. If one takes into consideration a combination of structural, ideational, and sociodemographic factors, in addition to incorporating misperceptions and reactions to the unforeseen consequences of prior policies, the "black box" of the state becomes much less mysterious. Moreover, reductionist theories that eschew analysis of French national identity miss a (perhaps *the*) central tension that permeates political discourse in France to this day.

As this case study illustrates, while there was consistent awareness of preferences for "cultural proximity" and "assimilability" among policymakers and the general public during the immediate postwar period, several factors served to reduce the salience of these factors in the construction of postwar grand strategy. The structural environment facing postwar France presented an acute sense of territorial threat in both military and economic terms. Similar to the German case, the acute external security threat served to prioritize economic development and reconstruction over concerns regarding societal security. Societal insecurity was also kept in check by the fact that migration flows in the early postwar period were dominated by Europeans (primarily Italians) who were deemed easily assimilable and represented little threat to French societal security. Moreover, the fact that these immigrants were easily assimilable reaffirmed the dominant beliefs of political elites in the power of liberal republicanism and the *modele français de l'integration*. Given these factors, there was little reason for societal insecurities to develop, at least to a degree that would affect the economics-dominated grand strategy of the early postwar period. As economic gains were realized and migration presented few sociopolitical problems (at the time), confidence among policymakers grew that migration could simply be another dimension of economic reconstruction, a belief that led to the transition from a government controlled program of worker recruitment, to one that established a period of laissez-faire application of existing programs.[115] The unanticipated consequences of this transition to laissez-faire policy (which led to recruitment from new and less culturally proximate migrant-sending nations) would then establish the conditions that have driven French politics since the late 1960s.

If French grand strategy from 1945–68 was dominated by economic interests, the period following can be characterized as an attempt to craft a new, more balanced grand strategy that sought to maximize security on both external and societal dimensions. How has France dealt with the problem of finding a stable equilibrium? Like the United States, defending societal security in France is complicated by the fact that the national identity is dominated by two dimensions set in binary opposition. On the one hand, liberal republicanism has been the cornerstone of French political identity since the Revolution. On the other hand, the presence of an increasing number of ethno-culturally diverse foreigners has generally swayed popular opinion toward what Miriam Feldblum has termed "neo-national" membership and policies that "reconfigure cultural, national, and transnational boundaries to ensure closure."[116] France is quite unique, however, in the fact that it has sought to address the identity question directly through public discourse and the establishment of government commissions and state-sponsored analyses of French nationhood. However, because of the incongruous nature of the two primary dimensions of French national identity, the referent object of "societal security" has been ambiguous and makes crafting policy that secures societal concerns deeply problematic.

Maxim Silverman characterized French migration policy as a two-pronged approach based on "control and integration."[117] Whereas European integration and multilateralism formed much of the basis of its control strategy, the question of integration has been much more problematic. It is the integration of the existing foreign population in France that has sparked the expansive debate regarding immigration, citizenship, and French national identity. Because trading-state economic liberalism has maintained its dominant position in the grand strategy of advanced industrial states, dealing with societal security concerns reflects an acutely political rather than instrumental problem for policymakers. Often, analysts have portrayed the political problems of societal security in terms of party politics, of a struggle between Leftist liberals and Le Pen's radical Right. However, the turbulent rhetoric of the 1980s and 1990s was not characterized by societal actors "capturing" the state and directing resultant policies, but rather of a state-centric attempt by administrations on both the Left and the Right to balance competing dimensions of the identity conflict and to craft a new identity to reach a mainstream consensus. Although those on the political fringe have sought to exploit France's identity crisis to forward their specific political agendas, Lionel Jospin revealed policymakers' desire to defuse the political problem when he stated that he would like immigration "to be removed from the realm of French passions."[118] This desire to defuse, rather than exploit, the political tensions inherent in identity politics is also evident in the government's establishment of the Commission des Sages in the 1980s, as well as subsequent state-sponsored studies that sought to identify a stable consensus-building position. In the French case, as in Germany, Great Britain, and the United States, policymakers have often attempted to "finesse" conflicting dimensions of national identity through the use of symbolic policy. In the case of the French citizenship debates, this took the form of manipulating the requirement for a positive declaration of desire to obtain French citizenship. It can be said that the Pasqua Law of 1993 is remarkable not so much because of its implementation of more restrictive measures to control immigration, but rather because jus soli was maintained as the fundamental basis of French citizenship during a period where openness was not supported by public opinion and the government in power was conservative. Here, retaining the symbolic act of voluntarism on the part of the applicant was used to defuse calls for a move away from France's liberal republican tradition that has been a fundamental dimension of French identity. The decision by lawmakers to again revise the Nationality Code in 1997 and remove this highly symbolic provision would seem strikingly incongruous with public consensus and may likely provoke a new round of debate on the issue of national identity in the new millennium.

In his seminal work on citizenship and nationhood, Rogers Brubaker juxtaposes the traditions of national identity in France and Germany.[119] Although the liberal republican tradition among France's political elite has certainly dominated definitions of French nationhood, the challenges of diverse immigration flows have revealed a latent ethno-cultural dimension reminiscent of German romanticism. This latent romanticism is reflected in the writings of Ernest Renan, who, while proclaiming the virtues of French republicanism, also refers to the nation as "a soul, a spiritual principle" and promotes French cultural absolutism.[120] Contemporary migration has brought these latent tensions to the surface, making societal security politically salient even when the referent objects of these security concerns are manifestly unclear and vociferously contested. Until a stable consensus is reached on how societal security is to be defined, French grand strategy may display a higher degree of inconsistency, periodic turbulence, and suboptimal outcomes. Ethnic rioting in November 2005 suggests that issues of societal security and national identity will remain prominent in French social and political discourse in the coming years.

CHAPTER SIX

National Security and Immigration in Great Britain

We should not engage in flagellation over our glorious past. I, for one, am proud of our imperial heritage.

— GERALD HOWARD, Tory MP, October 11, 2000

We do not denigrate British history. There is a very important role for a common national culture and a common civic nationality. But we are requesting this common culture needs to be discussed and renegotiated.

— BHIKHU PAREKH, Chair of the Commission of the Future of a Multiethnic Britain, October 11, 2000

Few issues stir the passions of Britons as much as immigration, and Great Britain's half-century of political turbulence surrounding the immigration question show few signs of abating. After an emergency Downing Street summit on immigration called by Tony Blair in April 2004, shadow home secretary David Davis described the government's immigration system as being "in complete shambles."[1] New "get tough" measures to control migration have taken the form of increased carrier- and employer sanctions rules, more restrictive processing of asylum claims, and emerging concerns about the potential migration generated by EU expansion. Addressing parliament in 2004, Tony Blair remarked, "It is important that we recognize that there is a potential risk from these accession countries. We will take whatever measures are necessary to make sure that the 'pull factor' which might draw people here is closed off."[2] However, restrictionist sentiment sparks an equally fervent response among Britons favoring a more liberal posture: "Most asylum seekers I have met have been treated abysmally in their own countries and are stigmatised and treated as less than human by the UK system and its officials. It makes me ashamed to be British when I read the ignorance of some of the comments on boards such as this and some of the editorials written by educated people who should know better."[3]

It has been suggested that the United Kingdom represents a deviant case in comparison to other advanced industrial states because it has "steadfastly ignored the economic consequences of immigration, even when (as is often the case) these would almost certainly be positive."[4] Extant explanations of policy outcomes in Britain have generally centered on three types of causal variables: localized interests and domestic politics, ideational factors, and institutional dynamics. Domestic-centered approaches have stressed the fact that the costs and benefits of migration are not evenly distributed nationally because migrants are not evenly dispersed geographically. The demands of immigrants for public goods and services establish competition with native populations and spurs anti-immigrant sentiment. As such, "societal preferences are filtered through the political system that weighs support for and opposition to immigration according to local and national conditions."[5] This sentiment moves from the local to the national level when such competition is levied in swing districts, as politicians capitalize by playing the "immigration card." However, if the public economic costs of migration were the primary component driving immigration restrictions in Britain, volume and geographic concentration, not type, of migration should drive policy. Yet this is clearly not the case in Britain during the post–WWII period.

Others have argued that predominant ideas concerning race drive political outcomes in Britain.[6] Some emphasize that political elites actively manipulated public opinion to further their own political preferences.[7] Others suggest that elites depoliticized race in the 1960s due to party consensus and apprehensions regarding the divisiveness of the race / immigration question, then repoliticized them in the 1970s and 1980s.[8] Even a cursory glimpse of the empirical evidence supports an active role for race in the construction of migration policy in Britain during the post–WWII era; however, models that focus solely on race as an explanatory variable can't explain why Britain maintained an open migration regime from 1948–62, leaving the country exposed to potentially massive levels of international migration. Moreover, race scholars tend to define British nationhood in primordial terms where racial criteria remain a fixed component of national identity. This point of view can obfuscate the fact that notions of a liberal and/or "multicultural" Britain have had vociferous proponents throughout the period and have had an influence on both discourse and policy during the late twentieth century.

A third alternative explanation of policy emphasizes the influence of institutions and the political effects of "path dependence" that institutions can foster.[9] Specifically, in the post–WWII period the 1948 British Nationality Act, "created an institutional structure that limited subsequent policy options and militated against its own replacement."[10] However, path dependency does little to explain the factors that created the 1948 act in the first place. The "path dependence" model can only account for political "stickiness"—it does not provide a model of interests and politics; rather, it only explains the institutional constraints that can affect the particular shape a policy outcome takes.

Indeed, each of these perspectives captures part of the story, yet leaves important elements unexplained. The Threat and Rally Hypotheses offer a means to explain policy outcomes that subsumes extant theories and suggests that the dimensions identified by existing studies are strongly influenced by geopolitical structure and national identity. Using the Threat and Rally Hypotheses, early cold war policies, including the 1948 British Nationality Act, are explained by high degrees of geopolitical threat and policymakers' reliance on its traditional imperial grand strategy. As structural conditions changed over time, emphasis on external security gradually ceded to a growing emphasis on societal security. This produced policy outcomes largely shaped by contrasting idioms of national identity—both civic and ethnic. What may be surprising when examining the empirical evidence through the lens of a three-dimensional statist paradigm is that Britain is less of an "outlier" than a cursory glance of policy might initially suggest.

Civis Britannicus Sum

Whereas variables reflecting geopolitical threats and/or economic interests are not difficult to operationalize, the "societal security" dimension can be analytically troublesome. Ole Wæver defines societal security as "the sustainability, within acceptable conditions for evolution, of traditional patterns of language, culture, association, and religious and national identity and custom."[11] Rogers Brubaker incorporated this "national identity" perspective in his seminal examination of policy development in France and Germany; however, when applying it to the case of Great Britain, one is immediately struck with a profound difficulty—who exactly are "the British?"[12]

British nationhood, formed through the incremental union of England, Scotland, Wales, and Ireland, can be traced to the sixteenth century with the initial union of England and Wales under Henry VIII in 1536. Because no primordial national identity existed among the peoples to be integrated into the new British state, nation building was fostered in the eighteenth and nineteenth centuries on the principles of Protestantism, liberalism, and empire.[13] Indeed, the presence of a common enemy, France, complemented this sense of Protestant unity in Great Britain and pushed British nationalism forward. Similar to American nationalism during the early cold war period, British nationalism during these formative stages was driven by negative rather than affirmative forces of national identity. Whereas commonality among the English, Welch, Scots, and Irish was tenuous and based largely on a sense of shared political and material interest in the face of external threat, lines of distinction between Britons and their enemy the French were much more concrete.[14] Britons were defined as much by what they *were not* as they were by a strong sense of what they *were*.[15] Protestantism was one facet that highlighted the difference between Britons and the Catholic French.

Related to the notion of Protestant toleration is Britain's self-perception as a center of Enlightenment liberalism.[16] Liah Greenfeld suggests that, "The dominant view . . . defined the nation in terms of the individual dignity, or liberties, of its members, and anything that inhibited the exercise of these liberties was anti-national."[17] Thus, in addition to religion, the idea of the equality of rational individuals served as a founding myth that united people under a civic conception of nationhood.

Although primarily a means of maximizing security amid geopolitical threat, imperial designs also carried with them strong implications for national identity. Although Protestantism and liberalism established the civic dimensions of British nationhood, Britain's quest for advancing its empire served to entrench an ethnic and racial component. In his extensive analysis of the construction of modern British national identity, Richard Weight writes, "Imperial expansion made Britishness a more racist consciousness. . . .

Because they regarded themselves as a benevolent civilizing force in the world, the British convinced themselves that they were not nationalists like the Europeans but patriots; . . . In reality, Victorian imperialism was a more virulent form of British nationalism than ever before."[18] Indeed, some of those same elements of political liberalism that pushed for the equality of man served to create a sense of racial hierarchy that gave a moral purpose to British imperialism. Reflected in the writings of Edward Tylor and Benjamin Kidd, late-Victorian sciences sought to prove that non-Europeans were less evolved, biologically and culturally, and thus were unable to govern themselves properly or develop their own territories. Other writers took these racial ideals even further, describing colonial subjects as fearsome cannibals and beasts who were hardly human, reflected in the writings of W. Winwood Reade, Richard Marsh, and Rudyard Kipling's "The White Man's Burden."[19]

Also important when considering the roots of British national identity related to the age of imperialism is how migration was understood. Whether the impetus for imperialism was material rationalism or "moral" racialism, migration was a necessary instrument of the process of empire building. However, migration was understood solely in terms of British emigration to colonial territories, not on immigration from these sources. Consistent with the "white man's burden," emigration supported the idea of British superiority and must be considered core element of British nationalism associated with its imperial identity.

Although some can argue that no "true" British identity exists, British nationhood is inherently intertwined with historical developments relating to the establishment of Protestantism, political liberalism, and imperial designs. However, rather than providing a foundation for a unified sense of national self, these core elements of British nationhood are inherently contradictory, creating an internal tension and ambiguity that renders issues of societal security quite volatile and fluid.

Using this definition of British nationhood to define societal security, what patterns should we expect in British migration policy after World War II if the Threat and Rally Hypotheses are valid? Given the labor requirements of the early cold war period, migration policy should be liberal in order to maximize reconstruction and material production, and should also be consistent with Britain's foreign-policy objectives. As perceptions of external threat decline, societal security issues should generally gain in relative significance and we should witness moves toward increasing degrees of closure as external threats decline.

Security and Empire in the Early Cold War Period

Postwar Britain was severely damaged, cash strapped, and vulnerable. In 1945, Britain's monetary reserves were nearly depleted and the country was already heavily in debt.[20] Compounding this situation was the fact that even though Britain carried a balance-of-payments surplus within the sterling area, it had a significant deficit with the dollar area, creating a "dollar shortage."[21] Moreover, like most European nations following the war, Britain's economy faced labor shortages. In 1946, government forecasts estimated a labor shortage of some 600,000 to 1.3 million workers, and although 335,000 POWs were employed in Britain in 1945 to fill manpower shortages, a government survey done in 1946 estimated that 600,000–1.3 million workers were needed to avoid a crisis of vital services.[22] Key industries, such as coal mining, textiles, agriculture, steel, and construction, were all seriously affected by labor shortages, and declining productivity would certainly negatively affect the reconstruction effort. These dire labor statistics were further compounded by estimates that suggested the working age population in Britain would decline by 200,000 by 1959.[23]

Early attempts by the British government to deal with its domestic labor shortage were manifest primarily in efforts to bring in labor from continental Europe and also Ireland. The Polish Resettlement Act of 1947 permitted settlement for some 120,000 Polish servicemen who served under British command during World War II.[24] Additional measures were taken to secure needed manpower in the short run. The European Volunteer Workers Program of 1947 facilitated the entry of approximately 180,000 workers to Great Britain, granting twelve-month work permits to European workers to fill specific shortages in the labor market.[25] However, these were not the only—nor the most significant—policy outcomes related to migration in the early cold war period.

Understanding Britain's unique perspective on security is crucial to understanding how migration fit within British grand strategy. During World War II and continuing in its aftermath, British policymakers did not make a strong differentiation between defense of the territory and defense of "the people" and the British national identity that unifies them. On May 19, 1940, Prime Minister Winston Churchill made this connection explicitly clear, stating, "After this battle in France abates its force, there will come the battle for our island—for all that Britain is and all that Britain means."[26] Not only was Britain's territorial security threatened, but also the security of Britain's place as a world power was facing formidable challenges—a crucial facet of British identity since the dawn of the Pax Britannica. In 1954, Oliver Franks, British Ambassador to the United States, declared that without the Commonwealth Britain could not continue as a Great Power, a view that incorporated both economic and ideational (societal) dimensions.[27]

The relationship with the United States was crucial, not only in understanding why British national identity was considered threatened by policymakers, but also in understanding the policy choices made. Ironically, this relationship would serve to concurrently create perceptions of threat and also reduce perceptions of threat. On the one hand, the United States was a key ally for Britain, and this "special relationship" can be seen to have reduced perceptions of geopolitical threat, at least relative to its continental European neighbors, France and Germany. This alliance provided not only a firm defense commitment, but also much needed Marshall Plan aid and asymmetric tariff bargains with the United States.[28] On the other hand, the United States represented the ascendant challenger to Britain's reign as a dominant world power.[29] During World War II, British leaders defined the "special relationship" as an alliance of roughly equal partners in the war against Nazi Germany. However, as the war drew to a close, it soon became apparent that US dominance would be the defining characteristic in the coming years. At the Yalta Conference in February 1945 U.S. efforts to avoid Soviet perceptions of a US–UK bloc allied against the Soviets resulted in the abrogation of the spheres of influence agreement that Churchill negotiated with Stalin prior to the conference.[30] Even though Britain remained a part of the "Big Three," American efforts to establish relations with the Soviets often resulted in British marginalization, thus threatening their sense of place as a dominant world power.

THE BRITISH NATIONALITY ACT OF 1948

In terms of reconstruction as a security imperative, bolstering Commonwealth unity represented a natural cornerstone of postwar grand strategy in Britain. Trade opportunities and acquisition of raw materials within the sterling area provided a financial buffer against Britain's accumulated wartime debt and the financial requirements needed to rebuild its war-torn infrastructure. Canada accounted for more than 40 percent of Britain's exports, while Australia and New Zealand provided dollar-free sources of meat, wheat, timber, and dairy produce.[31] Moreover, where Britain experienced a significant current account deficit vis-à-vis the dollar area, the British colonies experienced huge surpluses from 1950–54. This, coupled with Britain's trade surplus within the sterling area, was crucial in keeping Britain solvent. From 1939–58, a period when sterling was legally inconvertible, payments were settled on a multilateral basis within the sterling area, while British economic policy discriminated against the dollar area. Because of this pattern of trade, Britain's role as the central banker of the sterling area, and the fact that member countries' currencies were pegged to a fixed sterling rate, sterling balances increased in London financial institutions. In 1945 sterling balances were seven times as large as gold and dollar reserves.[32] These increasing balances provided the needed reserves necessary to finance 57 percent of Britain's balance of payments deficit in 1947, 50 percent in 1949, 35 percent in 1950, and 55 percent in 1953.[33] Given the political and economic benefits of its imperial relationships, there is little wonder why Clement Atlee's Labour government made the preservation of its empire the dominant mode of its postwar grand strategy.

In 1945, Prime Minister Mackenzie King introduced the Canadian Citizenship Act that "made Canadian citizenship paramount and British citizenship merely a fringe benefit."[34] For the first time citizens of a Commonwealth country were defined in terms that differentiated them from other subjects of the British Crown.[35] The symbolic importance of this change was not lost on policymakers in London who considered Commonwealth cohesion to be the essential foundation of post–WWII grand strategy and Canada was considered one of the pillars of the Commonwealth.[36] Reaffirming a commitment to the core of the Commonwealth was even more important given the prospect of impending independence in India, and the economic pressures to scale back commitments in Greece, Turkey, and the Middle East.[37]

Although economic and logistical constraints warranted that the scope of the empire be scaled back, policymakers remained convinced that maintaining cohesion within the Commonwealth was imperative to its strategic, political, and economic survival.[38] Reaffirming a sense of Commonwealth identity was seen as indispensable to achieve this goal: "The Canadian initiative's potential for encouraging [Canadian unilateralism and Dominion nationalism] made it of paramount importance that a common status be created for all British subjects."[39] The policy instrument used to forge this unity was the British Nationality Act, enacted on July 30, 1948. Through its six categories of citizenship, the act established a regime that allowed Commonwealth states to define their own citizenship, but that such definitions could not take place without reference to the United Kingdom. The act provided nearly identical rights for individuals that fell within either of the two primary categories—Citizens of the United Kingdom and Colonies (CUKCs) and Citizens of Independent Commonwealth Countries (CICCs). Richard Weight suggests that, "by legally codifying the concept of a far-flung British family, the Act was in a sense the high point of British imperialism."[40]

The British Nationality Act addressed the geopolitical, economic, and societal dimensions of postwar security in the United Kingdom. In a postwar environment of acute geopolitical threat (both in terms of potential Soviet expansionism *and* the ascendant American challenge to British hegemony), the act was intended as a strong statement of British commitment to the maintenance of the empire and to the equality of all of its members. Although the act did not specifically address the issue of migration as a remedy for postwar labor requirements, the need for unity within the Commonwealth was crucial to British economic interests by reinforcing ties with its key sources of exports, dollar-free imports, and capital accumulation. In addition, even though labor recruitment was not part of the legislation enacted in 1948, the British Nationality Act afforded Commonwealth citizens the right to enter the UK. This open migration regime allowed for market-forces to drive migration patterns consistent with Britain's labor needs and ongoing shifts in the business cycle. Though not an active labor recruitment policy, laissez-faire treatment of migration must be considered consistent with the economic interests of the country in a time of acute threat. Lastly, the symbolism of the British Nationality Act was intended to make a statement not only to the world around them, but also to Britons themselves. It was a statement intended to reinforce British identity and affirm British nationhood.

Taken in such a context, the British Nationality Act appears quite consistent with the Threat Hypothesis. Migration policy conformed to the economic and foreign-policy interests of the state in an environment of external threat. The empirical evidence is less supportive of the Rally Hypothesis. Even though the British Nationality Act established equality among Commonwealth citizens of diverse racial and ethnic stock, the Conservative Party opposed its passage on the basis that "coloured" people could not "become British."[41] This sensitivity to the racial dimension of societal security is also reflected the de facto discriminatory application of policies rather than in de jure changes in the policies themselves. These included manipulation of the issue and endorsement of travel documents in sending countries on the Indian subcontinent, the Caribbean, and Africa.[42] Representatives of the British government were encouraged to "use discretion" in issuing travel documents to those who were not closely connected to the British Isles through the descent of both parents. Moreover, additional de facto strategies were implemented to further support limitations on travel documents for racially "undesirable" migrants, including (1) changing rules regarding the proof necessary to document an applicant's connection to the UK; (2) attempts by government officials to manipulate the cost of passage from the Caribbean to the UK; and (3) the implementation of propaganda campaigns that sought to discourage emigration by suggesting severe employment and living conditions awaited migrants seeking entry into the UK.[43]

Clearly, the structural environment of the early cold war period produced a limited "rally-effect." Rather, sensitivity to societal difference remained an issue. However, consistent with the Threat Hypothesis, foreign and economic policy dimensions (focused on colonial relations) trumped societal security issues in an environment of acute external threats. De facto "policies" were deemed necessary by British policymakers because they sought to build and maintain cordial relations within the commonwealth. Adopting openly discriminatory measures to prevent the settlement of "colored" people in the United Kingdom would certainly not be conducive to good relations abroad.[44] Zig Layton-Henry suggests, "The imposition of immigration controls, particularly if seen to be racist, would have threatened Britain's moral authority as leader, or at least *primus inter pares*, of the Common-wealth."[45] However, the legacy of the British Nationality Act would soon become evident, as it changed the global patterns of migration within the Commonwealth.

Changing Circumstances and Unintended Consequences

Consistent with the imperial tradition, migration was based on a system of British *emigration*, not Commonwealth *immigration* to the United Kingdom. During colonization British nationals were sent abroad to both administer economic growth in the commonwealth and extend the domain of British culture and identity. In the period from 1846 to 1924, emigrants accounted for 41 percent of the British population at the turn of the century.[46] In the decade following World War II (1946–57), labor flows in Britain resulted in net emigration of roughly 300,000 with annual emigration levels averaging 125,000 per year.[47] However, the combination of a changing structural se-curity environment and changing patterns of migration that resulted from earlier policy decisions contributed to both an increase in perceptions of societal security and increasingly restrictionist policy outcomes. The first of these measures was the Commonwealth Immigrants Act of 1962 that placed restrictions on Commonwealth migration for the first time since the passage of the British Nationality Act.

STRUCTURAL ENVIRONMENT AND STRATEGIC RELATIONSHIPS

Several factors pushed the British to redefine their security interests during the late 1950s. The first was a shift from a grand strategy based on imperial cohesion toward one that was based on dependency on NATO alliances, particularly the Anglo-American "special relationship." This transition be-gan with decolonization in India, Burma, and Ceylon in the 1940s, and was pressed by domestic economic difficulties encountered in Britain in the mid-1950s. In the wake of the sterling crisis of 1955, a joint memorandum to Prime Minister Eden by Harold Macmillan and Walter Monckton sug-gested that the amount of money spent on defense of imperial holdings placed a prohibitive burden on the British economy. Later that year, another memorandum authored jointly by the Treasury office, the Ministry of Defense, and the Foreign Office, recommended that in order to maintain the strength of the national economy, nonessential overseas commitments must be shed.[48] The prohibitive cost increasingly pushed policymakers toward a more receptive position vis-à-vis decolonization. Moreover, Britain's participation in the General Agreement on Tariffs and Trade (GATT), gradually shifted foreign economic policy from imperial preferences to one based on internationally freer trade.[49]

In addition to the costs involved with an imperial-based grand strategy, maintaining the empire strained key strategic alliances, especially its "special relationship" with the United States. The Truman Doctrine defined the cold war in largely ideological terms, between oppressive regimes that rely on terror and oppression and the defenders of liberty. To counter Soviet expansionism, the principle of self-determination became one of the rallying cries of the cold war. It also became a point of contention between the Americans and the British who sought to maintain their grasp on the empire. Frank Heinlein notes that, "The British empire found itself in a world in which colonialism was 'increasingly unpopular and the use of force to maintain it no longer practical politics'—at least if Britain wanted to retain the support of its allies."[50] In order to avoid the material and political costs of maintaining its commitment to an imperial grand strategy, British policymakers gradually shifted their thinking about the importance of close ties within the Commonwealth—at least among its more peripheral members.

If the material and political costs of empire represented the underlying structural causes of a change in British grand strategy, the Suez Crisis was the proximate cause that pressed policymakers to rethink not only colonial policy, but also Britain's place in world politics. In 1954, Britain committed to the withdrawal of eighty thousand troops stationed at the Suez Canal through the Anglo-Egyptian Treaty. British military presence was strongly resented by the Egyptians, and the Treaty was an attempt to maintain Western ownership of the Canal while also appeasing public sentiment in Egypt. However, on July 26, 1956, Nasser announced the nationalization of the Suez Canal in breach of the Treaty, a decision that prompted a military response from the UK. Unfortunately for the British, the invasion received little support on the home front, the Soviets invaded Hungary and made increasingly threatening gestures to the west, and there was a run on the pound sterling, prompting a tremendous drain on British reserves to support the value of its currency. Rather than supporting the British attempt to resecure the Canal, the Americans withheld support for the British unless they withdrew their forces. Although British casualties were light— twenty-two dead and ninety-seven wounded—Britain's reputation, and perhaps more importantly, its self-image, were more significant casualties of the Suez Crisis.[51]

The Suez Crisis made two things clear to the Macmillan government. First, it showed how precarious Britain's financial situation truly was. Second, it made it abundantly clear that it was dependent on the United States and that its "special relationship" was not a union of equals, but rather, was clearly a hierarchical relationship with Britain serving as the junior partner. The world had changed, and British grand strategy would have to change accordingly. Whereas Commonwealth unity was the basis of its grand strategy in the immediate cold war period, grand strategy in the late 1950s was based on the foundation of collective security through NATO, dependence on the United States, and a nuclear basis for military defense.

These changes signaled an acceptance of Britain's dependence on the United States and its place under the American nuclear umbrella. Although this was certainly damaging to the grandeur of British imperial national identity, there is reason to believe that this shift placed Britain in a relatively less precarious security situation, one that should have eased geopolitical threats somewhat. More important, from the perspective of migration's role in grand strategy, was the acceptance that British grand strategy would no longer be based on the cohesion of the Commonwealth. Colonial relations relied less on the need to stress the equality and unity of the Commonwealth, and more on an acceptance of the process of decolonization. In addition to these changes in geopolitical environment, the unanticipated consequences of post–1948 migration would serve as the other major force in driving societal insecurities and shaping policy outcomes.

POST–1948 NEW COMMONWEALTH IMMIGRATION

Increasing numbers of immigrants from New Commonwealth countries resulting from the free movement rights afforded by the BNA generated societal insecurities in Britain during the 1950s. A Working Party Report issued

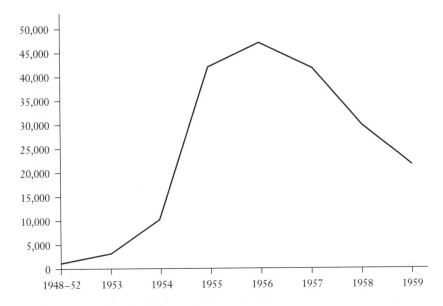

Figure 6.1.   Colonial Migrants to Britain, 1948–1958

SOURCE: Adapted from Kathleen Paul, *Whitewashing Britain: Race and Citizenship in the Postwar Era* (Ithaca, NY: Cornell University Press, 1997), 132. Copyright © 1997 by Cornell University. Used by permission of the publisher, Cornell University Press.

in 1955 concluded that, though current flows had not caused domestic instability economically or socially, allowing flows to continue unchecked could likely make the situation more critical.[52] As it had been during the decade from 1945–55, de facto measures were the preferred course of action in responding to unwanted New Commonwealth immigration. In India and Pakistan, measures were taken to prevent the emigration of individuals with low education or limited financial resources, and government bonds or cash-deposits were required to prove adequate financial resources. Moreover, those claiming that they were traveling to Britain to pursue their education were required to provide proof of admission to bona fide educational institutions and show adequate financial resources to cover expenses during their stay. Because of these measures, immigration from India decreased by 44 percent (from 6,200 to 2,930) and immigration from Pakistan decreased by 40 percent (from 4,690 to 1,860) from 1958–59.[53] Overall, New Commonwealth immigration fell from a high of 46,850 in 1956 to 21,600 in 1959, a 46 percent drop (Figure 6.1). However, even though numbers were decreasing political pressures to address New Commonwealth immigration in the UK began to increase.

Both domestic conditions and events abroad were crucial in shaping the evolving attitudes towards immigration and the priorities of the state. Domestically, racial disturbances in Birmingham and Liverpool in 1948, Deptford in 1949, and Camden in 1954 preceded the more virulent race riots in Birmingham and London in 1958.[54] These events increased perceptions that changing ethnic demographics in the UK had volatile political consequences if not effectively managed.[55] Given that existing flows were not sizable in relation to the overall population in Britain, the perception of societal threat that they generated was based more on fears of the size of future flows if trends continued unabated rather than on the size of current flows. The riots heightened a sense of societal threat, but pushing for rigorous border controls to stem New Commonwealth migration would suggest to the colonies that the British government was pandering to a racist populace.[56] As pressures to avoid insulting colonial leaders declined during the late 1950s, such tensions would become less problematic for policymakers.

Events abroad also shaped the influx of New Commonwealth immigration after 1948. In the United States, the McCarran-Walter Act of 1952 separated the West Indies from Britain's visa quota, a change that greatly reduced visa quotas for the region. Colonials of the British Crown could no longer apply for a US visa under the quota allocated to the United Kingdom. This had the effect of increasing migration pressures from the Caribbean to the UK, as the costs of migration to the US rose relative to migration to Britain.

Taken together, the changing patterns of migration that resulted from the 1948 British Nationality Act and the changing strategic position of the United Kingdom altered the existing balance between geopolitical, economic, and societal dimensions of security. Where migration was used in the 1940s and 1950s as a symbolic tool of British statecraft intended to foster cohesion within the empire, migration in the 1960s emerged as a new threat to security's societal dimension. On the one hand, the rising numbers of immigrants from sources deemed less socially proximate increased threats to Britain's racial component of national identity, while government policies enacted to stem such flows and discriminate on the basis of race threatened Britain's liberal base. This mix of impulses drove policy outcomes throughout the 1960s, 1970s, and 1980s.

Reformulating Grand Strategy in Britain

Public opposition to New Commonwealth migration was reflected in public opinion polls beginning in 1958 that showed consistent support for the implementation of immigration controls.[57] The societal dimension of grand strategy shifted accordingly, moving from de facto racialization to a more overt defense of a racially defined conception of British national identity. Migration policy soon exhibited more explicit preferences for European migrants over New Commonwealth migrants and a distinct desire to emphasize state control in meeting these goals. De jure restriction of movement within the Commonwealth, once thought incongruous with both colonial relations and a British national identity that sought to maintain its liberal and imperial benevolence within the empire, began in 1962 with the passage of the Commonwealth Immigrants Act.

Although not necessarily implementing a rigid system of closure, the 1962 act was a significant first step away from the notion of freedom of movement for all subjects of the Crown. The new law introduced immigration control for Commonwealth citizens whose passport originated outside the UK and established a three-tiered system of entry vouchers. Voucher preferences were based on: (1) those with employment arrangements in place ("A" voucher); (2) those whose skills were in demand in the United Kingdom ("B" voucher); and (3) others ("C" voucher), with preference given to war veterans.[58]

The Commonwealth Immigrants Act responded primarily to the material and societal dimensions of grand strategy, while foreign-policy dimensions no longer dominated migration policy decisions. In contrast to the foreign-policy dominated British Nationality Act of 1948, which created blanket openness within the Commonwealth, the Commonwealth Immigrants Act reflects the government's first attempt to specifically shape migration flows to conform to economic conditions in Britain and the labor needs of the country. However, the provisions of the act also strongly reflect a racialized sense of societal security, in that exceptions were made for Irish migration while seemingly focused on stemming New Commonwealth migration, especially from the Indian subcontinent. The act was a direct response to a perceived threat from increased migration (or even the potential for increased migration) from the subcontinent, a migrant-sending region perceived to be

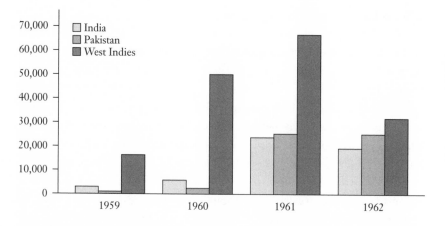

Figure 6.2.   New Commonwealth Migration to Great Britain, 1959–1962

SOURCE: Adapted from Sheila Patterson, *Immigration and Race Relations in Britain, 1960–1967* (London: Oxford University Press, 1969), 3.

racially and culturally distant from the home country. From 1959 to 1960, migration from India increased from 2,950 to 5,900 (Figure 6.2). The next year these figures jumped to 23,750. Pakistani migration increased from 850 in 1959 to 2,500 in 1960. In 1961 these figures rose sharply to 25,100.

The rising numbers of New Commonwealth migrants represented a threat that made control appear essential; however, the nature of the threat was also a function of perceptions of cultural/racial proximity. However, an important question must be raised: Why would British policymakers feel more threatened by trends in migration from the Indian subcontinent than from the West Indies, even though overall numbers from the Caribbean were much higher overall and showed a similar spike during the years just prior to the Commonwealth Immigrants Act? Although racial differences marked most New Commonwealth migration as less desirable than migration from Old Commonwealth countries or other European nations, migrants from the West Indies were seen as relatively more able to assimilate than those from the subcontinent. An Interdepartmental Working Party found increasing migration from India and Pakistan to be "particularly disturbing, since many of these people do not speak English, and they are among the more difficult groups to assimilate."[59] This notion of "assimilability" was a primary concern and was partly based in terms of the volume of migration flows, but more importantly, the racial and cultural composition of such flows.[60] In addition to the question of cultural proximity and "assimilability," migration volume (or potential volume) also figured prominently in the perception of threat. During debates leading to the implementation of immigration controls in 1962, it was frequently pointed out that the migration potential from the subcontinent was far greater than from the West Indies.[61] The population of West Indies source nations was some 3.5 million, and the subcontinent was home to some 550 million potential migrants. Thus, threat was perceived as much by perceptions of potential flows as to the raw numbers of existing flows. In June 1961 a Gallup poll found that 67 percent of the public favored immigration restrictions.[62]

In addition to poll data, the nature of the perceived threat is also manifest in subsequent adjustments made to the Commonwealth Immigration Act. Employment vouchers were originally issued on a "first-come, first-served" basis. However, during the first year of implementation it became clear that Indians and Pakistanis were disproportionately applying for all three categories of employment vouchers. By the end of 1963, applicants from the subcontinent garnered approximately 40 percent of "A" vouchers, 60 percent of "B" vouchers, and 66 percent of "C" vouchers.[63] Moreover, the deluge of applicants from India and Pakistan significantly contributed to the backlog of voucher processing. Since processing was based on the "first-come" basis, the heavy proportion of applications from the subcontinent ensured that vouchers would be dominated by these source countries for several years as the bureaucratic apparatus made its way through the considerable backlog, which by mid-1965 numbered some 300,000 applications in the "C" category alone. On July 31, 1963, the minister of labor suggested that some modification of the "first come, first served" basis "was necessary to maintain a reasonable distribution of vouchers throughout the Commonwealth."[64] The solution was to mandate that no Commonwealth country could receive more than 25 percent of the available "C" vouchers, thereby directly affecting the volume of migration from the Indian subcontinent. In August 1965, a Labour Government White Paper tightened the 1962 controls by establishing a ceiling on New Commonwealth immigration at 8,500 per annum, and abolishing the "C" voucher category altogether.[65]

Initially the controls appeared to be effective in gaining control of New Commonwealth immigration. In the first six months after the implementation of the act, net immigration from New Commonwealth countries fell from 94,890 to 8,290, less than one-tenth the original level.[66] Touting such reductions went far to allay public concern regarding rising migration trends and enabled policymakers to appear responsive to public demands. However, although the act served to address societal concerns in the short run, it may have exacerbated rather than alleviated British perceptions of societal threat in the long run. Prior to 1962, Asian migrants to Britain were predominantly male and were largely sojourners rather than permanent immigrants.[67] However, because open migration within the Commonwealth was no longer permitted, the act encouraged more permanent migration, and it was increasingly more common for a migrant to be accompanied by his wife and children. Thus, ironically, the act may have served to contribute more to the construction of a multiracial Britain rather than to the societal security of a culturally homogenous polity. The act also exacerbated sensitivity to clandestine migration, an issue that gained salience in policy discourse in 1965 and has driven migration discourse ever since. On March 9, 1965, the Prime Minister argued that "evasion was almost fatally eroding the Act," even though evasion statistics were admittedly unreliable.[68] As the state increased its desire to control flows, evasion of such controls by migrants was considered a valid argument for stricter control of immigration.

DEFENDING THE LIBERAL DIMENSION OF BRITISH NATIONHOOD

The contentious debate surrounding the implementation of migration controls in 1962 does not reflect the "path-dependence" of the British Nationality Act so much as it reflects the multiple traditions of British nationhood. Although the rise of Enoch Powell gave voice to racialized societal insecurities driven by changes in migration patterns, the shift from imperial grand strategy was not intended to reflect a British desire to abort its self-perception as an enlightened, liberal society.[69] The age of imperialism was no doubt based on an implicit racialized sense of national identity, yet was also based on the strong belief in liberal virtues such as equality, liberty, and the inherent rights of the individual. Although the Commonwealth Immigrants Act clearly differentiated migration preferences based on racial criteria, most Britons were loath to project overt racism. What emerged from this tension paralleled similar dynamics in the United States and France. Policies were enacted to both project an image of racial toleration and to promote domestic social stability by reducing racial tensions that were produced by demographic changes brought about by postwar immigration.

The United States served as the primary model for Britain in two ways. First, the racial tensions and the social upheaval that accompanied the civil rights movement were seen as inherently threatening to a stable social order. In 1968, Enoch Powell made the connection explicitly clear: "The tragic and intractable phenomenon which we watch with horror on the other side of the Atlantic but which is there interwoven with the history and existence of the States itself, is coming upon us here by our own volition and our own neglect."[70] A more measured assessment, put forth by the Race Relations Board in 1967, confirmed the general sentiment that Britain would face similar difficulties as the United States unless racial discrimination and successful integration of minorities was addressed by the government.[71] However, the United States also served as the model for creating institutions to deal with racial tensions and the promotion of toleration.[72] To offset (or balance) the overly racist elements of the Commonwealth Immigrants Act, the British government enacted the Race Relations Act of 1965 and subsequent extensions of the act in 1968. The acts sought to address racism in employment and housing by establishing a legal structure of administrative conciliation backed by civil law, which was thought to be more conducive to compliance than provisions based on a system of criminal sanctions.[73] The acts represented a compromise between Liberals and Conservatives on the issue of identity, and set in motion the first institutions that projected a multicultural basis for British nationhood that accompanied the series of measures that addressed ethno-cultural societal insecurities through increasing restrictionism.

CONTINUED RESTRICTIONISM

The passage of the Commonwealth Immigrants Act of 1968 would serve as a more conspicuous indicator of the rise of societal security on the policy agenda than its 1962 precursor. The 1968 Act introduced the notion of "patriality" to migration policy and British grand strategy, defined as those who were tied to the United Kingdom through family or settlement.[74] As stipulated in the 1968 legislation, only "patrial" CUKCs remained free from immigration controls while others were regulated via an entry voucher system, with initial levels set at fifteen hundred heads of household.[75] This ensured that descendants of white colonists would be able to immigrate to the UK while Asian passport holders found considerable obstacles, even in cases where spouses were already residing in the UK. This policy trend continued with the Immigration Act of 1971 that further increased societal closure.

The 1971 Act consolidated the two classes of immigration control— "alien" and "Commonwealth citizen"—and removed most privileges previously accorded to Commonwealth citizens. The act granted the government complete control over immigration with the exception of patrials, who would remain free of all controls. Moreover, employment vouchers were replaced by work permits that did not carry the right of permanent residence nor the right of entry for dependents under the family reunification provisions of existing British law. Patrials maintained the right of unrestricted entry and permanent settlement, and they were also the only group classified as "nationals" and able to take advantage of free movement within the EEC.[76] The specific terms of the act suggest that societal security was gaining in salience. Policy became increasingly directed toward controlling the racial makeup of migration flows rather than simply toward overall volume. Although the political rhetoric surrounding the passage of the act promoted curbing migration flows in general, the act actually served to increase the number of people entitled to enter Britain without restriction, though these were composed primarily of people of European extraction who, it was believed, posed little sociopolitical difficulty because of their "special ties of blood and kinship."[77]

FROM EMPIRE TO EUROPEAN COMMUNITY, 1968–1973

The Immigration Act of 1971 marks a significant shift in the security agenda of Great Britain. Merging the categories of "British subject" and "alien" closed the symbolic divide between citizens of the empire and "foreigners."[78] This, combined with Britain's decision to join the EC, signaled Britain's shift from a grand strategy predicated on empire to one that was increasingly linked with its European neighbors. The timing of this dual shift was nearly simultaneous. On the same day that the 1971 Immigration Act came into law (January 1, 1973), Britain implemented its Treaty of Accession to the

European Community (EC). In accordance with the provisions of the treaty, Britain accepted the principle of free movement for EC member citizens. The free market provisions of EC membership replaced the free market provisions of the Commonwealth, while free migration within the union would be consistent with British racialized preferences regarding immigrants. This conclusion is supported by the fact that while fears of the migration potential from the Indian subcontinent drove British policymakers to adopt restrictive policy in 1962, ceding control over European migration, a region with some 200 million people, generated very little public concern or debate, at least initially. Resistance to European integration centered on the potential loss of sovereignty as opposed to fears about immigration.[79]

THE BRITISH NATIONALITY ACT

The British Nationality Act of 1981 (BNA) has been described as "a major milestone and a critical break with Britain's imperial past."[80] The British Nationality Act can be seen as the first articulation of a definitive citizenship concomitant with an emerging national identity contained solely within the geographical confines of the United Kingdom.[81] Although the act can been seen as a turning point in British nationhood, the new immigration rules "were really only footnotes to a work that had, to all intents and purposes, already been completed."[82] The BNA, which supplanted the 1948 act, established three categories of citizenship: (1) patrials, defined as UK citizens; (2) British dependent territory citizens; and (3) British overseas citizens.[83] The status of "British subject," which had long been synonymous with "Commonwealth citizen," was for the most part abolished.[84] Moreover, the act not only attempted to establish a new geocentric definition of identity, but also moved the basis for British identity in line with its continental neighbors as European integration proceeded: "The measure continued the principle of differential rights first begun in the 1971 Act by abolishing the ancient Anglo-Saxon tradition of jus soli, that is, citizenship deriving from the place of a person's birth, and implementing the principle of citizenship by descent, that is, the Continental European practice of jus sanguinis. This was to bring Britain in line, it was claimed, with European partners as they moved towards deeper integration within the European Union under the Maastricht Treaty."[85]

In addition to its basic covenants regarding who is and who is not a British citizen, the British Nationality Act of 1981 also sought to shore up loopholes that could be exploited by those wishing to evade controls. This included the establishment of the "primary purpose rule" which prohibited entry of fiancées or spouses of British women citizens unless they could prove that the primary purpose of the marriage was not to garner settlement rights. Such provisions put incredibly high burdens of proof on spouses-to-be. When a court ruling in 1985 deemed the law to be sexually discriminatory, Britain opted simply to make it equally difficult for men to bring in their foreign wives rather than to open itself to a potential immigration loophole.[86] Subsequent legislation continued the British trend not only toward showing overt racialized preferences regarding migrants, but also in establishing rigid control over migrant flows, especially when it concerned attempts to circumvent British sovereignty over matters of entry. In 1987, the government passed the Carrier Liability Act that assessed penalties on carriers who transported undocumented aliens.

DEALING WITH ASYLUM: DISTINGUISHING BOGUS FROM BONA FIDE

As was the case with other European countries, as the front-door channels to legal immigration closed, migrants desiring entry into the United Kingdom sought to exploit other channels of entry—primarily the asylum channel. Regulating migration for the asylum channel is particularly troublesome for liberal democracies, since normative liberal ideals are codified within the legal institutions of the state and articulated in both national and international law.[87] However, in the case of the United Kingdom, "the trajectory of British asylum policy shows no dramatic twists and turning points, no epic battle between the foundational principles of liberal nation-state, human rights and sovereignty."[88] In Britain the Home Office has virtually uncontested authority on immigration and asylum policies, and the courts in general defer to its authority.[89]

The Tamil crisis of 1985 served to shift the focus of the societal security agenda from immigration policy to refugee and asylum policy.[90] The question of asylum policy and the need to distinguish bogus from bona fide has dominated migration discourse in the UK throughout the 1990s and into the new millennium. Increasing sensitivity to economic migrants exploiting

Britain's asylum provisions were exacerbated by reports that circumvention was increasingly organized and that illegal aliens apprehended by authorities were attempting to avoid deportation by applying for asylum. In 1995, two-thirds of the illegal aliens detected by authorities applied for asylum to prevent deportation.[91] As was the case with standard immigration control, asylum policy was largely driven by racial/cultural factors in addition to concerns for human rights. Interestingly, the asylum debate arose at a time when actual asylum flows were quite minimal. According to Amnesty International figures, annual asylum applications during the period from 1980–88 rarely exceeded the five-thousand mark, and overall applications numbered less than thirty-eight thousand for the period.[92] Although overall numbers were low, the sensitivity to asylum claimants emanating from Sri Lanka is strikingly consistent with overall British policy regarding migration from the subcontinent. Christian Joppke notes, "There was an instant reflex to brand the Tamils, who began arriving in larger numbers in 1985, as economic migrants or bogus refugees. Not without reason, since they came from a region in which the "pressure to immigrate" was the highest and which was accordingly targeted by the government to strike down family-based immigration: the Indian sub-continent."[93]

Continuing the trend begun in the late 1980s, asylum applications to the United Kingdom increased sharply at the close of the cold war (Figure 6.3). In response, Britain adopted the Asylum and Immigration Appeals Act of 1993 (AIAA) that sought to address the rise in asylum applications while also addressing continental criticisms that existing British asylum procedures were draconian. At this point, the political tension was not between societal security interests and colonial relations (as it was in the 1940s and 1950s), but between identity and EU relations, consistent with the emerging European-based grand strategy. Although the AIAA established the right of in-country appeals for asylum seekers, it also extended state powers to deal with manifestly non bona fide applicants.[94] Policymakers believed that asylum had become a means for circumventing legal immigration controls, and the AIAA was intended to reduce the probability of abuse by economic migrants.[95] The act removed the right of appeal for refused short-term visitors and students and also introduced fast-track procedures for processing "manifestly unfounded" asylum claims.[96] Fast-track processing led to a dramatic increase in the number of asylum applications refused, from 16 percent in 1993 to

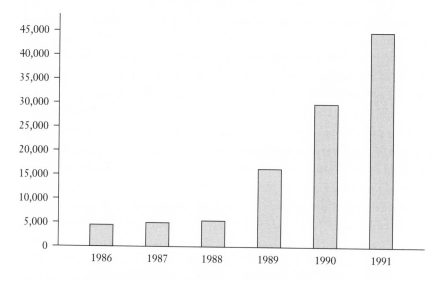

Figure 6.3. Asylum Applications in Great Britain, 1986–1991

SOURCE: Adapted from Zig Layton-Henry, "Britain: The Would-Be Zero Immigration Country," in *Controlling Immigration: A Global Perspective*, ed. W. Cornelius, P. Martin, and J. Hollifield (Stanford: CA, Stanford University Press, 1994), 278.

75 percent in 1994, while the number of those admitted under the "exceptional leave to remain" provisions declined from 77 percent in the first half of 1993 to 21 percent in the first quarter of 1994. In addition, the number of asylum seekers detained by the government doubled during those years, from 300 in 1993 to 600 in 1994.[97]

During the 1990s the British government not only sought to reduce the number of asylum seekers, but also their access to public entitlements. Regulations went into effect on February 5, 1996, that required asylum applicants to submit their application at the port of entry in order to be eligible for welfare benefits while awaiting a decision on their application. Moreover, rejected applicants were not allowed to receive benefits during the appeal of their claim.[98] It was estimated that denying welfare benefits to asylum seekers who applied inside the United Kingdom reduced the number of applicants by 42 percent between 1995 and 1996.[99] However, reports that immigrant smuggling had become active in assisting non bona fide asylum claimants to circumvent the system of controls kept asylum policy in the political discourse. A task force established to deal with migrant smuggling discovered that "asylum kits" were being sold in Sri Lanka at a cost of £3,000–£10,000. Migrants were first flown with their real passports to a place such as Dubai, where they transferred to a flight to Britain using forged visas. During passage, all documentation was discarded, ensuring that upon arrival their asylum claim could not be quickly dismissed (under provisions such as the "safe-country" policy). In July, 1998, Home Secretary Jack Straw expressed the government's concern with such developments: "I am seeing a great growth of people abusing the asylum system simply to evade immigration control or because they are economic migrants in this country."[100] On July 27, 1998, an Immigration and Asylum White Paper was issued that would limit asylum applicants to one appeal if their application was denied. The proposed legislation also stipulated that rejected applicants would be administratively removed rather than deported, a change that would eliminate the appeal of deportation orders and expedite processing.[101]

The limit of asylum applicants to only one appeal became law with the implementation of the 1999 Immigration and Asylum Act (IAA) that took effect on April 1, 2000.[102] In the continued effort to eliminate the "draw" of public entitlements to potential economic migrants abroad, the IAA also substituted vouchers for cash assistance to those asylum applicants who had properly submitted their claim. With applications for asylum up sharply in 1999 (to 71,160), public opinion polls suggested that public concern regarding migration was at its highest levels in two decades.[103] The new law did not close all existing loopholes in current asylum policies and procedures, but it did make a strong statement to the public that the government was seriously responding to their concerns regarding societal security.[104] The IAA also served to project government resolve in stemming the increasing flow of illegal immigrants. The provisions of the IAA included fines for cargo truck drivers who transport illegal aliens. Government estimates in 2000 suggested that as many as 2,000 undocumented immigrants were transported from France to Great Britain each year on trucks. When on British soil, many of these immigrants subsequently applied for asylum to avoid deportation.[105] The IAA provided for fines in the amount of £2,000 per illegal foreigner apprehended in a vehicle.

It was believed that clandestine immigration and refugee/asylum flows were increasingly linked, as the former would invariably lead to the latter as a means to regularize immigration status in the UK. Public concern necessitated a government response to both migration sources. In addition to carrier sanctions against airlines, the British government also established a program of employer sanctions. Included in the 1996 Asylum and Immigration Act were employer sanctions provisions that called for fines up to £5,000 per worker hired for employers found to have hired illegal aliens over the age of sixteen.[106] These provisions went into effect on January 27, 1997, following a Home Affairs Ministry notification mailed to 1.1 million British employers in December 1996. However, like the employer sanctions provisions established in the United States, an emphasis was placed on reducing undesired "harassment" of business. Although employers were required to check documents of applicants to verify their eligibility to work in the UK, British authorities did not require employers to judge the authenticity of documents provided to them by applicants. A government spokesman remarked, "We are not expecting employers to act as migration officers. We wouldn't expect an employer to detect a good forgery, for example. That is our business."[107] These de facto safeguards insured that Britain's employer sanctions laws performed more of a symbolic rather than instrumental function, similar to that in the United States.[108] In 1997, the newly elected Labour government went even further in weakening the instrumental strength of British employer sanctions, stating publicly that the government would not enforce the recently enacted provisions.[109] The strong de jure stance of government control was thus accompanied by de facto application that retained the image of government responsiveness to societal concerns while avoiding adding negative externalities to British business.

INTRA-EU MIGRATION

Migration from EC countries had long been preferable to NCW immigration, and as such, less politically problematic for British policymakers. However, it soon became evident that maintaining the racial-cultural composition of European flows depended on the ability of European Community member states to control their external borders from non-EC migrants ("third-country nationals"). The difficulties encountered by continental nations in controlling flows have caused Britain to question ceding its sovereignty over control to its territory.[110] Zig Layton-Henry argues that the

British in particular, "feel that immigration policy is too important to be left to the European Commission because of its implications for each country's security, national identity and culture."[111] Because of concern regarding potential migration inflows, Britain abstained from joining the Schengen group, fearing that abolishing internal checks would put British control at the mercy of other European states. This would be especially troubling with cases such as Italy and Spain, where control over migrant inflows has been elusive.[112]

Britain is often pointed to as one of the most defensive nations with regards to its societal security and sovereignty. Its initial hesitancy to join in the process of European integration (beginning with the Rome Treaty), and later, its refusal to join the Schengen group are often cited as examples of Britain's emphasis on social control, as well as an indicator of policymakers' belief in Britain's increased ability to manage flows autonomously due to its advantageous geographic position.[113] Yet, a close examination of British policies reveals a much more nuanced reality. Disjunctures between de jure articulation of government policies and the de facto application of policies highlight not only the conflicting interests of the state, but also the political maneuvering of policymakers attempting to craft a comprehensive grand strategy, making use of restrictive rhetoric and symbolic policies to square the circle between conflicting security logics.

Migration and Security after 9/11

The events of 9/11 merged societal security interests with military-security interests—both pressing for policies of closure and for integration of the existing immigrant population in Britain. In November 2001, the British government established a state of public emergency in response to the September 11 bombings. Under this state of emergency, increased powers were granted to law enforcement to detain suspected terrorists. In addition, the new security environment prompted government action to better control migration into the country. As has long been the case, focus has been placed on tightening the asylum channel and obtaining assistance from nongovernmental agents to help stem the flow of illegal immigrants into the country. The first major policy development following September 11 was the Nationality, Immigration and Asylum Bill, which came into effect on

November 8, 2002. The new law increased existing carrier and employers sanctions laws by increasing incarceration periods for those convicted of organizing the smuggling of illegal immigrants into Britain. In addition, the law restricts the appeals period for those seeking asylum and permits the government to detain asylum seekers for up to six months and also prohibits nationals of EU countries (and accession countries) from applying for asylum in the United Kingdom.[114] Moreover, the Tony Blair government proposed a new system of "safe havens" for processing asylum claims. Under the plan, British immigration officers would intercept potential asylum applicants prior to entry into the United Kingdom and then send them to safe haven camps outside Great Britain to be administered by the UNHCR. Home Secretary David Blunkett argued, "At the moment we have an absurd situation. If we can't send [refugees] back, or can't facilitate them going anywhere, they disappear into our economy." He added that safe havens would, "rapidly reduce the number of economic immigrants using asylum applications as a migration route."[115] Restrictionism focused on the refugee/asylum channel of entry resulted in both high rejection rates followed by declining applications. Of the 85,865 asylum applicants that applied in 2002, only 8,100 were granted refugee status. In the first quarter of 2003, asylum applications dropped by 33 percent compared to the number of applications in the same period in 2002. Moreover, the government began to forcibly remove failed asylum seekers, and in 2002 some 13,000 rejected applicants were deported.

In order to reduce a major artery of illegal immigration flows and a major source of asylum applicants, the British government has also sought cooperation from the French government. Britain contributed half of the cost for increased security fencing at the Channel Tunnel, and has added extra police and video surveillance cameras. More significantly, perhaps, was Britain's success in garnering French acceptance to close the Sangatte Red Cross Center, a suspected staging point for illegal immigrants and asylum seekers, in December 2002. British Home Secretary David Blunkett optimistically declared, "This agreement not only closes Sangatte . . . [but] it will also shut office the routes used by illegal immigrants to get to the UK from France. It effectively pushes our border controls across the channel to the French coast, where stronger controls and tighter security will mean we can prevent illegal immigrants from getting to the UK in the first place."[116]

Although the post–9/11 environment has been characterized by a sharp increase in restrictionism in migration policy, securing the borders has not been the sole interest reflected in Britain's emerging grand strategy. Migration policy was also shaped to conform to the national economic interest and to continue Britain's attempts to better integrate its immigrant population in the interest of social stability. In response to the needs of an economy increasingly based on skilled labor and services, Britain began the Highly Skilled Migrant Program in January 2002. Applicants that possess an advanced degree, have at least three years of work experience, and can verify that they have earned at least £40,000 a year are eligible to enter the country without a prior job offer as required under the normal work permit system. The program also made it easier for foreign students who received their degree in the United Kingdom to remain in the country after graduation. In 2002, approximately three thousand immigrants were admitted under the program, and in 2005 applications were averaging about five hundred per week.[117]

In terms of social integration, the Nationality, Immigration and Asylum Act of 2002 is largely consistent with the approach taken by its continental European neighbors. The act encourages the social integration of new immigrants by requiring citizenship applicants to take English language classes and to demonstrate a thorough knowledge of British society. By pressing migrants to speed assimilation through the acquisition of language skills and cultural familiarity, the act serves to reduce factors that serve to increase perceptions of social distance and societal threat. At the same time, it also serves to create bridges for migrants to reduce perceptions of marginalization and to speed their transition to productive member of British society and the economy.

The events of September 11 no doubt contributed to an environment where restrictionism became the dominant theme of government policy. However, evidenced by government policy regarding highly skilled labor recruitment and provisions that aim to foster social cohesion, grand strategy has not displayed a myopic fixation on the connection between migration and global terrorism. Rather, the focus of policy has been directed at those dimensions of migration that generate fear. In local elections held in Spring 2003, asylum policy dominated much of the political debate. Concerns about asylum were no doubt exacerbated by reports that of the 2,530 Algerians whose application for asylum was rejected in 2001, only 125 returned to Algeria. Moreover, the Algerian Refugee Council in London acknowledged that it believed that there were known terrorists among the Algerians now living in the United Kingdom.[118] A February public opinion poll showed that 85 percent of respondents felt that the government did not have adequate control over asylum and immigration.[119] Restrictive policy has not been applied to all migration flows, but has only been directly sharply at this element of migration that has generated fears. Although certainly more restrictive than the 1980s, the influence of grand strategy on migration policy has resulted in outcomes intended to address fears while gaining maximum benefits from migration flows. In this sense, Britain's approach to migration in the new millennium is convergent with the approaches taken by other advanced industrial democratic states, including the United States, France, and Germany.

Britain in an Era of Transition

The empirical evidence gives us reason to believe that Britain may be less of an outlier than has been suggested by scholars. In many ways, its grand strategy is notably consistent with the other advanced industrial democracies, though intervening variables may sometimes obfuscate those similarities. From a military-political standpoint, early cold war security interests focused efforts on speeding postwar recovery and maximizing economic strength. However, over the past half-century its grand strategy has shifted from one based on empire to one predicated on regional integration and collective security and development. During this period, maintaining its sense of British identity, evident largely in the discourse surrounding immigration policy, has also shown a consistent logic. Since 1945, migration policy in the UK has been characterized not so much by restrictionism, but rather by an increasing desire for control. Moreover, and more importantly, this emphasis on control has shown distinctly racial and sociocultural patterns, as the nature of restrictionist policy has been directed toward specific migrant streams rather than as a response to migration in general. Whereas Irish and other West European migration was accepted (if not encouraged), restrictionist policies were directed specifically to address migration from New

Commonwealth countries. This same proclivity also drives British positions concerning the question of the movement of "third-country nationals" within the European Union, including the refusal to join the Schengen group. Although emergent policy patterns associated with migration policy are readily identifiable in the period examined herein, understanding the forces driving such trends is considerably more difficult to explicate and has garnered a considerable literature.

The increasingly ethno-nationalist evolution of British migration policy mirrors its evolving security agenda. As maintenance of empire was replaced by European integration and collective security (NATO) as the means to security and the external threat of Soviet expansionism declined over time, the security agenda of the state changed as well. Like Germany and France, "reestablishing" national identity has moved up the security agenda, placing emphasis not only on defining national citizenship, but also in the allocation of resources directed at controlling migrant flows.[120] It has also shaped Britain's involvement in migration-related provisions of EU membership. Although not willing to join the Schengen group's "open-border" policies, it remains interested in the cooperative efforts to control clandestine immigration within the Schengen group. However, societal security, while increasingly salient, must compete with the economic dimension of Britain's security agenda. Britain has been more assertive with regard to societal security, but at several points has displayed a desire to diffuse societal insecurities through the use of symbolic policies. Like the United States, the UK has implemented a de jure policy of employer sanctions to reduce the economic draw to potential migrants. Yet, safeguards implemented in these policies, such as a reluctance to hold employers accountable for verifying the authenticity of documents provided by employment applicants, reduce their instrumental efficacy, though the symbolic value of the laws remain intact.

This argument does not suggest that a multiracial Britain is politically impossible—quite to the contrary, it would seem inevitable. Concomitant with Britain's turn toward restrictionism in the early 1960s was a process that sought to address British racism and, more broadly, to "reimagine" British national identity in the wake of the empire's demise. Initially, these attempts focused on establishing antidiscrimination laws and institutions to promote notions of a multiethnic Britain. In October 2000, a report released by the Runnymede Trust on "The Future of Multi-Ethnic Britain" received a mixed response, suggesting that postimperial British nationhood remains a work in progress.[121] The grand strategy model presented herein acknowledges that national identities are malleable, especially in times of upheaval as was the case with Britain during decolonization. In such times societal security remains a salient political variable, though one that is often contested and /or characterized by internal tensions and ambiguities. As is the case with the United States, Germany, and France, British nationhood has endured a process of reimagining the national identity under pressures generated by international migration. Moreover, consistent with the other advanced industrial states examined herein, the state has become increasingly savvy of the politics associated with migration and the myriad ways that conflicting dimensions of the national interest can be reconciled in policy. The continually evolving global economy has generated new interests associated with the successful management of migration, yet as the evidence drawn from the late twentieth century has shown us, we are a long way from a borderless world.

CHAPTER SEVEN

Conclusion

Security, Sovereignty, and International Migration

Change is, by definition, threatening.

—LEON BRITTAN, *Globalization vs. Sovereignty?*

In the early 1990s, Myron Weiner argued that the features of population movement "suggest the need for a security/stability framework for the study of international migration that focuses on state policies toward emigration and immigration as shaped by concerns over internal stability and international security."[1] The present book attempts to do just that by simultaneously addressing two central questions: (1) What role does international migration and border control play in national security? (2) How do security interests affect the timing and form of immigration and border control policies? Although sizeable literatures have been developed on the issues of security (primarily political scientists and historians) and immigration (in social sciences, humanities, and law), these have, for the most part, proceeded along largely separate paths. Only recently has scholarship begun exploring the relationship between the two.[2] The purpose of this book is to illustrate the important linkages that exist between national security and international migration, and perhaps more importantly, to establish the first steps in theorizing state behavior that stems from this interaction.

A More Comprehensive Framework of Security

"National security" has generally been defined in very limited terms, consisting primarily of issues related to interstate military conflict. As the post–cold war environment presents a more complex security system, we are beginning to see new thinking about security that is better able to more accurately capture the new dynamics at play in world politics. Barry Buzan argues, "Understanding the national security problem requires a wide-ranging understanding of the major levels of analysis and issue sectors that comprise the field of International Studies. Although the term 'national security' suggests a phenomenon on the state level, the connections between that level and the individual, regional and systems levels are too numerous and too strong to deny."[3] Some security scholars may be reluctant to embrace the more comprehensive and complex characterizations of security because they threaten the orthodox view that the realm of "high politics" must remain distinct from the realm of "low politics." The security paradigm proposed herein is intended to provide a theoretical framework that allows some sense of how "high" and "low" politics are in many ways interdependent. Although they may exist in an anarchic global system, nations are not always in a state of conflict. We are then left with an important question: What drives politics when geopolitical (military) threats decline? Constraining our thinking about security solely within the domain of "high politics" provides no tools to address this question.

The theoretical framework offered in this book provides a means to identify both external and internal facets of security, and to explore the relationships between them. Taken together, the Threat and Rally Hypotheses provide a rationale for why societal security interests decline in relative importance in the formation of state grand strategy when geopolitical military threats are acute, and also how and why these priorities change as the structural environment shifts over time. The framework provides a means to accurately describe, and perhaps predict, the changing priorities of grand strategy that emphasize some combination of external and internal security interests. It also illustrates how the geopolitical security environment can shape national identity. Some critics have suggested that the concept of "societal security" is flawed because it imposes a rigid, "near positivist" view of identity on society: "Identity is not a fact of society; it is a process of negotiation among people and interest groups."[4] The concept is not utilized in this fashion within the context of the framework offered herein—in fact, it is quite the opposite. What is important to recognize in questions regarding national identity is that, even though it may, in fact, be in a continuous state of flux as a result of public deliberation, it is rare (I would argue, nonexistent) that proponents of any particular type of national identity conceive of it in such fluid terms. Rather, individuals and groups simply have competing views of a largely static conceptualization—or are arguing for the replacement of an existing dominant idiom to be replaced with a new dominant, largely static concept. For example, the ethno-nationalist rhetoric of social conservatives in France, such as Jean-Marie Le Pen, conceives of an enduring French society based largely on issues of ethnicity and culture. In contrast, social liberals staunchly defend the civic-nationalist concept of *laïcité* and have passed laws restricting religious dress in public schools in order to maintain continuity of a national identity conceived of in terms of ideology and common interests. Each has an idealized vision of French nationhood that provides an enduring sense of purpose, place, and meaning.

Even though contrary and conflicting conceptions of nationhood may be present in a society, a dominant idiom of national identity can be identified at a given point of time and may remain dominant across a given period. When examining internal, "societal security" interests, this does not suggest that a dominant idiom is presupposed—reifying it as an object of security. Rather, it suggests that policymakers are responsive to perceptions of the dominant national identity, may also influence popular conceptions of national identity by leading public discourse, and are compelled to respond to threats against this identity with new policy. Even though national identity may be evolving over time, societal security interests are reflected in policy outcomes at specific points in time. The available empirical evidence suggests that these dynamics are applicable to both generally civic-oriented nations, such as the United States, France, and Great Britain, and generally ethnic-oriented nations, such as Germany.

Although national identity is often conceived in primordial terms that presuppose enduring qualities over time, the empirical evidence presented herein suggests that conceptions of nationhood—in terms of deciding who "we" are—can be affected by the presence or absence of an external enemy as well as other elements of the structural environment, including patterns of international migration. Samuel Huntington argues, "To define themselves, people need an other." Extending this logic to society writ large, he adds, "National unity is enhanced as potentially divisive internal antagonisms are suppressed in the face of a common enemy."[5] Clearly, we can expect an increased likelihood of the opposite effect when external enemies decline. Many policymakers are keenly aware of these social dynamics and the "energizing force" that external enemies can have on internal social cohesion.[6] As the cold war drew to a close, an advisor to Soviet leader Mikhail Gorbachev remarked, "We are doing something really terrible to you—we are depriving you of an enemy."[7] Patterns of international migration can also challenge conceptions of national identity, depending on the volume and composition of flows. As the available evidence makes clear, large-scale immigration flows can have a profound effect on social demographics in receiving countries, and this effect can be magnified if immigrant birthrates are significantly higher than the native population, as is the case in the United States and Western Europe.

A Structural Statist Model of Immigration and Border Policymaking

In addition to providing a more comprehensive view of security, this book also offers a theory of immigration and border policymaking that brings together domestic and international variables under an overarching structural framework. As outlined in Chapter 2, the conventional wisdom regarding immigration policy formation is that it is largely a function of domestic interest groups. Generally, international and/or structural variables receive scant, if any, attention in explaining policy outcomes, and the state is generally viewed as epiphenomenal to the process of domestic politics.

The policymaking framework offered in this book suggests that structural (that is, international) factors matter, and the state does indeed have agency in the formation of immigration and border policy. As the empirical evidence shows, the state plays a crucial role in determining national interests, providing information, and shaping public discourse—all of which affect political processes and policy outcomes, both directly and indirectly. Utilizing a statist theoretical framework allows us to focus on these factors and highlights how interests and policy preferences are often the product of issue-linkage.

Immigrant advocates may question the security framework offered here on the grounds that it "securitizes" migration. Individuals and groups seeking to mobilize support for more open immigration and border policies frequently lament any association of immigration with national security, since that may provide a compelling rationale for increased closure that can be exploited by those seeking more restrictive policies. Although such logic may enter public discourse surrounding immigration and border policy, recognizing migration's security implications does not necessarily require states to close their door to immigrants. This book is not intended to argue a position on policy—either more open or more restrictive—as some other recently published security-oriented works have sought to do.[8] Rather, the language of security is utilized because it best captures the dynamics of existing sentiment and interests at play in policy formation. Policy discourse over the past half-century has often taken on a distinct security logic, and the language of security is needed to accurately describe such phenomena. This has become even more pronounced after 9/11, where effective control over international migration has distinct implications for homeland security. However, utilizing a security framework to reflect this dynamic certainly does not purport to suggest that all immigrants are terrorists or security threats.

Some may dismiss the statist paradigm by suggesting that such a framework merely reflects the state as another player in the game of domestic politics.[9] As such, existing societal models are seen as sufficient to reflect the inclusion of state interests, including foreign-policy interests related to immigration and border policy. Indeed, in some ways the state does seem to act as a distinct interest group within the domestic sphere. However, there is a distinct difference between it and other domestic actors vying for political influence on policy outcomes. Whereas domestic interest groups—whether business lobbies, ethnic lobbies, labor unions, or legal immigrant advocacy organizations—tend to be single-issue oriented and define preferences accordingly, the state instead tends to forward a "national interest" that represents an aggregation of these domestic interests. It is rare to find the state beholden to the policy interests of a single domestic interest group. Rather, the state's position most often displays a preference to balance competing interests within the context of the larger foreign and domestic policy environment at a given point in time. As such, the state cannot be considered a "competing" interest group in the same sense that it is used within the context of most existing societal models of policy formation.

It is also likely that some critics will object to the statist paradigm on the grounds that it "black boxes" the state and, as such, obfuscates as much as it illuminates. By design, a statist framework avoids close analysis of the myriad parts at play in the domestic political arena and admittedly creates a "black box" wherein such processes take place. For some political scientists, this represents an unconscionable act. If overstated, however, such criticism is highly misguided. Too often, it seems, choices made regarding method and/or level of analysis are defended or attacked on the basis of a given school of thought instead of a recognition that such choices all offer both advantages and disadvantages. Regrettably there is no "perfect" social science theory. Instead, analysts must make choices based on their stated goals of inquiry and accept the limitations of scope that may be inherent within their choices. Clearly, by "black boxing" domestic political processes, a statist model will have a disadvantage in being able to account for the nuances involved in the domestic political arena. This is, however, exactly the point. Statist models do so precisely to take advantage of the advantages higher levels of analysis/abstraction offer in terms of explaining outcomes.

In choosing a methodological approach for social scientific inquiry, scholars are faced with a trade-off between *precision* (with regards to the level of detail) and *parsimony*. Clearly, the statist approach utilized herein does not provide a high degree of precision in terms of accounting for the actions and outcomes of the myriad forces at play in the domestic political arena. It does, however, provide a high level of parsimony. This parsimony allows us to see "the forest before the trees" and offers more potential in terms of predictive capacity. Although it does not profess to be able to anticipate the precise types of policies or the exact timing of policy development, the security framework provides a tool that can give us insight into the general type of policies that may be initiated given a particular security environment. The framework provides a better fit than domestic politics models for policy development that includes multiple cases of states exposed to high levels of international migration and/or migration pressures. It can also account for policy development along a broader time frame.

Although political science theories tend to be presented in terms of "competing" explanations, the security paradigm is not intended to replace societal models, nor does it profess to be imminently superior to them. Rather, my aim is to offer an explanation that (1) illuminates variables and processes heretofore unaccounted for in the existing literature, and (2) may be useful in providing insights helpful to models based on subnational levels of analysis. In terms of the latter objective, the Threat and Rally Hypotheses offer an explanation for the ebb and flow of nativism, nationalism, and the identity politics often associated with them. Understanding such forces may enable analysts to better explain why domestic interest groups may be more or less successful at a particular time, independent of collective action dynamics. The statist model also offers an explanation of the state's role in setting agendas and shaping discourse that can certainly affect the strategic interaction of domestic interest groups.

Another advantage of the structural, statist framework presented herein is that it provides insights into the relationship between international and domestic politics. Although limited in its ability to describe the intricacies of domestic politics, it allows us to better see how factors related to international migration and border regimes affect international politics and world order more generally and are, in turn, affected by these changes. Among these are the issues of globalization and sovereignty.

Migration, Borders, and Societal Sovereignty

Looking at the larger picture, observing how states have struggled with the issue of migration reveals much about contemporary sovereignty and the role borders play in the world political economy. The perception that we are witnessing unprecedented systemic change has spawned a cottage industry of scholarly work dealing with the subject of sovereignty.[10] Some have argued that current processes of globalization, the rise of nonstate political actors, and the proliferation of human rights norms suggest that sovereignty is in decline.[11] Others have added that these processes of globalization are eroding the fundamental basis of international society—state sovereignty—and that its decline represents a revolutionary transformation in the Westphalian structure of the international system.[12]

The connection between the various facets of sovereignty—especially interdependence (control over transborder flows), Westphalian (maintenance of borders and territory), and domestic sovereignty (relationship between government and people)—makes focusing only on some of these dimensions outside of the context of the other dimensions problematic.[13] Domestic sovereignty is maximized when the government is able to provide (1) territorial security (defense of Westphalian sovereignty) and (2) the material resources and knowledge to maintain economic growth. Yet this again creates a tension; maximizing domestic and Westphalian sovereignty within a trading-state system requires ease of factor mobility as well as trade, elements that would appear to weaken interdependence sovereignty. However, easing interdependence sovereignty in terms of labor mobility has been associated with rising societal insecurities and compromising Westphalian and domestic sovereignty.

What appears to be happening as the trading-state grand strategy has emerged as the dominant program among advanced industrial democracies is that contemporary approaches to defending territorial sovereignty have exhibited a growing awareness of sovereignty's societal dimensions and an increasing desire for stability in this emerging domain. Andrew Linklater has proposed that "the social bond which has linked the members of each modern European state together but also separated them from other states and the rest of humankind is being challenged by subnational groups and eroded by the advance of regional organizations and globalization. These pressures combine to challenge the exclusionary nature of sovereignty and traditional ideas about community and citizenship."[14] To some these processes represent an opportunity to move beyond nationalist identities. Andrew Linklater suggests that "the steady weakening of the old bonds linking citizens to the state creates unprecedented opportunities for new forms of political community attuned to the principles of cosmopolitan democracy and transnational citizenship."[15]

Empirical evidence drawn from the United States and Europe, however, suggests that a large portion of the populations in these states find these developments unsettling, if not outright threatening.[16] James Rosenau points out that "to the extent that people have a need for community and a sense of independence, then to that extent the achievement and maintenance of *sovereignty for their nation* [serves] important human longings."[17] In a world of unprecedented migration, the implications of this societal dimension of sovereignty (and its link to domestic sovereignty) become evident. "When it is no longer clear who makes up the nation, a state's internal sovereignty and the existence of the state itself is threatened."[18] Control over migration, both in the forms of citizenship and border control policies, is thus not only an aspect of what Stephen Krasner refers to as interdependence sovereignty, but it is intimately linked with domestic sovereignty and Westphalian sovereignty.

The rise of "societal sovereignty," thus, adds another dimension to an already complex amalgam of ideas and norms that constitute modern sovereignty. The result of this evolution is that "the social organization of the world . . . has become much more complex. Bordering has become much more multifaceted, in terms of both geographic and non-geographic forms, as well as of social, political, and economic character."[19] Some point to the process of globalization as one based on the gradual eradication of borders (and thus, some have argued, sovereignty); however, in actuality borders have in many ways *increased* in their sociopolitical importance. On the one hand, borders serve as important symbolic points of economic connection between trading partners as opposed to symbols of separation among advanced industrial countries in Europe and America. The self-limiting of interdependence sovereignty, however, does not suggest that these borders cease to exist but rather that they display a "softer shell"—a semipermeable membrane as opposed to a wall.[20] Emphasizing the symbolic qualities of borders as points of connection instead of separation as well as articulating the benefits to be had from such openness and interdependence play an important role in maintaining regimes.

On the other hand, although borders do serve as important symbols of economic connection, they also remain significant because they provide social closure and symbolic separation between peoples and cultures. Borders, together with the institution of citizenship, designate both inclusion and exclusion and define the sociopolitical community. Traditional means of "imagining the community"—ethnicity, language, culture—remain salient markers of societal inclusion (and exclusion), even amid academic discourse on the emerging multicultural society and the rise of regional integration regimes that also have an identity-building component as in the case of the European Union.[21] Our global age is characterized by a central tension—whereas markets are highly elastic and responsive to change, social identities are not. Borders are important in maintaining economic ties and serve as symbolic "points of connection," but maintaining stable national identities requires at least the image of the border as highly resilient—a "hard shell" rather than the "soft shell" characterized in economic discourse.

The empirical evidence presented in this book suggests that societal insecurities are most pronounced when generated by a sense that "societal sovereignty" is being violated.[22] Sovereignty within nation-states is conceived of as an inviolable compact between state and society—a view shared whether one is predisposed to either civic or ethnic nationalism. There is widespread consensus that deliberations regarding identity are held within the domain of the polity—liberal policies that extend rights to noncitizens or allow entry into the community (whether as a citizen or as a nonnaturalized denizen of the territory) are established as manifestations of the nation's liberal facet of identity.[23] Conversely, the adoption of restrictive legislation established to reduce the degree and speed of societal change reflects a belief that polities have the moral authority to enact such policies in order to maintain their own societal conception of self.

What do these developments tell us about the nature of sovereignty more generally? First and foremost, sovereignty is an institution—a set of norms and rules that include normative statements regarding authority and international recognition. It is often seen as the "immoveable cornerstone" of world order. However, when viewed as a disaggregated collection of distinct dimensions, the institution of sovereignty displays a remarkable degree of flexibility. As Stephen Krasner has pointed out, sovereignty has never been absolute, though it is often presented in such terms.[24] Rather than being in a state of decline, what we see today is simply an increased awareness of sovereignty's various dimensions and the gains to be reaped by making trade-offs between them. Sovereignty is, and always has been, a dynamic institution, though the exact types of sovereignty bargains executed by individual states have varied at different times. In the contemporary period, state behavior has been marked by two distinct sovereignty bargains: (1) in the economic realm, interdependence sovereignty is willingly ceded in order to bolster Westphalian and domestic sovereignty; (2) in the societal realm,

Westphalian sovereignty has been increasingly ceded in order to bolster interdependence sovereignty (control over migration flows), domestic sovereignty (the relationship between government and polity), and societal sovereignty (identity). Although these two bargains lead to opposite impulses with regard to interdependence sovereignty (control over flows), this tension can be (and evidence suggests largely is) addressed both by the use of symbolic policies intended to craft the image of secure borders and social identities, and by a predominant belief that neoliberal economic policies will, in the long run, serve to mitigate migration pressures that are the source of societal insecurities in receiving states.

The 9/11 terrorist attacks in New York City and Washington, DC, will no doubt serve to further complicate the "sovereignty bargains" exacted in the coming years. These events made the connection between international migration and the construction of global terror networks clear to the public and policymakers alike. In terms of sovereignty, the 9/11 event certainly raised the stakes concerning the importance of interdependence sovereignty as a prerequisite to defending other aspects of sovereignty.

Policy Implications

Although the purpose of this book is to provide an accurate account of the political forces that shape state responses to international migration rather than to forward policy prescriptions, the findings presented do suggest significant implications for policy. Two implications seem to be particularly salient: (1) in the absence of absolute security, domestic stability increasingly depends on the state's ability to forward a strong image of control over flows as an instrument of sovereignty; (2) in a world where control over flows is increasingly important, both instrumentally and politically, forces press states to shift immigration and border policy from the purely domestic domain to one increasingly operating in the international domain.

GRAND STRATEGY: ADDRESSING THE THREE FACETS OF SECURITY

One of the great illusions of governance is that of security. Regardless of the types of policies enacted or their magnitude, the fact is that we are *never* completely secure. Security is thus a *relative* issue. Moreover, security has different facets, each with its own inherent logic. At times, the policy interest of these various facets may converge. However, the opposite is also true, and often the policy interests of the various facets diverge. States increasingly find themselves in a situation wherein security interests simultaneously press for both more openness toward international migration and more closure. Taken together, the policy implications of this study suggest that complete security is not necessary or necessarily desirable if it is relevant only to one facet of national security. For example, whereas a fortified garrison state may maximize security against foreign invasion or terrorist infiltration, the cost to societal security would be prohibitive, as civil liberties would necessarily be sacrificed at the altar of such a garrison state. Instead, "effective" security would focus on the following: with regard to military defense and/or homeland security, because security addresses perceptions of security as much, if not more so, than instrumental security, policy would be established to (1) reduce the probability of a successful large-scale terrorist attack on home soil over the long-term, and (2) reduce the probability of multiple small-scale attacks in the short-term. In terms of economic security, policy is likely to remain committed to the liberal market-driven approach maintained since Bretton Woods. Clearly, the restrictive aspects of policy necessary to maximize homeland security interests conflict with economic security interests that favor increased openness. In these initial post–9/11 years, high levels of threat perception along the homeland security dimension have pushed policy to prioritize those interests over economic interests. However, if successful in achieving these limited homeland security goals, it is likely that policy will gradually scale back the most restrictive aspects since these have negative consequences for security's economic and/or societal dimensions. In the United States, for example, the absence of major terrorist activity in the next decade will likely erode support for the more restrictive aspects of the USA Patriot Act—a move that will allow for freer movement (forwarding macroeconomic interests) and less government intrusiveness into the lives of the citizenry (forwarding societal interests).

In terms of responding to societal security interests related to the issue of immigration and border control, the evidence suggests that responding to this sense of threat requires that policy project a strong image of state control. It is this image of control—not necessarily the actual curtailment of immigration flows—that most directly responds to societal insecurities.

This is particularly the case for countries that have already experienced a considerable amount of immigration and have moved toward a more ethnically heterogeneous society—such as those included in this book. Newer countries to immigration—such as those in the Nordic region of Europe that have a higher degree of ethno-racial homogeneity—will likely experience a more focused opposition to an increase in immigration volume, not just on the appearance of control, at least in the short to medium run. As demographic transformation takes place over time, however, it becomes less and less clear who is a newcomer and who is one of "us." It is at this point that the symbolic importance of policy takes increasing precedence over its more instrumental aspects. At issue is the defense of societal sovereignty.

Taken together, the implications for immigration and border policy more generally suggest the importance of conceiving of policy responses in terms of grand strategy rather than piecemeal. Of course, the complexity of international migration makes pursuing a grand strategy approach quite challenging for policymakers. However, it is in the understanding of the various implications of migration flows on the various facets of security that will enable policymakers to craft policy that increases the probability of increased aggregate gains (and/or minimizes aggregate costs). The most obvious example of this type of new thinking involves the creation of temporary-worker regimes. Germany's experience with temporary labor provides an important lesson about the likelihood that temporary labor's tendency to create permanent immigration and the potentially negative implications this has on societal security, even when economic benefits are achieved. This is not to say that temporary-labor recruitment is no longer a policy option—simply, that the policies and procedures associated with such a program require careful planning, effective administration, and continued oversight. A grand strategy approach presses for more attention to be given to root causes and issue linkage—a perspective that will hopefully mitigate the probability of unanticipated negative consequences of policy.

INTERDEPENDENCE AND MULTILATERALISM

A grand-strategy perspective is more conducive to achieving an accurate view of the complex processes of migration and their myriad economic, social, and political effects. From such a vantage point, international migration can be seen as one of the many phenomena that forward the condition of complex interdependence among nations.[25] Migration has historically been viewed in largely domestic terms—a cornerstone of Westphalian sovereignty. Increasingly, however, there is growing recognition of both domestic and international factors that shape migration pressures—both push and pull.[26] Moreover, there appears to be growing recognition that effective management requires policy to be directed not solely at one element, but both. Consequently, there are increasing pressures for policymakers to move away from a purely unilateral approach and to be more open to bilateral and multilateral regimes to govern the movement of people across borders. Demetrios Papademetriou, director of the Migration Policy Institute in Washington, DC, noted, "In many ways, the age of unilateralism in border controls may be over."[27]

In an address to the Senate Judiciary Committee on March 4, 2003, John Ashcroft explained that "close working relationships with international allies" would allow the United States to "leverage our anti-terrorism efforts throughout the world."[28] In another address, Ridge added, "By working together we can better reach our common goals of ensuring the security and prosperity of our citizens."[29] Not only has governmental dialogue become increasingly marked by references to the need for increased cooperation and coordination among nations to better manage migration, but we have also seen an increase in bilateral and multilateral programs. In the United States, these have been marked by new initiatives to create "Smart Borders" with its neighbors and NAFTA partners, Canada and Mexico. Included in these initiatives are programs to establish harmonization on the use of biometric identification data, procedures for expedited entry for prescreened frequent travelers (NEXUS), integrated border-enforcement teams (IBETs), information-sharing procedures, and coordination of refugee and asylum policies, among others. At this point, cooperation between countries in North America has been primarily bilateral rather than multilateral, marked by cooperation rather than policy harmonization, and the level of cooperation is higher between the United States and Canada than between the United States and Mexico.[30] Moreover, political discourse has remained sensitive to the issue of sovereignty. As John Manley, then Canadian deputy prime minister, once remarked, "Working closely with the United States does not mean turning over to them the key to Canadian sovereignty."[31]

This sentiment was echoed by George W. Bush, who remarked, "You pass your laws, we'll pass our laws."[32] Nevertheless, the direction of policymaking is unmistakable, as cooperation and coordination between and among nations increasingly becomes the new norm.

Multilateral cooperation on issues of migration and border policy is deeper among countries that comprise the European Union, as there is more experience with such cooperation. A conference of EU policymakers, government officials, and migration experts and analysts held in 2004 released a statement that suggested that "the processes of immigration and immigrant integration in Europe are now too significant to be left to guide themselves. Migration is now a social and economic phenomenon of the first order, with positive and negative potential that European countries cannot afford to ignore. Furthermore, Europe has now reached a point where differences between the immigration experiences of European countries and the 'traditional countries of immigration' are growing smaller. No country of the developed world is—or need be—alone in facing the challenge of managing migration."[33] One of the most notable achievements in terms of multilateral cooperation since the Treaty of Rome (1957) is the Schengen Agreement that called for a common visa policy, policy harmonization to deter illegal immigration, and the creation of an automated Schengen Information System (SIS).[34] Another example of cooperation can be found in the Dublin Convention that established common procedures for the handling of asylum claims.[35]

Increased bilateralism and multilateralism is not limited only to regional cooperation and collaboration, though incentives for regional cooperation may be greater than for countries less geographically proximate. Nevertheless, in addition to increased regional cooperation in Europe and North America, we also see evidence of increased transatlantic cooperation.[36] This is especially the case since 9/11, as the need for cooperation as a means to increase control and security became manifest. Cresencio Arcos, director of international affairs at the U.S. Department of Homeland Security, remarked, "Homeland security can't stop at a nation's border. The same threats are present for all of us and we must work together to meet them. . . . No one country can be truly safe without the cooperation and like-minded commitment of others."[37] Rey Koslowski notes that the U.S. Department of Homeland Security and the European Commission "have been taking international cooperation into sensitive areas of state sovereignty dealing with border controls, government surveillance, data collection and exchange that before September 11, 2001 would have been unthinkable."[38]

If increased bilateral and multilateral cooperation on migration and other transborder flows can effectively increase state control, there is also reason to expect a potential impact on foreign policy more generally. In the aftermath of the 9/11 terrorist attacks the Bush administration crafted the Bush Doctrine as the defining feature in the emergent war on terrorism. The logic was clear: fight terrorists abroad so that we don't have to fight them at home. The logic of the Bush Doctrine was used to legitimate military action abroad in Afghanistan and Iraq. The potential foreign-policy blowback of such an approach has already been felt, both in terms of U.S. relations with the Muslim world, and in terms of strained relations with key allies, especially Germany and France.[39] Effective border management may serve to mitigate the need for Bush Doctrine foreign policy without sacrificing homeland security interests—in fact, such an approach may be vastly superior in terms of end results.

If multilateral information sharing regarding terrorists and related organizations can be cultivated and control mechanisms at the borders can effectively screen friend from foe, there is reason to expect higher levels of security without necessarily having to "fight them at home." Homeland security would shift from a logic of military defense to one of international law enforcement and border management. Interdiction prior to organization or execution of strategic terrorist objectives could mean that the "war" would be averted without necessarily cultivating a "fight." Of course, the levels of control necessary to achieve such an end are at this point in time quite unprecedented. At its foundation, such an approach would require first and foremost a vast network of information and intelligence sharing, as well as coordinated analysis. To effectively screen out the "bad guys" we must first be able to positively identify who such individuals are. Several analyses of the 9/11 terrorist attacks, including the 9/11 Commission Report, concluded that America's vulnerability was compounded by a failure of intelligence. Intelligence regarding the plot was available, though fragmented throughout the wider intelligence community. The result was a failure to "connect the dots" necessary to effectively anticipate and interdict the terrorists before they could execute their plan.[40] In the United States, moves have been made to "reinvent" the intelligence system—a development that might be considered the first compulsory step in establishing the new security regime. President Bush remarked:

> All the institutions of our government must be fully prepared for a struggle against terror that will last into the future. Our goal is an integrated, unified national intelligence effort. Therefore, my administration will continue moving forward with additional changes to the structure and organization of our intelligence agencies. . . . All these reforms have a single goal: We will ensure that the people in government responsible for defending American and countering terrorism have the best possible information to make the best decisions.[41]

Some of the first moves included the creation of the Terrorist Threat Integration Center (TTIC), given the mission of integrating the existing intelligence gathered by the numerous agencies that collect such data, including the Central Intelligence Agency (CIA), the Federal Bureau of Investigation (FBI), and those associated with the military. A new Terrorist Screening Center (TSC) was later established to provide 24/7 access for law enforcement and security personnel to this integrated intelligence. A more comprehensive reorganization was initiated with the passage of the Intelligence Reform and Terrorism Prevention Act of 2004. The act mandated, among other things, the creation of a new National Counterterrorism Center (NCTC) that would replaced the existing TTIC, and that management of the U.S. intelligence community be integrated under the guidance of a new National Intelligence Director (NID). In 2005, the former U.S. ambassador to the United Nations John Negroponte was named to serve as the first NID. The NCTC was charged with the task of coordinating U.S. government actions plans regarding terrorism, concentrating analytical expertise on foreign and domestic terrorism in one location, preparing the President's Terrorist Threat Report (PTTR), and coordinating the prioritization of interagency law enforcement and counterterrorism response to emergent threats.

Attempting to create a new border regime that effectively filters terrorists without unduly constraining cross-border flows represents a monumental undertaking. Beginning with intelligence reorganization necessary to better identify potential threats to national security, the task is formidable for the intelligence community historically has proven itself to be reluctant to embrace change—especially that which threatens its organization sovereignty.[42] Some intelligence experts remain skeptical of the U.S. intelligence community's ability to embrace needed change. Amy Zegart remarked, "I believe it will take another catastrophic terrorist attack at a minimum [to bring about true reform], and even that may not be enough—because the barriers to reform are so deeply entrenched and so high."[43] Moreover, bureaucratic inertia is not limited to U.S. agencies, but must be faced by all nations seeking to manage cross-border flows to maximize gains and minimize risk. And that is just the beginning of a new regime that may direct immigration and border management in the coming years—one likely to be more expansive in scale and scope, as well as increasingly international in orientation.

Indeed, this presents an entirely new dimension to the politics of immigration and border policymaking—one already characterized by high levels of complexity. However, the stakes are higher than ever and there is little room for error. The apprehension and arrest of Ahmed Ressam was indeed a fortunate occurrence, however national security cannot depend on good fortune. How states manage immigration has a tremendous impact on all our lives—politically, socially, economically, and in terms of homeland security and defense. Understanding the practical and political processes at play is necessary in order to proceed in creating informed policy and maximizing national security.

Reference Matter

Notes

CHAPTER ONE

1. "Trail of a Terrorist," *PBS Frontline*, http://www.pbs.org/wgbh/pages/front line/shows/trail/.

2. All nineteen had visas to enter the United States. However, eight of the terrorists had passports that "showed evidence of fraudulent manipulation, and another five had "suspicious indicators." None of the hijackers filled out their visa applications correctly, and three lied on their application forms. National Commission on Terrorist Attacks, *The 9/11 Report: The National Commission on Terrorist Attacks upon the United States* (New York: St. Martin's Press, 2004); Stephen Flynn, *America the Vulnerable: How Our Government is Failing to Protect Us from Terrorism* (New York: HarperCollins, 2004).

3. Steven A. Camarota, "The Open Door: How Militant Islamic Terrorists Entered and Remained in the United States, 1993–2001," *CIS Paper No. 21* (Washington, DC: Center for Immigration Studies, 2002); Committee on International Relations, U.S. House of Representatives, "Preventing the Entry of Terrorists into the United States," Hearing before the Subcommittee on International Terrorism, Nonproliferation, and Human Rights, No. 108–90, second session (February 13, 2004).

4. Charles Kindleberger, *The World in Depression, 1929–39* (Berkeley: University of California Press, 1973).

5. David Ricardo, *Works* (Cambridge: Cambridge University Press, 1955); Paul R. Krugman and Anthony J. Venables, "Globalization and the Inequality of Nations," *Working Paper #5098* (Cambridge, MA: NBER, 1995); Paul R. Krugman and Maurice Obstfeld, *International Economics* (Reading, MA: Addison-Wesley, 1997).

6. Richard Rosecrance, *The Rise of the Trading State* (New York: Basic Books, 1986), 46.

7. Rosecrance, *Trading State*.

8. See Hans Morgenthau, *Politics Among Nations* (New York: Alfred A. Knopf, 1957). Cf. Paul Kennedy, *The Rise and Fall of the Great Powers* (London: Unwin-Hyman, 1988); Jack Snyder, *Myths of Empire* (Ithaca, NY: Cornell University Press,

1991); Charles Kupchan, *The Vulnerability of Empire* (Ithaca, NY: Cornell University Press, 1994); Richard N. Rosecrance, "Overextension, Vulnerability, and Conflict: The 'Goldilocks Problem' in International Strategy," *International Security* 19, no. 4 (1995); Chalmers Johnson, *Blowback: The Costs and Consequences of American Empire* (New York: Metropolitan Books, 2000).

9. Cf. John Mueller, *Retreat from Doomsday: The Obsolescence of Major War* (New York: Basic Books, 1989); Thomas C. Schelling, "The Role of Nuclear Weapons," in *Turning Point: The Gulf War and U.S. Military Strategy*, ed. L. Ederington and M. Mazarr (Ithaca, NY: Cornell University Press, 1994); Nina Tannenwald, "The Nuclear Taboo: The United States and the Normative Basis of Nuclear Non-Use," *International Organization* 53, no. 3 (spring 1999).

10. Arthur A. Stein, "The Hegemon's Dilemma," *International Organization* 38, no. 3 (spring 1984).

11. Stephen D. Krasner, "State Power and the Structure of International Trade," *World Politics* 28, no. 3 (1976): 322–23; see also Robert O. Keohane, "The Theory of Hegemonic Stability and Changes in International Economic Regimes, 1967–1977," in *Change in the International System*, ed. O. Holsti, R. Silverson, and A. George (Boulder, CO: Westview Press, 1980); Robert G. Gilpin, *War and Change in World Politics* (Cambridge: Cambridge University Press, 1981); Bruce M. Russett, "The Mysterious Case of Vanishing Hegemony," *International Organization* 39 (1985); and David A. Lake, *Power, Protection and Free Trade* (Ithaca, NY: Cornell University Press, 1988).

12. Robert O. Keohane, *After Hegemony* (Princeton, NJ: Princeton University Press, 1984).

13. OECD, *Global Economy*.

14. World Bank, *World Development Report* (Washington, DC: World Bank, 1999); World Trade Organization, *International Trade Statistics* (Geneva: WTO, 2000).

15. John Gerard Ruggie, *At Home Abroad, Abroad at Home: International Liberalization and Domestic Stability in the New World Economy* (Florence: European Union Institute, 1995); Benjamin J. Cohen, *The Geography of Money* (Ithaca, NY: Cornell University Press, 1998).

16. Saskia Sassen, *Losing Control? Sovereignty in an Age of Globalization* (New York: Columbia University Press, 1996), 40; James H. Mittelman, The *Globalization Syndrome: Transformation and Resistance* (Princeton, NJ: Princeton University Press, 2000), 21.

17. Wayne Cornelius, Takeyuki Tsuda, Philip L. Martin and James Hollifield refer to this phenomenon as the "Convergence Hypothesis"—that policies in immigrant-receiving states are increasingly similar and generally stress control provisions rather than facilitating international migration. See Wayne A. Cornelius, Takeyuki Tsuda, Philip L. Martin, and James F. Hollifield, eds., *Controlling Immigration: A Global Perspective*, 2d ed. (Stanford, CA: Stanford University Press, 2004).

18. Timothy J. Hatton and Jeffrey G. Williamson, *The Age of Mass Migration* (New York: Routledge, 1998).

19. Ronald Rogowski, "Commentary on 'Migration as International Trade,'" in "Reconsidering Immigration in an Integrating World," ed. C. Rudolph, *UCLA Journal of International Law and Foreign Affairs* 3, no. 2 (1998): 416.

20. Cf. H-O theory in Paul Krugman and Maurice Obstfeld, *International Economics,* 6th ed. (New York: Addison-Wesley, 2003); Robert A. Mundell, "International Trade and Factor Mobility," *American Economic Review* 47, no. 3 (1957). Kevin O'Rourke and Jeffrey G. Williamson, *Globalization and History: The Evolution of a Nineteenth Century Atlantic Economy* (Cambridge, MA: MIT Press, 1999); William J. Collins, Kevin O'Rourke, and Jeffrey G. Williamson, "Were Trade and Factor Mobility Substitutes in History?" in *Migration: The Controversies and the Evidence*, ed. R. Faini, J. de Melo, and K. Zimmermann (Cambridge: Cambridge University Press, 1999).

21. Rogowski, "Commentary."

22. Manuel Castells, *The Rise of the Network Society* (New York: Basil Blackwell, 1996).

23. OECD, *Global Economy*, 108.

24. Rosecrance, *Virtual State*, 11.

25. These are sometimes referred to as the "three-D" jobs—those that are dirty, dangerous, and demeaning.

26. Wayne A. Cornelius, *The Role of Immigrant Labor in the U.S. and Japanese Economies* (La Jolla, CA: Center for U.S.-Mexican Studies, 1998).

27. Michael S. Teitelbaum and Jay Winter, *A Question of Numbers: High Migration, Low Fertility, and the Politics of National Identity* (New York: Hill and Wang, 1998).

28. James P. Smith and Jeffrey S. Passel, eds., *The New Americans: Economic, Demographic, and Fiscal Effects of Immigration* (Washington, DC: National Academy Press, 1997).

29. A poll of prominent economists conducted by the CATO Institute showed that 81 percent of respondents believed that immigration has "very favorable" effects on aggregate economic growth. See Julian L. Simon, "Immigration: The Demographic and Economic Facts," *CATO Institute and National Economic Forum* (December 11, 1995).

30. See Howard F. Chang, "Immigration as International Trade: The Economic Gains from the Liberalized Movement of Labor," *UCLA Journal of International Law and Foreign Affairs* 3, no. 2 (1998); Richard Vedder, Lowell Gallaway, and Stephen Moore, *Immigration and Unemployment: New Evidence* (Arlington, VA: Alexis de Tocqueville Institution, 1994).

31. An excellent overview of the various disciplinary techniques applied to the study of migration can be found in Caroline Brettell and James F. Hollifield, eds., *Migration Theory: Talking Across the Disciplines* (New York: Routledge, 2000).

32. One of the most often cited is Peter Brimelow, *Alien Nation: Common Sense About America's Immigration Disaster* (New York: Harper, 1996).

33. Restrictionist sentiment based on this perspective is reflected in Samuel P. Huntington, *Who Are We? The Challenges to America's National Identity* (New York: Simon and Schuster, 2004).

34. Rosecrance, *Trading State.*

CHAPTER TWO

1. Georges Vernez, *National Security and Migration: How Strong the Link?* (Santa Monica, CA: RAND, 1996), 2.

2. United Nations, *Trends in Total Migrant Stock, 1995*, Doc. no. POP/1B/DB/95/1/REV.3 (New York: Population Division, Dept. of Economic and Social Affairs, United Nations Secretariat, 1995); United Nations, *International Migration, 2002*, Doc. no. ST/ESA/SER.A/219 (New York: Population Division, Dept. of Economic and Social Affairs, United Nations Secretariat, 2002).

3. United Nations, *World Population Monitoring 1997* (New York: United Nations, 1998), 14.

4. Ibid., 15.

5. Rey Koslowski, *Migrants and Citizens* (Ithaca, NY: Cornell University Press, 2000), 2.

6. Douglas S. Massey, Joaquin Arango, Graeme Hugo, Ali Kouaouci, Adela Pellegrino, and J. Edward Taylor, *Worlds in Motion: Understanding International Migration at the End of the Millennium* (Oxford: Oxford University Press, 1999); Stephen Castles and Mark Miller, *The Age of Migration: International Population Movements in the Modern World*, 2d ed. (New York: Guilford, 1998).

7. Monica Boyd, "Family and Personal Networks in International Migration: Recent Developments and New Agendas," *International Migration Review* 2, no. 3 (1989): 638–70; Harvey M. Choldin, "Kinship Networks in the Migration Process," *International Migration Review* 7 (1973): 163–76; Douglas T. Gurak and Fe Caces, "Migration Networks and the Shaping of Migration Systems," in *International Migration Systems: A Global Approach*, ed. M. Kritz, L. L. Lim, and H. Zlotnik (Oxford: Clarendon Press, 1992); John S. MacDonald and Leatrice D. MacDonald, "Chain Migration, Ethnic Neighborhood Formation, and Social Networks," in *An Urban World*, ed. C. Tilly (Boston: Little, Brown, 1974); Douglas S. Massey, Joaquin Arango, Jorge Durand, and Humberto Gonzalez, *Return to Aztlan: The Social Process of International Migration from Western Mexico* (Berkeley: University of California Press, 1987); Douglas S. Massey and Felipe Garcia Espana, "The Social Process of International Migration," *Science* 237 (1987): 733–38.

8. On the push-pull effects of economic disparity on international migration flows, see J. R. Harris and Michael P. Todaro, "Migration, Unemployment, and Development: A Two-Sector Analysis," *American Economic Review* 60 (1970): 126–42;

Paul R. Krugman and Maurice Obstfeld, *International Economics* (Reading, MA: Addison-Wesley, 1997); W. Arthur Lewis, "Economic Development with Unlimited Supplies of Labour," *Manchester School of Economic and Social Studies* 22 (1954): 139–91; Gustav Ranis and J. C. H. Fei, "A Theory of Economic Development," *American Economic Review* 51 (1961): 533–65; Michael P. Todaro, *Internal Migration in Developing Countries* (Geneva: International Labor Office, 1976); Michael P. Todaro and L. Maruszko, "Illegal Migration and U.S. Immigration Reform: A Conceptual Framework," *Population and Development Review* 13 (1987): 101–14; on population growth rates between developed and developing countries, see Paul Kennedy, *Preparing for the Twenty-First Century* (New York: Random House, 1993), 23.

9. Philip L. Martin, "Economic Integration and Migration: The Case of NAFTA," *UCLA Journal of International Law and Foreign Affairs* 3, no. 2 (1998): 419–41; Commission for the Study of International Migration and Cooperative Economic Development, *Unauthorized Migration: An Economic Development Response* (Washington, DC: Commission for the Study of International Migration and Cooperative Economic Development, 1990).

10. Michael S. Teitelbaum and Jay Winter, *A Question of Numbers: High Migration, Low Fertility, and the Politics of National Identity* (New York: Hill and Wang, 1998), 241.

11. Ibid., 3.

12. Ibid., 4.

13. Cf. Nathan Glazer and Daniel Patrick Moynihan, *Beyond the Melting Pot: The Negroes, Puerto Ricans, Jews, and Italians of New York City* (Cambridge, MA: MIT Press, 1963); Robert Park, "Human Migration and the Marginal Man," *American Journal of Sociology* 33 (1928): 881–93. See also Barbara Schmitter Heisler, "The Future of Immigrant Incorporation: Which Models? Which Concepts? *International Migration Review* 26, no. 2 (1992): 623–45; Alejandro Portes, "Children of Immigrants: Segmented Assimilation and Its Determinants," in *The Economic Sociology of Immigration*, ed. A. Portes (New York: Russell Sage, 1995); Alejandro Portes and Min Zhou, "The New Second Generation: Segmented Assimilation and Its Variants Among Post–1965 Immigrant Youth," *Annals of the American Academy of Political and Social Sciences* 535 (1993): 74–96; Martin Heisler, "Contextualizing Global Migration: Sketching the Socio-Political Landscape in Europe," in "Reconsidering Immigration in an Integrating World," ed. C. Rudolph, *UCLA Journal of International Law and Foreign Affairs* 3, no. 2 (1998): 575–76. See also Martin O. Heisler and Barbara Schmitter Heisler, "Citizenship—Old, New and Changing: Inclusion, Exclusion, and Limbo for Ethnic Groups and Migrants in the Modern Democratic State," in *Dominant National Cultures and Ethnic Identities*, ed. J. Fijalkowski, H. Merkins, and F. Schmidt (Berlin: Free University Press, 1991), 91–128.

14. Christopher Rudolph, "Globalization and Security: International Migration and Evolving Conceptions of Security in Statecraft and Scholarship," *Security Studies* 13, no. 1 (2003): 1–32.

15. Wayne A. Cornelius, Thomas J. Espenshade, and Idean Salehyan, eds., *The International Migration of the Highly-Skilled: Demand, Supply, and Development Consequences for Sending and Receiving Countries* (La Jolla: Center for Comparative Immigration Studies, University of California at San Diego, 2001); Cornelius et al., *Controlling Immigration.*

16. These include countries such as South Korea, Indonesia, Sri Lanka, the Philippines, India, Pakistan, Egypt, Morocco, Tunisia, China, Bangladesh, and Vietnam. See Nasra M. Shah and Fred Arnold, "Government Policies and Programs Regulating Labor Migration," in *Asian Labor Migration: Pipeline to the Middle East,* ed. Fred Arnold and Nasra Shah (Boulder, CO: Westview Press, 1986), 65–80; Manolo I. Abella, "Contemporary Labour Migration from Asia: Policies and Perspectives of Sending Countries," in *International Migration Systems: A Global Approach,* ed. Mary M. Kritz, Lin Lean Lim, and Hania Zlotnik (Oxford: Clarendon Press, 1992), 263–78; Graziano Battistella, "Philippine Overseas Labour: From Export to Management," *ASEAN Economic Bulletin* 12 (1995): 257–74; Graeme J. Hugo, "Labour Export from Indonesia: An Overview," *ASEAN Economic Bulletin* 12 (1995): 275–98; Laurie Brand, "Explaining the Development of Tunisian and Moroccan Emigration-Related Institutions" (paper presented at the Center for International Studies, University of Southern California, Los Angeles, February 27, 2002).

17. Jorge Castañeda quoted in Tom Zoellner, "Mexico Says Legalize Crossers or No Deal," *The Arizona Republic,* June 22, 2001.

18. "Sudan: UN Health Agency Survey Shows High Death Rates in Darfur Crisis," *UN News Center* (September 13, 2004), URL: <http://www.un.org/apps/news/storyAr.asp?NewsID=11908&Cr=sudan&Cr1=> (accessed February 15, 2005).

19. David Kyle and Zai Liang, "Migration Merchants: Human Smuggling from Ecuador and China," *CCIS Working Paper No. 43* (La Jolla: Center for Comparative Immigration Studies, University of California, San Diego, October 2001); David Kyle and Rey Koslowski, eds., *Global Human Smuggling: Comparative Perspectives* (Baltimore: Johns Hopkins University Press, 2001); Peter Andreas, *Border Games: Policing the U.S.-Mexico Divide* (Ithaca, NY: Cornell University Press, 2000); see also Nigel Harris, *The New Untouchables* (London: I. B. Tauris, 1995).

20. *Migration News* (August 1999).

21. Momentum, however, has been building along these lines. See James F. Hollifield, "The Politics of International Migration," in *Migration Theory: Talking Across the Disciplines,* ed. Caroline Brettell and James F. Hollifield (New York: Routledge: 2000).

22. Cf. Christian Joppke, ed., *Challenge to the Nation-State: Immigration in Western Europe and the United States* (Oxford: Oxford University Press, 1998); Cornelius et al., *Controlling Immigration*; Wayne A. Cornelius, "Appearances and Realities: Controlling Illegal Immigration in the United States," in *Temporary Workers or Future Citizens?* ed. M. Weiner and T. Hanami (London: Macmillan, 1998); Joseph Nevins, *Operation Gatekeeper: The Rise of the "Illegal Alien" and the Making of the*

U.S.-Mexico Boundary (New York: Routledge, 2002); Teresa Hayter, *Open Borders: The Case Against Immigration Controls* (Ann Arbor, MI: Pluto Press, 2004); Peter Duignan and Lewis Gann, eds. *The Debate in the United States Over Immigration* (Stanford, CA: Hoover Institution Press, 1998); Roy Beck, *The Case Against Immigration* (New York: W. W. Norton, 1996); Peter Brimelow, *Alien Nation* (New York: Random House, 1995).

23. Aristide R. Zolberg, "International Migration Policies in a Changing World System," in *Human Migration, Patterns and Policies*, ed. William H. McNeill and Ruth Adams (Bloomington: Indiana University Press, n.d.), 241–86; Myron Weiner, "On International Migration and International Relations," *Population and Development Review* 11, no. 3 (1985), 441–55.

24. Daniel Tichenor, *Dividing Lines: The Politics of Immigration Control in America* (Princeton, NJ: Princeton University Press, 2002), 20.

25. Cf. Brinley Thomas, *Migration and Economic Growth* (Cambridge: Cambridge University Press, 1973); Julian L. Simon, *The Economic Consequences of Immigration* (Oxford: Basil Blackwell and the Cato Institute, 1989); George Borjas, *Friends or Strangers* (New York: Basic Books, 1990); Philip L. Martin and Elizabeth Midgley, "Immigration to the United States: Journey to an Uncertain Destination," *Population Bulletin* 49, no. 2 (1994): 2–45.

26. James F. Hollifield, Daniel Tichenor, and Gary Zuk, "Immigrants, Markets, and the American State: The Political Economy of U.S. Immigration," in *Explaining Migration Policy*, ed. Marco Guigni and Florence Passy (Lanham, MD: Lexington Books, 2003); Tichenor, *Dividing Lines*.

27. Ashley S. Timmer and Jeffrey G. Williamson, "Immigration Policy Prior to the 1930s: Labor Markets, Policy Interactions, and Globalization Backlash," *Population and Development Review* 24 (1998): 739–72.

28. Cf. Manuel Castells, "Immigrant Workers and Class Struggles in Advanced Capitalism," *Politics and Society* 5, no. 1 (1975): 33–66; Stephen Castles and Godula Kosack, *Immigrant Workers and Class Structure in Western Europe* (Oxford: Oxford University Press, 1973); R. Miles, "Labour Migration, Racism and Capital Accumulation in Western Europe Since 1945," *Capital and Class* 28 (1986): 49–86; R. Miles, *Capitalism and Unfree Labour: Anomaly or Necessity?* (London: Tavistock, 1987); M. Nikolinakos, "Notes Toward a General Theory of Migration in Late Capitalism," *Race and Class* 17, no. 1 (1975): 5–18; Elizabeth McLean Petras, "The Global Labor Market in the Modern World Economy," in *Global Trends in Migration*, ed. M. Kritz, C. B. Keely, and S. Tomasi (New York: Center for Migration Studies, 1981).

29. Eytan Meyers, "Theories of International Immigration Policy: A Comparative Analysis" (paper presented at the Annual Meeting of the International Studies Association, Los Angeles, 2000), 6. See also Petras, "Global Labor Market"; Alejandro Portes, "Modes of Structural Incorporation and Present Theories of Labor Immigration," in *Global Trends in Migration*, ed. M. M. Kritz, C. B. Keely, and S. M. Tomasi (New York: Center for Migration Studies, 1981).

30. Outlined in Michael Piore, *Birds of Passage* (New York: Cambridge University Press, 1979).

31. Michael LeMay, *From Open Door to Dutch Door* (New York: Praeger, 1987); William Schugart, Robert Tollison, and Mwangi Kimenyi, "The Political Economy of Immigration Restrictions," *Yale Journal on Regulation* 51 (1986): 79–97; Keith Fitzgerald, *The Face of the Nation* (Stanford, CA: Stanford University Press, 1996).

32. Cf. Gary P. Freeman, "Modes of Immigration Politics in Liberal Democratic States," *International Migration Review* 29, no. 4 (winter 1995): 881–913; Leah Haus, "Openings in the Wall: Transnational Migrants, Labor Unions, and U.S. Immigration Policy," *International Organization* 49, no. 2 (1995); Philip L. Martin, "Good Intentions Gone Awry: IRCA and U.S. Agriculture," *Annals of the AAPSS* 534 (July 1994): 44–57; Jeannette Money, *Fences and Neighbors* (Ithaca, NY: Cornell University Press, 1999); Aristide R. Zolberg, "Reforming the Backdoor: The Immigration Reform and Control Act of 1986 in Historical Perspective," in *Immigration Reconsidered*, ed. V. Yans-McLaughlin (New York: Oxford University Press, 1990); William Schugart, Robert Tollison, and Mwangi Kimenyi, "The Political Economy of Immigration Restrictions," *Yale Journal on Regulation* 51 (1986): 79–97.

33. Mancur Olson, *The Logic of Collective Action* (Cambridge, MA: Harvard University Press, 1965).

34. Freeman, "Model of Immigration Politics," 885.

35. On the political effects of costs/benefits concentration, see James Q. Wilson, *The Politics of Regulation* (New York: Harper, 1980).

36. Freeman, "Modes of Immigration Politics," 886.

37. Money, *Fences and Neighbors*.

38. Cornelius et al., *Controlling Immigration*.

39. Cf. James G. Gimpel and James R. Edwards Jr., *The Congressional Politics of Immigration Reform* (Boston: Allyn and Bacon, 1999); Marc R. Rosenblum, "The Making of Immigration Policy: An Economic Interest Group Approach" (paper read at the Western Political Science Association Meeting, San Francisco, 1996); Carolyn Wong, "The Political Economy of U.S. Immigration Legislation: Congressional Votes in the Postwar Period" (paper read at the Annual Meeting of the American Political Science Association, Chicago, August 31–September 3, 1995).

40. Alan E. Kessler, "Globalization, Domestic Politics, and the 'Curious Coalitions' of Postwar American Immigration Reform" (paper presented at the Annual Meeting of the American Political Science Association, Atlanta, GA, 1999).

41. Hollifield, "Politics of International Migration"; Haus, "Openings in the Wall"; Leah Haus, "Labor Unions and Immigration Policy in France," *International Migration Review* 33, no. 3 (1999): 683–716.

42. E. E. Schattschneider, *The Semi-Sovereign People* (New York: Holt, Rinehart and Winston, 1942); Theda Skocpol, *Protecting Soldiers and Mothers* (Cambridge, MA: Harvard University Press, 1992).

43. Gimpel and Edwards, *Congressional Politics*.

44. Tichenor, *Dividing Lines.*

45. Kitty Calavita, *Inside the State: The Bracero Program, Immigration, and the INS* (New York: Routledge, 1992).

46. Andreas, *Border Games.*

47. See U.S. Commission on Immigration Reform, *U.S. Immigration Policy: Restoring Credibility* (Washington, DC: U.S. Commission on Immigration Reform, 1994).

48. James F. Hollifield, "Immigration and Republicanism in France: The Hidden Consensus," in *Controlling Immigration: A Global Perspective,* ed. W. A. Cornelius, P. L. Martin, and J. F. Hollifield (Stanford, CA: Stanford University Press, 1994).

49. Cf. James F. Hollifield, *Immigrants, Markets, and States* (Cambridge, MA: Harvard University Press, 1992); David Jacobson, *Rights Across Borders* (Baltimore: Johns Hopkins University Press, 1996); Yasemin Nuhoglu Soysal, *The Limits of Citizenship* (Chicago: University of Chicago Press, 1994); Virginie Guiraudon, "Citizenship Rights for Non-Citizens: France, Germany, and the Netherlands," in *Challenge to the Nation-State,* ed. C. Joppke (Oxford: Oxford University Press, 1998).

50. Jacobson, *Rights Across Borders.*

51. Christian Joppke, "Asylum and State Sovereignty: A Comparison of the United States, Germany, and Britain," *Comparative Political Studies* 30, no. 3 (1997); Jeannette Money, "Human Rights Norms and Immigration Control," in "Reconsidering Immigration in an Integrating World," ed. C. Rudolph, *UCLA Journal of International Law and Foreign Affairs* 3, no. 2 (1998): 497–525.

52. Rogers Brubaker, *Citizenship and Nationhood in France and Germany* (Cambridge, MA: Harvard University Press, 1992). Cf. John Higham, *Strangers in the Land: Patterns of American Nativism, 1860–1925* (New Brunswick, NJ: Rutgers University Press, 1955); Maldwyn Allen Jones, *American Immigration* (Chicago: University of Chicago Press, 1960); Ulrich Herbert, *A History of Foreign Labor in Germany, 1880–1980* (Ann Arbor: University of Michigan Press, 1990); Helga Leitner, "International Migration and the Politics of Admission and Exclusion in Postwar Europe," *Political Geography* 14, no. 3 (1995): 259–78; Hermann Kurthen, "Germany at the Crossroads: National Identity and the Challenges of Immigration," *International Migration Review* 29, no. 4 (1995): 914–38; Rogers M. Smith, "Beyond Tocqueville, Myrdal, and Hartz: The Multiple Traditions in America," *American Political Science Review* 87, no. 3 (1993): 549–66; Rogers M. Smith, *Civic Ideals: Conflicting Visions of Citizenship in U.S. History* (New Haven, CT: Yale University Press, 1997).

53. Brubaker acknowledges, however, that French citizenship is not based on pure jus soli, or automatic citizenship at birth for children born in France, regardless of parentage.

54. Alec G. Hargreaves, *Immigration, "Race" and Ethnicity in Contemporary France* (New York: Routledge, 1995); E. J. B. Rose et al. *Colour and Citizenship: A Report on British Race Relations* (London: Oxford University Press, 1969); Ian R. G. Spencer, *British Immigration Policy Since 1939* (London: Routledge, 1997); J. Solomos, *Race and*

Racism in Britain (Houndmills, England: Macmillan, 1993); M. Dummett and Ann Dummett, "The Role of Government in Britain's Racial Crisis," in *"Race" in Britain: Continuity and Change*, ed. C. Husbands (London: Hutchinson, 1982); Ira Katznelson, *Black Men, White Cities: Race, Politics, and Migration in the United States, 1990–30 and Britain, 1948–68* (London: Oxford University Press, 1973); Robert Miles, *Racism and Migrant Labour* (London: Routledge 1982).

55. Maxim Silverman, *Deconstructing the Nation* (London and New York: Routledge, 1992); Kathleen Paul, *Whitewashing Britain* (Ithaca, NY: Cornell University Press, 1997); B. Carter, C. Harris, and S. Joshi, "The 1951–1955 Conservative Government and the Racialization of Black Immigration," *Immigrants and Minorities* 6, no. 3 (1987); B. Carter, C. Harris, and S. Joshi, "Immigration Policy and the Racialization of Migrant Labour: The Construction of National Identities in the USA and Britain," *Ethnic and Racial Studies* 19, no. 1 (1996); Ann Dummett and Andrew Nicol, *Subjects, Citizens, Aliens and Others* (London: Weidenfeld and Nicholson, 1982); Paul Foot, *Immigration and Race in British Politics* (Baltimore: Penguin, 1965); Zig Layton-Henry, *The Politics of Race in Britain* (London: Allen and Unwin, 1984).

56. On multiple traditions of nationhood, see Rogers Smith, *Civic Ideals* (New Haven, CT: Yale University Press, 1997).

57. Subsequently refined and codified in German law by Kaiser Wilhelm II and Adolf Hitler during their periods of rule.

58. Benedict Anderson, *Imagined Communities* (London: Verso, 1983).

59. A notable exception is James F. Hollifield, "The Emerging Migration State," *International Migration Review* 38, no. 3 (2004): 885–912. To this point, international relations theory has been used primarily to explain policy development in individual cases, the foreign-policy implications of migration, and / or policy development for specific streams of migration rather than presenting a comparative theoretical framework for explaining state behavior toward migration. Cf. James F. Hollifield, "Migration and International Relations: Cooperation and Control in the European Community," *International Migration Review* 26, no. 2 (1992): 568–95; Rey Koslowski, *Migrants and Citizens* (Ithaca, NY: Cornell University Press, 1999); Mark J. Miller, "International Migration and Security: Towards Transatlantic Convergence," in *Immigration into Western Societies: Problems and Policies*, ed. Emek M. Uçarer and Donald J. Puchala (London: Pinter, 1997); Myron Weiner, "On International Migration and International Relations," *Population and Development Review* 11, no. 3 (1985): 441–55; Myron Weiner, ed., *International Migration and Security* (Boulder, CO: Westview Press, 1993); Christopher Mitchell, "International Migration, International Relations, and Foreign Policy," *International Migration Review* 23, no. 3 (1989): 681–708; Mark J. Miller and Demetrios G. Papademetriou, "Immigration and U.S. Foreign Policy," in *The Unavoidable Issue: U.S. Immigration Policy in the 1980s*, ed. Mark J. Miller and Demetrios G. Papademetriou (Philadelphia, PA: Institute for the Study of Human Issues, 1983); Marc R. Rosenblum, *The Intermestic Politics of U.S. Immigration Policy* (Boulder, CO: Lynne Rienner, 2004).

60. Robert G. Gilpin, "The Richness of the Tradition of Political Realism," in *Neorealism and Its Critics*, ed. Robert O. Keohane (New York: Columbia University Press, 1986), 301–21.

61. Hans J. Morgenthau, *Politics Among Nations: The Struggle for Power and Peace*, 6th ed. (New York: Alfred A. Knopf, 1985), 5.

62. For an overview, see Sean M. Lynn-Jones, "International Security Studies After the Cold War: An Agenda for the Future," *BCSIA Working Paper* (Cambridge, MA: Belfer Center for Science and International Affairs, Harvard University, December 1991); Stephen M. Walt, "The Renaissance of Security Studies," *International Studies Quarterly* 35, no. 2 (1991): 211–39. More generally, Miles Kahler shows that dominant models and schools of thought in international relations theory are largely the product of the specific international political climate in which they were developed. See Miles Kahler, "Inventing International Relations: International Relations Theory After 1945," in *New Thinking in International Relations Theory*, ed. Michael W. Doyle and G. John Ikenberry (Boulder, CO: Westview Press, 1997), 20–53.

63. Two primary variants emerged: "defensive" structural realism (neorealism) and offensive structural realism. On neorealism, see Kenneth N. Waltz, *Theory of International Politics* (Reading, MA: Addison-Wesley, 1979); on offensive structural realism, see John J. Mearshimer, *The Tragedy of Great Power Politics* (New York: W. W. Norton, 2001).

64. For an overview, see Michael Mastanduno, "Economics and Security in Statecraft and Scholarship," in *Exploration and Contestation in the Study of World Politics*, ed. Peter Katzenstein, Robert Keohane, and Stephen Krasner (Cambridge, MA: MIT Press, 1999), 185–214.

65. Lynn-Jones, "International Security Studies."

66. Gilpin, "Richness of the Tradition," 308.

67. Jacob Viner, "Power Versus Plenty as Objectives of Foreign Policy in the Seventeenth and Eighteenth Centuries," *World Politics* 1, no. 1 (1948): 1–29. Cf. Thucydides, *History of the Peloponnesian War*, trans. by John H. Finley Jr. (New York: Modern Library, 1951); E. H. Carr, *The Twenty Years' Crisis, 1919–1939*, 2d ed. (London: Macmillan, 1946); Morgenthau, *Politics Among Nations*.

68. Robert O. Keohane, *After Hegemony* (Princeton, NJ: Princeton University Press, 1984), 22.

69. He adds, "We easily lose sight of the fact that struggles to achieve and maintain power, to establish order, and to contrive the kind of justice within states, may be bloodier than wars among them." Kenneth N. Waltz, "Anarchic Orders and Balances of Power," in *Neorealism and Its Critics*, ed. Robert O. Keohane (New York: Columbia University Press, 1986), 99.

70. Samuel P. Huntington, "The Erosion of American National Interests," *Foreign Affairs* 76, no. 5 (1997): 28–29.

71. Cf. Barry Buzan, *People, States, and Fear: The National Security Problem in International Relations* (London: Wheatsheaf Books, 1983); Richard Ulman, "Redefining

Security," *International Organization* 8, no. 1 (1983); Alexander Wendt, "Identity and Structural Change in International Politics," in *The Return of Culture and Identity in IR Theory*, ed. Y. Lapid and F. Kratochwil (Boulder, CO: Lynne Rienner, 1997); Yosef Lapid and Friedrich Kratochwil, eds., *The Return of Culture and Identity in IR Theory* (Boulder, CO: Lynne Rienner, 1997).

72. Cf. Donald Horowitz, *Ethnic Groups in Conflict* (Berkeley: University of California Press, 1985); Walker Connor, *Ethnonationalism: The Quest for Understanding* (Princeton, NJ: Princeton University Press, 1994); Michael Ignatieff, *Blood and Belonging: Journeys Into the New Nationalism* (New York: Farrar, Straus and Giroux, 1994).

73. Alexander Wendt, *Social Theory of International Politics* (Cambridge: Cambridge University Press, 1999).

74. Yale Ferguson and Richard W. Mansbach, *Polities: Authority, Identity, and Change* (Columbia: University of South Carolina Press, 1996); and Yale Ferguson and Richard W. Mansbach, "The Past as Prelude to the Future: Identities and Loyalties in Global Politics," in *The Return of Culture and Identity in IR Theory*, ed. Yosef Lapid and Friedrich Kratochwil (Boulder, CO: Lynne Rienner, 1997), 21–44. Cf. Albert et al., *Identities, Borders, Orders*.

75. Ferguson and Mansbach, "Past as Prelude," 21; see also Ferguson and Mansbach, *Polities*.

76. David A. Lake and Donald Rothchild, eds., *The International Spread of Ethnic Conflict* (Princeton, NJ: Princeton University Press, 1998).

77. Samuel P. Huntington, *The Clash of Civilizations and the Remaking of World Order* (New York: Touchstone, 1996).

78. See Robert J. Lieber and Ruth E. Weisberg, "Globalization, Culture, and Identities in Crisis," *International Journal of Politics, Culture, and Society* 16, no. 2 (winter 2002): 273–96.

79. Horowitz, *Ethnic Groups in Conflict*; Anthony D. Smith, *National Identity* (Reno: University of Nevada Press, 1990).

80. Myron Weiner and Michael S. Teitelbaum, *Political Demography, Demographic Engineering* (New York: Berghahn Books, 2001).

81. Samuel P. Huntington, *Who Are We? The Challenges to America's National Identity* (New York: Simon and Schuster, 2004).

82. Weiner and Teitelbaum, *Political Demography*, 22. On societal sovereignty, see Christopher Rudolph, "Sovereignty and Territorial Borders in a Global Age," *International Studies Review* 7, no. 1 (spring 2005).

83. Ronald R. Krebs and Jack S. Levy, "Demographic Change and the Sources of International Conflict," in *Demography and National Security*, ed. Myron Weiner and Sharon Stanton Russell (New York: Berghahn Books, 2001), 62–105; Will H. Moore and David R. Davis, "Transnational Ethnic Ties and Foreign Policy," in *The International Spread of Ethnic Conflict*, ed. David Lake and Donald Rothchild (Princeton, NJ: Princeton University Press, 1998), 89–103; Weiner and Teitelbaum, *Political*

Demography, ch. 7; Gabriel Sheffer, "Ethnic Diasporas: A Threat to Their Hosts?" in *International Migration and Security*, ed. Myron Weiner (Boulder, CO: Westview Press, 1993), 264–85.

84. Ole Wæver, "Societal Security: The Concept," in *Identity, Migration, and the New Security Agenda in Europe*, ed. O. Wæver et al.(New York: St. Martin's Press, 1993), 23.

85. Several studies have pointed to the centrality of national identity in anti-immigration sentiment, most notably in the areas of sociology and political sociology. The general parameters are most often set in terms of citizenship laws (jus sanguinis versus jus soli conceptions of citizenship), or between historically settler and non-settler nations. Unfortunately, while the in-depth historical evaluation of national identities is useful in understanding the character of nativist sentiment, the degree of focus on identity alone is unable to capture the political conflicts and trade-offs that characterize contemporary migration politics. Moreover, assumptions about the "immigration traditions" in countries like the United States, Australia, and Canada also belie the conflicting impulses in the national identities of such "settler" states. Often, national identities are seen as fixed (or "primordial"), and while political discourse may seek to perpetuate such myths, this is certainly not the case among the advanced industrial democracies examined herein. Cf. Rogers Brubaker, *Citizenship and Nationhood in France and Germany* (Cambridge, MA: Harvard University Press, 1992); M. A. Jones, *American Immigration* (Chicago: University of Chicago Press, 1960); Desmond King, *Making Americans: Immigration, Race, and the Diverse Democracy* (Cambridge, MA: Harvard University Press, 2000); Doris M. Meissner, Robert D. Hormats, Antonio Garrigues Walker, and Shijuro Ogata, *International Migration Challenges in a New Era* (New York, Paris, and Tokyo: Trilateral Commission, 1993); Maxim Silverman, *Deconstructing the Nation* (London and New York: Routledge, 1992); William Alonso, "Citizenship, Nationality, and Other Identities," *Journal of International Affairs* 48, no. 2 (1995): 585–99; Zolberg, "Contemporary Transnational Migration"; Smith, *National Identity*.

86. Anthony D. Smith, *The Ethnic Origins of Nations* (Oxford: Basil Blackwell, 1986); Ole Wæver, Barry Buzan, Morten Kelstrup, and Pierre Lemaitre, eds., *Identity, Migration, and the New Security Agenda in Europe* (New York: St. Martin's Press, 1993).

87. Some extant studies dealing with the issue of migration policy formation have included—or appeared to include—an identity variable in their paradigms. However, identity is seen as simply a mobilizing force in competition between natives and immigrants over scarce resources, once again presenting the politics of migration in mostly economic terms with a strong interest-group element. Susan Olzak suggests that when two groups find themselves competing over the same economic niche, "niche overlap" triggers anti-immigrant pressures. Although some of these analyses suggest that they are in fact modeling the political struggle between economic and identity elements, they appear to be focused primarily on questions of economics,

utilizing identity only in its capacity to define and organize political action. See Susan Olzak, *The Dynamics of Ethnic Competition* (Stanford, CA: Stanford University Press, 1992); Helga Leitner, "International Migration and the Politics of Admission and Exclusion in Postwar Europe," *Political Geography* 14, no. 3 (1995): 259–78; Money, *Fences and Neighbors*; Waldinger, *Still the Promised City?*; Waldinger, "Social Capital or Social Closure?"; Roger Waldinger and Mehdi Bozorgmehr, eds., *Ethnic Los Angeles* (New York: Russell Sage, 1996).

88. Stephen M. Walt, *The Origins of Alliances* (Ithaca, NY: Cornell University Press, 1987).

89. For an overview, see Robert G. Gilpin, *The Challenge of Global Capitalism* (Princeton, NJ: Princeton University Press, 2000); Robert G. Gilpin, *Global Political Economy* (Princeton, NJ: Princeton University Press, 2001).

90. I have elsewhere referred to this only as the "Threat Hypothesis." Christopher Rudolph, "Security and the Political Economy of International Migration," *American Political Science Review* 97, no. 4 (2003): 603–20.

91. Thanks to both Jim Hollifield and Patrick Jackson for suggesting the inclusion of feedback loops in the model.

92. David Easton, *A Framework for Political Analysis* (Englewood Cliffs, NJ: Prentice-Hall, 1965).

93. John C. Torpey, "States and the Regulation of Migration in the Twentieth-Century North Atlantic World," in *The Wall Around the West*, ed. Peter Andreas and Timothy Snyder (Lanham, MD: Rowman and Littlefield, 2000), 35. See also John C. Torpey, *The Invention of the Passport: Surveillance, Citizenship and the State* (Cambridge: Cambridge University Press, 2000).

94. Philip L. Martin, "Germany: Managing Migration in the Twenty-First Century," in *Controlling Immigration: A Global Perspective*, 2d ed., ed. Cornelius et al. (Stanford, CA: Stanford University Press, 2004), 245. See also Philip L. Martin, B. Lindsay Lowell, and Edward J. Taylor, "Migration Outcomes of Guest Worker and Free Trade Regimes: The Case of Mexico-U.S. Migration," in *Managing Migration: Time for a New International Regime?* ed. Bimal Ghosh (Oxford: Oxford University Press, 2000); Douglas S. Massey and Zai Liang, "The Long-Term Consequences of a Temporary Worker Program: The U.S. Bracero Program Experience," *Population Research and Policy Review* 8, no. 3 (1989): 199–226.

95. On the effects of IRCA on migration flows, see Frank D. Bean, Georges Vernes, and Charles B. Keely, *Opening and Closing the Doors: Evaluating Immigration Reform and Control* (Lanham, MD: University Press of America, 1989); Michael Fix, *The Paper Curtain: Employer Sanctions' Implementation, Impact, and Reform* (Washington, DC: Urban Institute Press, 1991).

96. Hollifield, *Immigrants, Markets, and States*; Jacobson, *Rights Across Borders*.

97. Convention Relating to the Status of Refugees (July 28, 1951), quoted in Jeannette Money, "Human Rights Norms and Immigration Control," *UCLA Journal of International Law and Foreign Affairs* 3, no. 2 (1998): 509. Jeannette Money

counters the Liberal State Hypothesis by noting that, in the domains of family reunification and refugees, states retain significant power to control. In the domain of family reunification, the state retains the right to define the scope by which "the family" is defined (from the most narrow, spouse only, to a broader definition that includes extended family members). For refugees and asylum seekers, Money points out that states are not required to admit refugees—just constrained from deporting them to their home country. As such, "convention refugees" (covered by Article 33 of the 1951 Refugee Convention) and its protections are manifest only for asylum seekers, not refugees in third countries. Moreover, the state retains policy autonomy and authority to minimize the physical presence of refugees on national territory.

98. See, for example, Anne-Marie Burley and Walter Mattli, "Europe Before the Court: A Political Theory of Legal Integration," *International Organization* 47, no. 1 (1993): 41–76; Andrew Moravscik, *The Choice for Europe: Social Purpose and State Power from Messina to Maastricht* (Ithaca, NY: Cornell University Press, 1998); Alec Stone Sweet and Wayne Sandholtz, eds, *European Integration and Supranational Governance* (New York: Oxford University Press, 1998).

99. Although Gallya Lahav argues that supranationalism and/or intergovernmentalism do not necessitate more open policy, but rather can foster increased harmonization and cooperation based on increasing control mechanisms. Kathleen Newland and Demetrios Papademetriou come to a similar conclusion, noting that regime formation in the EU has generally taken the form of building better mousetraps (to control migration) rather than harmonizing member-state policies toward more liberal ends. See Gallya Lahav, *Immigration and Politics in the New Europe* (Cambridge: Cambridge University Press, 2004); Kathleen Newland and Demetrios G. Papademetriou, "Managing International Migration: Tracking the Emergence of a New International Regime," *UCLA Journal of International Law and Foreign Affairs* 3, no. 2 (1998): 637–57.

100. See Harry Eckstein, "Case Study and Theory in Political Science," in *Handbook of Political Science*, ed. N. Polsby and F. Greenstein (Reading, MA: Addison-Wesley, 1975); Alexander L. George, "Case Studies and Theory Development: The Method of Structured, Focused Comparison," in *Diplomacy*, ed. P. G. Lauren (New York: Free Press, 1979), 43–68; Arend Lijphart, "Comparative Politics and the Comparative Method," *American Political Science Review* 65, no. 3 (1971): 682–93; Arend Lijphart, "The Comparable-Case Strategy in Comparative Research," *Comparative Political Studies* 8 (July 1975): 158–77.

101. Drawing on Stephen Walt's operationalization; see his *Origins of Alliances*.

102. Thanks to Patrick Jackson for the term "routinization." On how routinization is helped and hindered using psychological theories, see Deborah Welch Larson, *Origins of Containment* (Princeton, NJ: Princeton University Press, 1986).

103. Marc Trachtenberg, *A Constructed Peace: The Making of the European Settlement, 1945–1963* (Princeton, NJ: Princeton University Press, 1999); John J. Mearshimer, *The Tragedy of Great Power Politics* (New York: W. W. Norton, 2001).

104. Andrew Moravscik, "Taking Preferences Seriously: A Liberal Theory of International Politics," *International Organization* 51, no. 4 (1997): 515–16.

105. Kenneth N. Waltz, "Reductionist and Systemic Theories," in *Neorealism and Its Critics*, ed. Robert O. Keohane (New York: Columbia University Press, 1986), 57.

106. Kenneth N. Waltz, "Reductionist and Systemic Theories," in *Neorealism and Its Critics*, ed. Robert O. Keohane (New York: Columbia University Press, 1986), 52; a rebuttal to this argument is offered by Andrew Moravscik in "Taking Preferences Seriously," 513–53.

107. Building on the work of Stephen Walt, see Walt, *Origins of Alliances*.

108. One form of this "globalization thesis" as applied to the issue of immigration and border control is the "Gap Hypothesis" offered by Wayne Cornelius, Takeyuki Tsuda, Philip L. Martin, and James Hollifield. See Cornelius et al. *Controlling Immigration*.

CHAPTER THREE

1. Michael Fix and Jeffrey S. Passel, *Immigration and Immigrants: Setting the Record Straight* (Washington, DC: Urban Institute, 1994), 3.

2. Desmond King, *Making Americans: Immigration, Race, and the Diverse Democracy* (Cambridge, MA: Harvard University Press, 2000), 1.

3. Howard F. Chang, "Immigration Policy, Liberal Principles, and the Republican Tradition," *Georgetown Law Journal* 85, no. 7 (1997): 2115.

4. Peter Brimelow, *Alien Nation* (New York: Random House, 1995).

5. Rogers M. Smith, "Beyond Tocqueville, Myrdal and Hartz: The Multiple Traditions in America," *American Political Science Review* 87, no. 3 (1993): 549–66.

6. Reed Ueda, *Postwar Immigrant America* (Boston: Bedford Books, 1994), 18. See also Gordon S. Wood, *The Creation of the American Republic, 1776–1787* (Chapel Hill: University of North Carolina Press, 1969), 609–15.

7. Peter N. Kirstein, *Anglo Over Bracero: A History of the Mexican Worker in the United States from Roosevelt to Nixon* (San Francisco: R. and E. Associates, 1977), 12; Manuel Garcia y Griego, "The Importation of Mexican Contract Laborers to the United States, 1942–1964: Antecedents, Operation and Legacy," *Working Papers in U.S.-Mexican Studies* 11 (San Diego: Program in United States-Mexican Studies, University of California, San Diego, 1980), 16.

8. Agricultural jobs were often referred to as "stoop labor," indicating their undesirable status.

9. Kitty Calavita, *Inside the State: The Bracero Program, Immigration, and the I.N.S.* (New York: Routledge, 1992), 218.

10. David M. Reimers, *Still the Golden Door: The Third World Comes to America* (New York: Columbia University Press, 1985), 51.

11. Calavita, *Inside the State*, 32. See also Eleanor Hadley, "A Critical Analysis of the Wetback Problem," *Law and Contemporary Problems* 21 (1956): 334–57.

12. This reference, originally appearing the January 1954 issue of the INS *Reporter*, is quoted in Ernesto Galarza, *Merchants of Labor: The Mexican Bracero Story* (Charlotte, SC: McNally and Loftin, 1964).

13. *New York Times* service broadcast, May 9, 1953, quoted in John Myers, *The Border Wardens* (Englewood Cliffs, NJ: Prentice-Hall, 1971), 79–80; and Calavita, *Inside the State*, 48.

14. Reimers, *Still the Golden Door*, 55. See also Juan Garcia, *Operation Wetback: The Mass Deportation of Mexican Undocumented Workers in 1954* (Westport, CT: Greenwood Press, 1980), 157–60.

15. U.S. Immigration and Naturalization Service, *Annual Report* (Washington, DC: INS, 1955), 15.

16. The remaining preference categories were based on family unification, a strategy that was originally thought to replicate the existing ethnic makeup of the nation (an approach that also guided the 1965 amendments to the INA).

17. Deborah Welch Larson, *Origins of Containment* (Princeton, NJ: Princeton University Press, 1985), 308–9.

18. Daniel Tichenor, *Dividing Lines* (Princeton, NJ: Princeton University Press, 2002), 207.

19. Aristide R. Zolberg, "From Invitation to Interdiction: U.S. Foreign Policy and Immigration Since 1945," in *Threatened Peoples, Threatened Borders*, ed. M. S. Teitelbaum and M. Weiner (New York: W. W. Norton, 1995), 154–55.

20. Cited in Zolberg, "Invitation to Interdiction," 123–24.

21. As stipulated in the 1952 act, the attorney general's "parole" power could be exercised to permit refugees to enter the country for emergency reasons or if it were "deemed strictly in the public interest." Since 1957, most refugees have entered the country via such parole provisions or by special statutory refugee status that were later adjusted to lawful status by acts of Congress.

22. Joel S. Fetzer, *Public Attitudes Toward Immigration in the United States, France, and Germany* (Cambridge: Cambridge University Press, 2000), 40.

23. Michael S. Teitelbaum and Myron Weiner, "Introduction: Threatened Peoples, Threatened Borders: Migration and U.S. Foreign Policy," in *Threatened Peoples, Threatened Borders*, ed. M. S. Teitelbaum and M. Weiner (New York: W. W. Norton, 1995), 15.

24. Quoted in Michael Barson, *Better Red than Dead: A Nostalgic Look at the Golden Years of Russia Phobia, Red-baiting, and Other Commie Madness* (New York: Hyperion, 1992).

25. <http://www.ins.usdoj.gov/graphics/aboutins/statistics/legishist/506.htm>

26. King, *Making Americans*, 229.

27. President's veto message, June 25, 1952, quoted in King, *Making Americans*, 241; see also Tichenor, *Dividing Lines*, 195.

28. Thomas Borstelmann, *The Cold War and the Color Line* (Cambridge, MA: Harvard University Press, 2002), 109.

29. Testimony of Nicholas deB. Katzenbach before the Subcommittee on Immigration and Naturalization, Senate Judiciary Committee, 89th Congress, 1st session, part 1, quoted in Tichenor, *Dividing Lines*, 215.

30. King, *Making Americans*, 246.

31. Borstelmann, *Cold War*, 194.

32. Larson, *Origins of Containment*.

33. *Congressional Record* (August 25, 1965), 21,812.

34. Frank D. Bean and Marta Tienda, *The Hispanic Population of the United States* (New York: Russell Sage Foundation, 1987).

35. King, *Making Americans*, 251.

36. These changes are both a function of increasing migration from Asia and Latin America and the increased fertility rates among these groups. See Jeffrey S. Passel and Barry Edmonston, "Immigration and Race: Recent Trends in Immigration to the United States," in *Immigration Policy Paper PRIP-UI-22* (Washington, DC: Urban Institute, 1992).

37. Census data published in the *Los Angeles Times* (October 20, 1999), A3.

38. Fetzer, *Public Attitudes Toward Immigration*.

39. Cheryl Shanks, *Immigration and the Politics of American Sovereignty* (Ann Arbor: University of Michigan Press, 2001), 234.

40. See Joseph Nevins, *Operation Gatekeeper: The Rise of the "Illegal Alien" and the Remaking of the U.S.-Mexico Boundary* (New York: Routledge, 2001).

41. Reimers, *Still the Golden Door*, 214. See also Frank D. Bean, Eduardo Telles, and Lindsay Lowell, "Undocumented Migration to the United States: Perceptions and Evidence," *Population and Development Review* 13, no. 4 (1987): 671–90.

42. Interagency Task Force on Immigration Policy, *Staff Report* (Washington, DC: U.S. Departments of Justice, Labor, and State, 1979), 2.

43. Ibid., 37.

44. Select Commission on Immigration and Refugee Policy, *U.S. Immigration Policy and the National Interest* (Washington, DC: U.S. Government Printing Office, 1981).

45. Vernon M. Briggs Jr., *Mass Immigration and the National Interest* (Armonk, NY: M. E. Sharpe, 1996), 156.

46. Nicholas Laham, *Ronald Reagan and the Politics of Immigration Reform* (Westport, CT: Praeger, 2000), 5.

47. Michael Fix and Paul T. Hill, *Enforcing Employer Sanctions: Challenges and Strategies* (Santa Monica, CA: RAND and the Urban Institute, 1990), 52–54.

48. John M. Abowd and Richard B. Freeman, eds., *Immigration, Trade, and the Labor Market* (Chicago: University of Chicago Press, 1991), 50.

49. Frank D. Bean and Michael Fix, "The Significance of Recent Immigration Policy Reforms in the United States," in *Nations of Immigrants: Australia, the United States, and International Migration*, ed. G. P. Freeman and J. Jupp (Melbourne, Australia: Oxford University Press, 1992), 55.

50. Tichenor, *Dividing Lines*, 246.

51. Russell, "Migration Patterns," 49.

52. See David A. Martin, "The Refugee Act of 1980: Its Past and Future," *Michigan Yearbook of International Legal Studies* (1982): 91–123.

53. Russell, "Migration Patterns," 49.

54. See Robert L. Bach, "The Cuban Exodus: Political and Economic Motivations," in *The Caribbean Exodus*, ed. B. B. Levine (New York: Praeger, 1982); Felix Masud-Piloto, *From Welcomed Exiles to Illegal Immigrants: Cuban Migration to the U.S.* (Lanham, MD: Rowman and Littlefield, 1996); Felix Roberto Masud-Piloto, *With Open Arms: Cuban Migration to the United States* (Totowa, NJ: Rowman and Littlefield, 1988).

55. Russell, "Migration Patterns," 51.

56. Ibid.

57. Shanks, *Immigration*, 234.

58. Peter Andreas, *Border Games: Policing the U.S.-Mexico Divide* (Ithaca, NY: Cornell University Press, 2000); Kitty Calavita, "The New Politics of Immigration: Balanced Budget Conservatism and the Symbolism of Proposition 187," *Social Problems* 43, no. 3 (1996): 284–306.

59. See George J. Borjas, *Friends or Strangers* (New York: Basic Books, 1990); George J. Borjas, "The New Economics of Immigration," *Atlantic Monthly*, 1996, 72–80; George J. Borjas, *Heaven's Door: Immigration Policy and the American Economy* (Princeton, NJ: Princeton University Press, 1999).

60. T. Alexander Aleinikoff, "United States Refugee Law and Policy: Past, Present, and Future," in *International Migration, Refugee Flows and Human Rights in North America: The Impact of Free Trade and Restructuring*, ed. A. B. Simmons (New York: Center for Migration Studies, 1996), 251–52.

61. Ibid., 255.

62. Defined as those countries that prima facie do not produce refugees.

63. Office of the President, *Accepting the Immigration Challenge: The President's Report on Immigration* (Washington, DC: U.S. Government Printing Office, 1994), v. INS policy responses to the president's report are detailed in U.S. Immigration and Naturalization Service, *Toward INS 2000: Accepting the Challenge* (Washington, DC: U.S. Government Printing Office, 1995).

64. U.S. Commission on Immigration Reform, *U.S. Immigration Policy: Restoring Credibility* (Washington, DC: U.S. Commission on Immigration Reform, 1994).

65. Office of the President, *Accepting the Immigration Challenge*, vi.

66. U.S. Immigration and Naturalization Service, *Status of Border Enforcement Evaluation: Preliminary Report* (Washington, DC: INS, 1955).

67. U.S. Commission on Immigration Reform, *U.S. Immigration Policy*, 13.

68. U.S. Immigration and Naturalization Service, *Operation Gatekeeper: Landmark Progress* (Washington, DC: INS, 1995), 2.

69. Andreas, *Border Games*, 94.

70. See *Los Angeles Times*, April 30, 2000, A1, A12.

71. U.S. Immigration and Naturalization Service, *Statistical Yearbook* (Washington, DC: U.S. Government Printing Office, 1998), 202.

72. Other than the smuggler's fees, if one is used, which have risen from $250 per person to as much as $1,500. See U.S. Immigration and Naturalization Service, *INS' Southwest Border Strategy* (Washington, DC: INS, 1999).

73. Audrey Singer and Douglas S. Massey, "The Social Processes of Undocumented Border Crossing," *Working Paper No. 27* (Los Angeles: Lewis Center for Regional Policy Studies, 1997).

74. See Philip L. Martin, "Economic Integration and Migration: The Case of NAFTA," in "Reconsidering Immigration in an Integrating World," *UCLA Journal of International Law and Foreign Affairs*, ed. C. Rudolph, 3, no. 2 (1998): 439–41.

75. See Andreas, *Border Games*; Binational Study of Migration, *Binational Study: Migration Between Mexico and the United States* (Mexico City and Washington, DC: Mexican Foreign Ministry and U.S. Commission on Immigration Reform, 1997).

76. Wayne A. Cornelius, "Appearances and Realities: Controlling Immigration in the United States," in *Temporary Workers or Future Citizens—Japanese and U.S. Migration Policies*, ed. Myron Weiner and Tadashi Hanami (New York: New York University Press, 1998), 392.

77. Between 1989 and 1995, the number of employers investigated for violations under the employer sanctions provisions of IRCA fell from 14,706 to 5,963, while fines levied against those in violation of the law fell from $6.2 million in 1992 to $4.1 million in 1995. Few criminal penalties have been handed down to employers. See Cornelius, "Appearances and Realities," 403.

78. Claudia Smith, "Operation Gatekeeper's Darker Side," *San Diego Union Tribune*, October 16, 1997.

79. Andreas, *Border Games*, 108.

80. "Gatekeeper Works: Despite Charges, Border Has Been Secured," *San Diego Union Tribune*, July 17, 1998, B-6.

81. The use of these images, many taken in 1992, by California governor Pete Wilson during his 1994 campaign ensured that these images remained in the public eye long after they had occurred, magnifying the image of border chaos.

82. Commission for the Study of International Migration and Cooperative Economic Development, *Unauthorized Migration: An Economic Development Response* (Washington, DC: Commission for the Study of International Migration and Cooperative Economic Development, 1990).

83. Doris Meissner, "Managing Migrations," *Foreign Policy* 86 (1992): 66–83; Doris M. Meissner, Robert D. Hormats, Antonio Garrigues Walker, and Shijuro Ogata, *International Migration Challenges in a New Era* (New York, Paris, and Tokyo: Trilateral Commission, 1993).

84. P. Martin, "Economic Integration and Migration."

85. Cornelius, "Appearances and Realities," 416.

86. Peter Andreas, "The Escalation of U.S. Immigration Control in the Post-NAFTA Era," *Political Science Quarterly* 113, no. 4 (winter 1998–99): 593.

87. Kevin R. Johnson, "Free Trade and Closed Borders: NAFTA and Mexican Immigration to the United States," *U.C. Davis Law Review* 27, no. 4 (1994): 937–78.

88. Peter Schuck, "The Great Immigration Debate," *The American Prospect* (1990): 100–18.

89. Thomas J. Espenshade and Maryann Belanger, "Immigration and Public Opinion," in *Crossings: Mexican Immigration in Interdisciplinary Perspective*, ed. M. M. Suarez-Orozco (Cambridge, MA: David Rockefeller Center for Latin American Studies, 1998), 371.

90. Dana Blanton, *Fox News/Opinion Dynamics Poll: Americans Still Strongly Supporting Bush, War*, November 2, 2001 (available online at http://www.foxnews.com/story/0,2933,37940,00.html) (accessed February 12, 2004).

91. Stephen A. Camarota, "The Open Door: How Militant Islamic Terrorists Entered and Remained in the United States, 1993–2001," *CIS Paper No. 21* (Washington, DC: Center for Immigration Studies, 2002).

92. USA Patriot Act, H.R. 3162; Enhanced Border Security and Visa Entry Reform Act, H.R. 3525.

93. Rey Koslowski, "Information Technology, Migration and Border Control" (paper presented at the Institute for Governmental Studies, University of California, Berkeley, April 25, 2002).

94. U.S. Department of Homeland Security, *Fact Sheet: US-VISIT Program*; URL: http://www.dhs.gov (accessed February 21, 2004).

95. *Migration News* (April 2005).

96. Jerry Kammer, "Foes Fear 'Amnesty,' Drains on Economy," *San Diego Union Tribune*, May 13, 2005; URL: http://www.signonsandiego.com/news/mexico/tijuana/20050513-9999-1n13immig.html (accessed May 17, 2005).

97. Alan Elsner, "McCain, Kennedy Introduce Immigration Reform Bill," *Reuters*, May 13, 2005; URL: http://www.reuters.com/newsArticle.jhtml?type=politicsNews&storyID=8476039 (accessed May 17, 2005).

98. Douglas S. Massey, "International Migration at the Dawn of the Twenty-First Century: The Role of the State," *Population and Development Review* 25, no. 2 (1999): 312.

99. Aristide Zolberg, "Reforming the Backdoor: The Immigration Reform and Control Act of 1986 in Historical Perspective," in *Immigration Reconsidered: History, Sociology, and Politics*, ed. Virginia Yans-McLaughlin (New York: Oxford University Press, 1990), 316.

100. Christopher Rudolph, "Sovereignty and Territorial Borders in a Global Age," *International Studies Review* 7, no. 1 (2005).

101. Massey, "International Migration," 318.

102. Ibid., 314. See also Thomas J. Espenshade and Charles A. Calhoun, "An Analysis of Public Opinion Toward Undocumented Immigration," *Population*

Research and Policy Review 12 (1993): 189–224; Thomas J. Espenshade and Katherine Hempstead, "Contemporary American Attitudes Toward U.S. Immigration," *International Migration Review* 30 (1996): 535–70.

CHAPTER 4

1. Rogers Brubaker, *Citizenship and Nationhood in France and Germany* (Cambridge, MA: Harvard University Press, 1992).

2. Ibid., 1.

3. Translation: "Law of the blood"

4. Brubaker, *Citizenship*, 168.

5. Joseph Nogee and Robert Donaldson, *Soviet Foreign Policy Since World War II* (New York: Macmillan, 1992), 96.

6. Quoted in Steven L. Spiegel and Fred L. Wehling, *World Politics in a New Era*, 2d ed. (New York: Harcourt Brace, 1999), 143.

7. Robert Hunter, *Security in Europe* (Bloomington: Indiana University Press, 1969).

8. Patrick Thaddeus Jackson, *Civilizing the Enemy: German Reconstruction and the Invention of the West* (Ann Arbor: University of Michigan Press, 2006).

9. Prepared remarks of George C. Marshall before Congress, January 18, 1948. Quoted in Jackson, *Civilizing the Enemy*, 107.

10. John A. Reed Jr., *Germany and NATO* (Washington, DC: National Defense University Press, 1987).

11. Spiegel and Wehling, *World Politics*, 318.

12. Ulrich Herbert, *A History of Foreign Labor in Germany, 1880–1990* (Ann Arbor: University of Michigan Press, 1990), 214.

13. Jurgen Fijalskowski, "Aggressive Nationalism, Immigration Pressure, and Asylum Policy Disputes in Contemporary Germany," *Occasional Paper No. 9* (Washington, DC: German Historical Institute, 1993), 7.

14. John Bendix, *Importing Foreign Workers: A Comparison of Germany and American Policy* (New York: Peter Lang, 1990), 45.

15. See Charles P. Kindleberger, *Europe's Postwar Growth* (Cambridge, MA: Harvard University Press, 1967), 181–82; Aristide R. Zolberg, "International Migrations in Political Perspective," in *Global Trends in Migration: Theory and Research on International Population Movements*, ed. M. M. Kritz, C. B. Keely, and S. Tomasi (New York: Center for Migration Studies, 1981), 17.

16. See Hermann Korte, "Labor Migration and the Employment of Foreigners in the Federal Republic of Germany Since 1950," in *Guests Come to Stay: The Effects of European Labor Migration on Sending and Receiving Countries*, ed. Rosemary Rogers (Boulder, CO: Westview Press, 1985), 36; James F. Hollifield, *Immigrants, Markets, and States* (Cambridge, MA: Harvard University Press, 1992).

17. URL: <http://www.iuscomp.org/gla/statutes/GG.htm#116> (accessed April 25, 2005).

18. P. N. Jones and M. T. Wild, "West Germany's 'Third Wave' of Migrants: The Arrival of the Aussiedler," *Geoforum* 23, no. 1 (1992).

19. Herbert Schlenger, *"Das Weltfluchtlingsproblem,"* in *Die Vertriebenen in Westdeutschland*, ed. E. Lemberg and F. Edding (Kiel, Germany: Ferdinand Hirt, 1959), 40–42.

20. Philip L. Martin, "Germany: Reluctant Land of Immigration," in *Controlling Immigration: A Global Perspective*, ed. Wayne A. Cornelius, Philip L. Martin, and James F. Hollifield (Stanford, CA: Stanford University Press, 1994), 198. Also available online at: <http://www.agecon.ucdavis.edu/Faculty/Phil.M/germany/germany.htm>

21. Rogers Brubaker, *Citizenship and Nationhood in France and Germany* (Cambridge, MA: Harvard University Press, 1992).

22. URL: <http://www.iuscomp.org/gla/statutes/GG.htm#116> (accessed April 25, 2005).

23. Brubaker, *Citizenship and Nationhood*, 168.

24. Friedrich Edding, "The Refugees as a Burden, a Stimulus and a Challenge to the West Germany Economy," *Research Group for European Migration Study No. IV* (The Hague: Nijhoff, 1951).

25. W. Abelshauser, *Wirtschaftsgeschichte der Bundesrepublik Deutschland 1945–1980* (Frankfurt: Suhrkamp, 1983), 20.

26. Herbert, *History of Foreign Labor*, 194.

27. Wesley D. Chapin, *Germany for the Germans? The Political Effects of International Migration* (Westport, CT: Greenwood Press, 1997), 7.

28. Edward Homze, *Foreign Labor in Nazi Germany* (Princeton, NJ: Princeton University Press, 1967), 232.

29. Ralf E. Ulrich, *"Vertriebene* and *Aussiedler*—The Immigration of Ethnic Germans," in *The Economic Consequences of Immigration to Germany*, ed. G. Steinmann and R. E. Ulrich (Heidelberg, Germany: Physica-Verlag, 1994). Kindleberger, *Europe's Postwar Growth*, 31.

30. Korte, "Labor Migration," 30.

31. Bendix, *Importing Foreign Workers*.

32. Herbert, *History of Foreign Labor*, 204.

33. Bendix, *Importing Foreign Workers*.

34. Ursula Mehrlander and Gunther Schultze, "Einwanderungskonzept fur die Bundesrepublik—Fakten, Argumente, Vorschlaege," *Geschprächskreis Arbeits und Soziales No. 7* (Bonn, Germany: Friedrich Ebert Stiftung, 1992).

35. Cf. Kindleberger, *Europe's Postwar Growth*; Knuth Dohse, *Ausländische Arbeitnehmer und Burgerliche Staat* (Hain, Germany: Konistein/Taunos, 1981); Philip L. Martin, *Guestworker Programs: Lessons from Europe.* (Washington, DC: International Labor Affairs Bureau, Department of Labor, 1980); Mark J. Miller and Philip L. Martin, *Administering Foreign-Worker Program: Lessons from Europe* (Lexington, KY: Lexington Books, 1982); Gunter Schiller et al. *Ausländische, Arbeitnehmer, und Arbeitsmarkt* (Nuremberg, Germany: IAB-BA, 1976).

36. Ibid., 25.

37. Herbert, *History of Foreign Labor*, 206.

38. Bendix, *Importing Foreign Workers*, 23.

39. Knuth Dohse, *Ausländische Arbeitnehmer und Burgerliche Staat* (Hain, Germany: Konistein/Taunos, 1981).

40. Albert O. Hirschman, "Exit, Voice, and the Fate of the German Democratic Republic," *World Politics* 45, no. 2 (1993): 179.

41. As noted by Klaus Bade, labor agreements were also established with Morocco (1963) and Tunisia (1965); however, flows from these sources were relatively insignificant. See Klaus J. Bade, "Transatlantic Emigration and Continental Immigration: The German Experience Past and Present," in *Population, Labour and Migration in the 19th- and 20th-Century Germany*, ed. K. J. Bade (New York: St. Martin's Press, 1987), 153.

42. Christoph Schmidt and Klaus F. Zimmermann, "Migration Pressure in Germany: Past and Future," in *Migration and Economic Development*, ed. K. F. Zimmermann (New York: Springer-Verlag, 1992).

43. P. Martin, "Germany," 200.

44. Korte, "Labor Migration," 31; P. Martin, "Germany," 201.

45. Korte, "Labor Migration," 39.

46. Hollifield, *Immigrants, Markets*.

47. Horst Reimann and Helga Reimann, "Federal Republic of Germany," in *International Labor Migration in Europe*, ed. R. E. Krane (New York: Praeger, 1979), 66.

48. Friedrich Heckmann, "Temporary Labor Migration or Immigration? 'Guest Workers' in the Federal Republic of Germany," in *The Effects of European Labor Migration on Sending and Receiving Countries*, ed. Rosemary Rogers (Boulder, CO: Westview Press, 1985), 70.

49. Ursula Mehrlander, *Soziale Aspeckte der Ausländerbeschäftigung* (Bonn, Germany: Verlag Neue Besellschaft, 1974), 39.

50. Bundesanstalt für Arbeit, *Erfahrungsbericht: Answerbung und Vermittlung Ausländischer Arbeitnehmer* (Nuremberg, Germany: Bundesanstalt für Arbeit, 1965), 11–12.

51. Herbert, *History of Foreign Labor*, 214.

52. Bendix, *Importing Foreign Workers*, 48.

53. Brubaker, *Citizenship and Nationhood*, 171. See also Ray Rist, *Guestworkers in Germany: The Prospects for Pluralism* (New York: Praeger, 1978).

54. Roger W. Böhning, "Guestworker Employment in Selected European Countries—Lessons for the United States?" in *The Border That Joins: Mexican Migrants and U.S. Responsibility*, ed. P. G. Brown and H. Shue (Totowa, NJ: Rowman and Littlefield, 1983).

55. Dohse, *Ausländische Arbeitnehmer*.

56. See Bendix, *Importing Foreign Workers*; Karl Herbst and Rolf Weber, *Beschäftigung Ausländischer Arbeitskrafte: Was der Arbeitgeber bei Answerbung, Vermittlung,*

Einstellung and *Beschäftigung Ausländischer Arbeitskrafte Beachten Sollte* (Cologne, Germany: Bundesvereinigung der Deutschen Arbeitbegerverbande, 1961); Hans Meenzen, "Ausländische Arbeiter nur Konjunkturpuffer? Der Einsatz südeuropaischer Arbeiter ist eine Westeuropaischer Dauererscheinung," *Industriekurier* 3 (December 1960).

57. Dohse, *Ausländische Arbeitnehmer.*

58. Korte, "Labor Migration," 48.

59. Ibid., 45.

60. Heinz Salowski, "Gesamptwirtschaftliche Aspeckte der Ausländerbeschaftigung," in *Beitrage des Deutschen Industrieinstituts No. 9* (Cologne, Germany: Deutsche Industrieverlag, 1971), 71.

61. Herbert, *History of Foreign Labor*, 233.

62. P. Martin, "Germany," 201.

63. Herbert, *History of Foreign Labor*, 230.

64. Sarah Collinson, *Europe and International Migration* (London and New York: Pinter, 1993).

65. Rogers, *Guests Come to Stay*, 14. See also Bundesanstalt für Arbiet, *Representative-Untersuchung '72: Beschäftigung Ausländischer Arbeitnehmer* (Nuremberg, Germany: Bundesanstalt für Arbeit, 1973); Ursula Mehrlander, *Soziale Aspeckte der Ausländerbeschaftigung* (Bonn, Germany: Verlag Neue Gesellschaft, 1974); Ursula Mehrlander, Roland Hofmann, Peter König, and Hans-Jurgen Krause, *Situation der Ausländischen Arbeitnehmer und Ihrer Familiengehörigen in der Bundesrepublik: Representativuntersuchung '80* (Bonn, Germany: Der Bundesminister für Arbeit und Socialordnung, 1981).

66. Bendix, *Importing Foreign Workers*, 44.

67. Friedrich Heckmann, "Temporary Labor Migration or Immigration? Guest Workers in the Federal Republic of Germany," in *The Effects of European Labor Migration on Sending and Receiving Countries*, ed. Rosemary Rogers (Boulder, CO: Westview Press, 1985), 73.

68. Herbert, *History of Foreign Labor*, 234–35.

69. P. Martin, "Germany," 202.

70. L. Funcke, *Daten und Fakten zur Ausländersituation* (Bonn, Germany: Beauftragte der Bundesregierung fur Ausländerfragen, 1985).

71. Stephen Castles, "The Guests Who Stayed—The Debate on 'Foreigners Policy' in the German Federal Republic," *International Migration Review* 19, no. 3 (1985): 519.

72. Ibid., 524.

73. These cities were defined as those whose foreign population constituted more than 12 percent of the total population.

74. Castles, "Guests Who Stayed," 524; see also P. Martin, "Germany."

75. William A. Barbieri Jr., *Ethics of Citizenship: Immigration and Group Rights in Germany* (Durham, NC: Duke University Press, 1998), 30.

76. Heintz Kuhn, "Stand und Wieterentwicklung der Integration der Ausländischen Arbeitnehmer und ihrer Familien in der Bundesrepublik Deutschland—Memorandum des Beauftragten der Bundesregierung," 1979.

77. Quoted in Castles, "Guests Who Stayed," 525.

78. Thomas Faist, "How to Define a Foreigner? The Symbolic Politics of Immigration in German Partisan Discourse, 1978–1992," in *The Politics of Immigration in Western Europe*, ed. M. Baldwin-Edwards and M. A. Schain (Essex, England: Frank Cass, 1994), 56–57.

79. Castles, "Guests Who Stayed," 525.

80. P. N. Jones, "West Germany's Declining Guestworker Population," *Regional Studies* 24 (1990): 223–33.

81. Other provisions included repayment of employees' pension insurance contributions without the usual two-year waiting period. See Castles, "Guests Who Stayed," 530.

82. P. Martin, "Germany."

83. Collinson, *Europe and International Migration*.

84. Castles, "Guests Who Stayed," 530.

85. Peter O'Brien, "Continuity and Change in Germany's Treatment of Non-Germans," *International Migration Review* 22, no. 3 (1998): 109–34. See generally Murray Edelman, *The Symbolic Uses of Politics* (Urbana: University of Illinois Press, 1964).

86. Helmut Quaritsch, *Recht auf Asyl* (Berlin: Duncker and Humblot, 1985), 41.

87. Christian Joppke, "Asylum and State Sovereignty: A Comparison of the United States, Germany, and Britain," *Comparative Political Studies* 30, no. 3 (1997): 277.

88. Michael S. Teitelbaum, "Political Asylum in Theory and Practice," *Public Interest* 76 (1984): 74–86.

89. Daniel Kanstroom, "Wer sind Wir wieder? Laws of Asylum, Immigration, and Citizenship in the Struggle for the New Germany," *Yale Journal of International Law* 18 (1993): 155–210.

90. Joppke, "Asylum and State Sovereignty," 274. See also Frank Rottmann, "Des Asylrecht des Art. 16 GG als liberal-rectsstaatliches Abwehrrecht," *Der Staat* 3 (1984): 337–68.

91. Faist, "How to Define," 52.

92. P. Martin, "Germany " (online version).

93. Christian Joppke, *Immigration and the Nation-State* (Oxford: Oxford University Press, 1999), 90.

94. Ursula Muench, *Asylpolitik in der Bundesrepublik Deutschland* (Opladen, Germany: Leske and Budrich, 1992).

95. P. Martin, "Germany" (online version).

96. Martin Baldwin-Edward and Martin Schain, "The Politics of Immigration: Introduction," *West European Politics* 17, no. 2 (1994): 4. See also W. R. Böhning,

"Integration and Immigration Pressures in Western Europe," *International Labour Review* 130 (1991). Joppke, "Asylum and State Sovereignty," 278.

97. Hans-Joachim Cremer, "Internal Controls and Actual Removals of Deportable Aliens," in *Immigration Controls: The Search for Workable Policies in Germany and the United States*, ed. K. Hailbronner, D. A. Martin, and H. Motomura (Providence, RI: Berghahn Books, 1997), 63–71.

98. P. Martin, "Germany," 213. See also Bernhard Blanke, *Zuwanderung und Asyl in Modernen Konkurrenzgesellschaften* (Opladen, Germany: Leske and Budrich, 1993); Jan Werner, *Die Invasion der Armen: Asylanten und illegalle Einwanderer* (Mainz, Germany: Von Hase/Koehler Verlag, 1992).

99. Forschungsgruppe Wahlen, *Politbarometer 11/91* (1991).

100. Thomas Kielinger and Max Otte, "Germany: The Pressured Power," *Foreign Policy* 91 (summer 1993): 40. Also cited in Wesley D. Chapin, *Germany for the Germans?* (Westport, CT: Greenwood Press, 1997), 62.

101. Klaus J. Bade, "Immigration and Social Peace in United Germany," *Daedalus* 123, no. 1 (winter 1994): 93. Also cited in Chapin, *Germany for the Germans?* 63.

102. Joppke, *Immigration and the Nation-State*, 92.

103. In 1993, this discretionary power granted to local officials was revoked.

104. *Migration News* (December 1997). Germany has two types of naturalization mechanisms. The first, naturalization by right (*Anspruch*), involves ethnic Germans returning to the homeland. The second, discretionary naturalization, deals with all nonethnic German applicants.

105. Castles, "Guests Who Stayed," 533.

106. *Migration News* (January 1998).

107. Quoted in *Migration News* (December 1997).

108. Christiane Lemke, "Citizenship Law in Germany: Traditional Concepts and Pressures to Modernize in the Context of European Integration," *Harvard Focus Europe* (spring 2001).

109. Ibid.

110. Quoted in *Migration News* (January 1998).

111. P. Martin, "Germany" (online version).

112. Kay Hailbronner, "New Techniques for Rendering Asylum Manageable," in *Immigration Controls: The Search for Workable Policies in Germany and the United States*, ed. K. Hailbronner, D. Martin, and H. Motomura (Providence, RI: Berghahn Books, 1997), 161.

113. Kay Hailbronner, "Asylum Law Reform and the German Constitution," *American University Journal of International Law and Policy* 9 (1994): 165.

114. Heribert Prantl, *Deutschland—Leicht Entflammbar* (Munich: Hanser, 1994).

115. Joppke, *Immigration and the Nation-State*, 94.

116. Hailbronner, "New Techniques for Rendering," 163.

117. Joppke, "Asylum and State Sovereignty," 274.

118. Peter Andreas, "Old Walls, New Walls: The Shifting Function of Border Controls in the United States and Western Europe" (paper presented at the Annual Meeting of the American Political Science Association, Atlanta, GA, 1999).

119. *Migration News* (July 2000).

120. Bundesgrenzschutz, *Jahresberichte des Bundesgrenzschutz, 1991–1998* (Bonn, Germany: Bundesgrenzschutz, 1999).

121. *Migration News* (October 1997).

122. Andreas, "Old Walls, New Walls," 17.

123. *Migration News* (July 2000).

124. Bundesministerium des Inneren, *Texte zur Inneren Sicherheit* (Bonn, Germany: Bundesministerium des Inneren, 1997), 66.

125. *Migration News* (July 2000).

126. Faist, "How to Define," 52.

127. *Migration News* (April 1997).

128. *Migration News* (July 1997).

129. Cf. Peter Andreas, "The Escalation of U.S. Immigration Control in the Post-NAFTA Era," *Political Science Quarterly* 113, no. 4 (1998): 591–615; Wayne A. Cornelius, "Appearances and Realities: Controlling Illegal Immigration in the United States," in *Temporary Workers or Future Citizens?* ed. M. Weiner and T. Hanami (London: Macmillan, 1998).

130. *Migration News* (July 1997).

131. Saskia Sassen, *Guests and Aliens* (New York: The New Press, 1999), 116.

132. *Migration News* (October 1997).

133. Andreas, "Old Walls, New Walls," 20.

134. *Migration News* (January 1995).

135. Dominique Schnapper, "The Debate on Immigration and the Crisis of National Identity," in *The Politics of Immigration in Western Europe*, ed. M. Baldwin-Edwards and M. A. Schain (Essex, England: Frank Cass, 1994), 137.

136. *Migration News* (August 2000).

137. Hermann Kurthen, "Germany at the Crossroads: National Identity and the Challenges of Immigration," *International Migration Review* 29, no. 4 (winter 1995): 914–38; Kees Groenendijk, "Regulating Ethnic Immigration: The Case of the *Aussiedler*," *Journal of Ethnic and Migration Studies* 23, no. 4 (October 1997): 461–82; Klaus F. Zimmermann, "Ethnic German Migration Since 1989: Results and Perspectives," *IZA Discussion Paper No. 50* (Bonn, Germany: *Forschungsinstitut zur Zukunft der Arbeit*, August 1999).

138. Barbara Dietz, "Ethnic German Immigration from Eastern Europe and Former Soviet Union to Germany: The Effects of Migrant Networks," *IZA Discussion Paper No. 68* (Bonn, Germany: *Forschungsinstitut zur Zukunft der Arbeit*, November 1999).

139. *Migration News* (August 2000).

140. *Migration News* (December 2000).

141. *Migration News* (April 1995).

142. In a 1997 report released by the DIW Economics Research Institute in Berlin, analysts suggested that Germany needs immigrants in order to stabilize its population and labor force. They recommended levels from 340,000 to 680,000 annually, though it is notable that the study singled out the need for immigrants from central and eastern Europe (those of closer cultural proximity), suggesting an acute sense for the "societal security" preferences of the state. *Migration News* (March 1997).

143. *Migration News* (July 1996).

144. *Migration News* (January 1995).

145. Ibid.

146. *Migration News* (December 2000). Information on the position paper available online at <http://www.cdu.de>

147. *Migration News* (June 2000).

148. *Migration News* (May 2000).

149. *Migration News* (June 2000).

150. *Migration News* (May 2000).

151. *Migration News* (November 2000). Poll information available online at <www.emnid.tnsofres.com>.

152. *Migration News* (July 2000).

153. *Migration News* (April 2002).

154. See Konrad Milenski, "New Immigration Act: A Weapon Against 'Dangerous Aliens,'" trans. Mary Boyd (available online at URL: http://www.goethe .de/kug/ ges/rch/thm/en155925.htm).

155. Castles, "Guests Who Stayed," 528.

156. Schnapper, "Debate on Immigration," 129.

157. Faist, "How to Define," 51.

CHAPTER FIVE

1. Xavier Lannes, *L'immigration en France dupuis 1945* (The Hague: Martinus Nijhoff, 1953), 9.

2. Quoted in Harold F. Gosnell, *Truman's Crises: A Political Biography of Harry S. Truman* (London: Greenwood, 1980), 351.

3. Alfred Sauvy, "Evaluation des besoins de l'immigration francaise," *Population* 1 (January–March 1946): 91–98.

4. Catherine Wihtol de Wenden, *Les immigres et la politique* (Paris: Presses de la Fondation Nationale des Sciences Politiques, 1988).

5. See James F. Hollifield, *Immigrants, Markets, and States* (Cambridge, MA: Harvard University Press, 1992); James F. Hollifield, "Immigration and Republicanism in France: The Hidden Consensus," in *Controlling Immigration: A Global Perspective*, ed. W. A. Cornelius, P. L. Martin, and J. F. Hollifield (Stanford, CA: Stanford

University Press, 1994); James F. Hollifield, "Ideas, Institutions and Civil Society: On the Limits of Immigration Control in France," in *Mechanisms of Immigration Control: A Comparative Analysis of European Regulation Policies*, ed. G. Brochmann and T. Hammar (Oxford: Berg, 1999); Patrick Weil, *La France et ses etrangers: l'adventure d'une politique de l'immigration* (Paris: Calmann-Levy, 1991).

6. Rogers Brubaker, *Citizenship and Nationhood in France and Germany* (Cambridge: Harvard University Press, 1992), 184.

7. Ibid., 111.

8. Hollifield, "Ideas, Institutions," 10.

9. See Ernest Renan, "What Is a Nation?" in *Modern Political Doctrines*, ed. A. Zimmern (Oxford: Oxford University Press, 1939). Maxim Silverman suggests, however, that while Renan sought to rationalize French identity in contrast to German romanticism, the dichotomy of French nationhood permeates his lecture: "He talks of the eighteenth century as a return to the spirit of antiquity in the way in which the words 'fatherland' and 'citizen' recovered their former meaning; he compares this process with the attempt to 'restore to its original identity a body from which one had removed the brain and the heart; he calls the nation 'a soul, a spiritual principle'; he talks of ancestors, of the heroic past of glory, sacrifice and suffering, of the past in the present and determining the future. . . . This is not the imagery of the rational Enlightenment; it is the imagery of romanticism." See Maxim Silverman, *Deconstructing the Nation* (London and New York: Routledge, 1992), 20. Others have been less critical of Renan, accepting the notion of cultural heritage as intellectual and moral, rather than biological. Cf. Dominique Schnapper, *La France de l'Integration: Sociologie de la Nation en 1990* (Paris: Gallimard, 1991).

10. Brubaker, *Citizenship and Nationhood*, 112.

11. See Georges Mauco, *Les Etrangers en France* (Paris: Colin, 1932).

12. Robert Debre and Alfred Sauvy, *Des français pour la France, le probleme de la population* (Paris: Gallimard, 1946).

13. Georges Tapinos, "L'immigration etrangere en France, 1946–1973," *Institut National d'Etudes Demographiques No. 7* (Paris: Presses Universitaires de France, 1975), 16.

14. Sarah Collinson, *Europe and International Migration* (London and New York: Pinter, 1993).

15. Carliene Kennedy-Brenner, *Foreign Workers and Immigration Policy: The Case of France* (Paris: OECD, 1979); See also Wihtol de Wenden, *Les immigres et la politique*, 108–9.

16. Silverman, *Deconstructing the Nation*, 41.

17. Jean-Pierre Dormois, *The French Economy in the Twentieth Century* (Cambridge: Cambridge University Press, 2004).

18. Gary P. Freeman, *Immigrant Labor and Racial Conflict in Industrial Societies* (Princeton, NJ: Princeton University Press, 1979), 82.

19. Robert Schuman, "Declaration of 9 May 1950," in *The Origins and Development of the European Community*, ed. David Weigall and Peter Stirk (Leicester, England: Leicester University Press, 1984), 58–59.

20. John McCormick, *The European Union* (Boulder, CO: Westview Press, 1996).

21. Text of treaty available online at http://europa.eu.int/eur-lex/en/treaties/dat/C_2002325EN.003301.html (accessed May 18, 2005).

22. For an analysis of the economic challenges facing French economic reconstruction, see Charles P. Kindleberger, "The Postwar Resurgence of the French Economy," in *In Search of France*, ed. S. Hoffmann (Cambridge, MA: Harvard University Press, 1963).

23. CGP, "Premier rapport de la commission de la main-d'oeuvre (Octobre 1946)," *Documents relatifs a la premiere session du Conseil du Plan, 16–19 mars 1946* (Paris: Imprinte Nationale, 1946), 23, 26; see also Jean-Jacques Carre et al. *French Economic Growth* (Stanford, CA: Stanford University Press, 1975).

24. Hollifield, *Immigrants, Markets*, 55.

25. Kennedy-Brenner, *Foreign Workers*.

26. Charles P. Kindleberger, *Europe's Postwar Growth* (Cambridge, MA: Harvard University Press, 1967); see also Hollifield, *Immigrants, Markets*, ch. 5.

27. Cf. Debre and Sauvy, *Des français pour la France*; Sauvy, "Evaluation des besoins de l'immigration francaise"; D. Vincent, "Vieillissement de la population, retraites et immigration," *Population* 2 (1946): 213–44.

28. Silverman, *Deconstructing the Nation*, 41.

29. CGP, "Premier rapport de la commission de la main-d'oeuvre"; see also Jacques Doublet, "L'immigration des travailleurs etrangers permanents en France," *Droit Social* 5 (1965): 292; and Lannes, *L'immigration en France depuis 1945*, 14–15.

30. Patrick Weil, *La France et ses etrangers: l'adventure d'une politique de l'immigration* (Paris: Calmann-Levy, 1991).

31. See Philip Ogden, "International Migration in the Nineteenth and Twentieth Centuries," in *Migrants in Modern France: Population Mobility in the Later 19th and 20th Centuries*, ed. P. E. Ogden and P. E. White (London: Unwin Hyman, 1989); and Tapinos, " L'immigration etrangere en France, 1946–1973."

32. See France, "L'accord de l'immigration Franco-Italien," *Notes Documentaires et Etudes no. 584* (Paris: La Documentation Francaise, 1947).

33. INSEE, *Recensement de la population de 1990: nationalites, resultats du sondage au quart* (Paris: INSEE, 1992); Freeman, *Immigrant Labor*, 79; see also Pierre Bidebery, "Bilan de vingt annees d'immigration, 1946–1966," *Revue Française des Affaires Sociales* 21 (1967).

34. Freeman, *Immigrant Labor*, 73.

35. French minister of social affairs Jean-Marcel Jeanneney, quoted in Ministere des Affaires Sociales et de la Solidarite Nationale, *1981–1986: Une Nouvelle Politique de l'Immigration* (Paris: La Documentation Francaise, 1986), 10; see also

James F. Hollifield, "Immigration and Modernization," in *Searching for the New France*, ed. J. F. Hollifield and G. Ross (New York: Routledge, 1991); and Leon Gani, *Syndicats et traveilleurs immigres* (Paris: Editions Sociales, 1972).

36. Hollifield, "Immigration and Modernization," 122; Hollifield, *Immigrants, Markets*, 63; Leon Gani, *Syndicats et traveilleurs immigres* (Paris: Editions Sociales, 1972), 44–55.

37. Freeman, *Immigrant Labor*, 84.

38. Hollifield, *Immigrants, Markets*, 151.

39. Silverman, *Deconstructing the Nation*, 48; see also Collinson, *Europe and International Migration*, 54.

40. Jeannette Money, *Fences and Neighbors: The Political Geography of Immigration Control* (Ithaca, NY: Cornell University Press, 1999), 120–23; see also Philip Ogden, "Immigration, Cities and the Geography of the National Front in France," in *Foreign Minorities in Continental European Cities*, ed. G. Glebe and J. O'Loughlin (Stuttgart, Germany: Franz Steiner Verlag Wiesbaden, 1987); Philip Ogden, "International Migration in the Nineteenth and Twentieth Centuries," in *Migrants in Modern France: Population Mobility in the Later 19th and 20th Centuries*, ed. P. E. Ogden and P. E. White (London: Unwin Hyman, 1989); Paul White, "The Migrant Experience in Paris," in *Foreign Minorities in Continental European Cities*, ed. G. Glebe and J. O'Loughlin (Stuttgart, Germany: Franz Steiner Verlag Wiesbaden, 1987); Paul White, "Immigrants and the Social Geography of European Cities," in *Mass Migration in Europe: The Legacy and the Future*, ed. R. King (New York: John Wiley and Sons, 1995).

41. Hargreaves, *Immigration, "Race,"* 19.

42. On the rise and effects of Islamic immigration to France, cf. Thomas Gerholm and Yngve George Lithman, eds. *The New Islamic Presence in Western Europe* (London: Mansell, 1988); Gilles Kepel, *Les banlieues de l'Islam*. Paris: Seuil, 1987); Michel Oriol, "Sur la transposabilite des cultures populaires en situations d'emigration," *L'Immigration en France: le choc des cultures* (L'Arbresle Centre, France: Documentations Thomas More, 1987); Michel Oriol, "Islam and Catholicism in French Immigration," in *Immigration in Two Democracies: French and American Experiences*, ed. D. L. Horowitz and G. Noiriel (New York: New York University Press, 1992); Jean Leca, "L'Islam, l'etat et la societe en France: de la difficulte de construire un object de rechereche et d'argumentation," in *L'Islam en France*, ed. B. Etienne (Paris: CNRS, 1991); O. Roy, "Islam in France: Religion, Ethnic Community or Ethnic Ghetto?" in *Muslims in Europe*, ed. B. Lewis and D. Schnapper (London: Pinter, 1994).

43. Freeman, *Immigrant Labor*, 82–83; Money, *Fences and Neighbors*, 109; Kennedy-Brenner, *Foreign Workers*.

44. Cf. Corentin Calvez, "Extraits du Rapport de Corentin Calvez sur le probleme des travailleurs etrangers," *Hommes et Migrations* 768 (1969): 1–13; Maurice Schumann, "La politique francaise d'immigration," *Revue de la Defense Nationale* 25

(1969): 933–40; Michel Massenet, "Les travailleurs etrangers en France: Un renfort necessaire ou one source de conflits?" *Hommes et Migrations* 793 (1970): 19–25.

45. Massenet, "Les travailleurs etrangers en France," 19–25

46. Schumann, "La politique francaise d'immigration," 940.

47. Calvez, "Extraits du Rapport de Corentin Calvez," 2.

48. Silverman, *Deconstructing the Nation*, 75–76.

49. Calvez, "Extraits du Rapport de Corentin Calvez," 315.

50. Freeman, *Immigrant Labor*, 93–94.

51. Hollifield, *Immigrants, Markets*, 68.

52. Ibid., 69.

53. Hollifield, "Immigration and Republicanism," 155; see generally Weil, *La France et ses etrangers.*

54. Silverman, *Deconstructing the Nation*, 77; Sarah Collinson adds, "Concern over social and political costs associated with these large immigrant populations had been growing for several years before the clamp-down." See Collinson, *Europe and International Migration*, 54.

55. Alain Girard et al. "Attitudes des francaise a l'egard de l'immigration etrangere: nouvelle enquete d'opinion," *Population* 29, nos. 4–5 (1974): 1015–64; for a comparative analysis of public attitudes regarding immigration, see Joel S. Fetzer, *Public Attitudes Toward Immigration in the United States, France, and Germany* (Cambridge: Cambridge University Press, 2000).

56. Hargreaves, *Immigration, "Race,"* 18.

57. Daniel Kubat, "France: Balancing Demographic and Cultural Nationalism," in *The Politics of Migration Policies*, ed. D. Kubat (New York: Center for Migration Studies, 1993), 174–75.

58. Originally, these funds were only available to unemployed workers, but were later extended to all workers that met the five-year residence criterion.

59. Andre Lebon, "Return Migration from France: Policies and Data," in *The Politics of Return*, ed. D. Kubat (Rome: Centro Studi Emigrazione, 1984).

60. Weil, *La France et ses etrangers.*

61. James Hollifield notes that illegal immigration was particularly evident in the service sector, as the number of immigrants working in service-related jobs increased from 58,800 in 1973 to 92,400 in 1979, suggesting, "a substantial portion of the increase was due to some form of 'extralegal' migration." See Hollifield, "Immigration and Modernization," 148 n. 89.

62. Hollifield, "Ideas, Institutions," 65–66.

63. Weil, *La France et ses etrangers.*

64. Alec Hargreaves attributes the ability of Asian refugees to avoid nativist hostilities in France on the fact that they were "clearly perceived as victims of political intolerance and because Vietnamese nationals in particular were held to have valuable entrepreneurial skills." See Hargreaves, *Immigration, "Race,"* 20.

65. Hollifield, "Ideas, Institutions," 20–21; David A. Martin, "The New Asylum Seekers," in *The New Asylum Seekers: Refugee Law in the 1980s*, ed. David A. Martin (Dordrecht, Germany: Nijhoff, 1988).

66. OFPRA, *Bilan de trieze annees de fonctionnement de l'OFPRA (1981–1993)* (Fontenay-sous-Bois, France: OFPRA, 1994).

67. Andre Lebon, *1986–1987: Le point sur l'immigration et la presence etrangere en France* (Paris: La Documentation Francaise, 1988), 19–21.

68. Hargreaves, *Immigration, "Race,"* 21; see also OFPRA, *Bilan de trieze annees de fonctionnement de l'OFPRA (1981–1993)*; Catherine Wihtol de Wenden, "The French Response to the Asylum Seeker Influx, 1980–93," *Annals of the American Academy of Political and Social Science* 534 (July 1994): 81–90.

69. Hollifield, *Immigrants, Markets*; David Jacobson, *Rights Across Borders: Immigration and the Decline of Citizenship* (Baltimore: Johns Hopkins University Press, 1996).

70. D. Martin, "New Asylum Seekers," 13; see also Collinson, *Beyond Borders*, 59–87.

71. Collinson, *Beyond Borders*; Satvinder S. Juss, "Sovereignty, Culture, and Community: Refugee Policy and Human Rights in Europe," in "Reconsidering Immigration in an Integrating World," ed. C. Rudolph, *UCLA Journal of International Law and Foreign Affairs* 3, no. 2 (1998): 463–95.

72. Virginie Guiraudon, "Citizenship Rights for Non-Citizens: France, Germany, and the Netherlands," in *Challenge to the Nation-State: Immigration in Western Europe and the United States*, ed. C. Joppke (Oxford: Oxford University Press, 1998), 302.

73. Ad Hoc Group on Immigration, *Conclusions of the Meeting of the Ministers Responsible for Immigration* (London: Ad Hoc Group on Immigration, 1992).

74. Demetrios G. Papademetriou, *Coming Together or Pulling Apart?* (Washington, DC: Carnegie Endowment for International Peace, 1996), 96–97.

75. See, for example, Hollifield, "Ideas, Institutions," 67.

76. BVA poll was published in *Paris-Match*, November 29, 1985, cited in Hargreaves, *Immigration, "Race,"* 151.

77. BVA poll was published in *Paris-Match*, December 14, 1989, cited in Hargreaves, *Immigration, "Race,"* 151.

78. Hargreaves, *Immigration, "Race,"* 175.

79. See Catherine Wihtol de Wenden, "Immigration Policy and the Issue of Nationality," *Ethnic and Racial Studies* 14, no. 3 (1991): 327–28; cf. Patrick Ireland, *The Policy Challenge of Ethnic Diversity* (Cambridge, MA: Harvard University Press, 1994), ch. 2; see also Guillaume Malaurie, "France: Le risque de la contagion," *L'Express*, February 9, 1990.

80. At the other end of the spectrum, 81 percent of respondents answered that Italians and Spaniards "integrated well," followed by Poles (75 percent), Portuguese (70 percent), and Pieds-noirs (66 percent). See MRAP (Mouvement contre le

Racisme et pour l'Amitie entre les Peuples), *Vivre ensemble avec nos différences* (Paris: Editions Differences, 1984), 20.

81. Between 1986 and 1987, explusions nearly doubled, from 848 to 1,746; however, these figures are insignificant in relation to the total foreign population in France. Moreover, removals to the frontier increased only from 12,364 in 1986 to 15,837 in 1987; the number of those who were refused admission increased from 51,436 in 1986 to 71,063. See Christopher T. Husbands, "The Mainstream Right and the Politics of Immigration in France: Major Developments in the 1980s," *Ethnic and Racial Studies* 14, no. 2 (1991): 187.

82. See "General Declaration of Policy" to the National Assembly, April 9, 1986, reprinted in *Actualités Migrations* 125 (April 21, 1986): 1.

83. Brubaker, *Citizenship and Nationhood*, 151–52.

84. Hargreaves, *Immigration*, *"Race,"* 169.

85. There were some conditions, including (1) residence in France for the five-year period prior to declaration; (2) those convicted of committing certain criminal offenses were automatically excluded; and (3) the state reserved the right to exclude those deemed to be of unacceptable morals or who are inadequately assimilated.

86. Hollifield, "Ideas, Institutions," 69.

87. Feldblum, *Reconstructing Citizenship*; Ireland, *Policy Challenge*; S. Wayland, "Mobilising to Defend Nationality Law in France," *New Community* 20, no. 1 (1993): 93–110.

88. Silverman, *Deconstructing the Nation*, 145.

89. See Dominique Schnapper, "La Commission de la Nationalite, une instance singuliere," *Revue europeenne des migrations internationals* 4, nos. 1–2 (1988): 15.

90. Hargreaves, *Immigration*, *"Race,"* 171.

91. Alec G. Hargreaves, "The French Nationality Code Hearings," *Modern and Contemporary France* 34 (July 1988): 1–11.

92. Marceau Long, *Etre Français, Aujourd'hui et Demain? Rapport de la Commission de la Nationalité presente par M. Marceau Long au Premier Ministre* (Paris: La Documentation Française, 1988); see also Feldblum, *Reconstructing Citizenship*, 105.

93. Hargreaves, *Immigration*, *"Race,"* 173.

94. Feldblum, *Reconstructing Citizenship*, 102.

95. Gerard Noiriel, "Immigration: Amnesia and Memory," *French Historical Studies* 19, no. 2 (1995): 380.

96. CSA poll originally published in *La Vie* (November 28, 1991), cited in Hargreaves, *Immigration*, *"Race,"* 157.

97. Feldblum, *Reconstructing Citizenship*, 123–28.

98. *Migration News* (November 1994).

99. Hollifield, "Ideas, Institutions," 78.

100. The proposed law exempted European migrants, as well as those from thirty other designated countries.

101. Ibid., 81–84.

102. Patrick Weil, *Mission d'etude des legislations de la nationalité et de l'immigration* (Paris: La Documentation Francaise, 1997).

103. *Migration News* (September 1997).

104. Hollifield, "Ideas, Institutions," 86.

105. Weil, *Mission d'etude des legislations de la nationalité et de l'immigration*.

106. *Migration News* (January 1998).

107. *Migration News* (January 1997).

108. *Migration News* (January 1998).

109. Hargreaves, *Immigration, "Race,"* 151.

110. *Migration News* (January 2000).

111. *Migration News* (April 2003).

112. *Associated Press Worldstream* (July 10, 2003).

113. Money, *Fences and Neighbors*, 148.

114. Ibid.

115. Freeman, *Immigrant Labor*.

116. Miriam Feldblum, "Reconfiguring Citizenship in Western Europe," in *Challenge to the Nation-State*, ed. C. Joppke (Oxford: Oxford University Press, 1998), 232.

117. Silverman, *Deconstructing the Nation*.

118. *Migration News* (May 1998).

119. Brubaker, *Citizenship and Nationhood*.

120. Silverman, *Deconstructing the Nation*, 20–21.

CHAPTER SIX

1. "Tories Urge Immigration Inquiry," *BBC News* (April 7, 2004) (available online at URL: http://news.bbc.co.uk/1/hi/uk_politics/3606843.stm).

2. "EU Countries Fear Mass Migration from the East," *Deutsch Welle* (April 22, 2004) (available online at URL: http://www.dw-world.de).

3. Among numerous public comments posted on a BBC Web site in the wake of the April 2004 immigration summit that addressed the issue of asylum fraud. See "Is Britain's Immigration System Working?" *BBC News*, April 14, 2004 (available online at URL: http://news.bbc.co.uk/1/hi/talking-point/3603273.stm).

4. Gary P. Freeman, "Britain, the Deviant Case," in *Controlling Immigration: A Global Perspective*, ed. W. A. Cornelius, P. L. Martin, and J. F. Hollifield (Stanford, CA: Stanford University Press, 1994), 298.

5. Jeannette Money, *Fences and Neighbors* (Ithaca, NY: Cornell University Press, 1999), 101.

6. Cf. E. J. B. Rose et al., *Colour and Citizenship: A Report on British Race Relations* (London: Oxford University Press, 1969); Ian R. G. Spencer, *British Immigration Policy Since 1939* (London: Routledge, 1997); J. Solomos, *Race and Racism in Britain* (Houndmills, England: Macmillan, 1993); M. Dummett and Ann Dummett, "The

Role of Government in Britain's Racial Crisis," in *"Race" in Britain: Continuity and Change*, ed. C. Husbands (London: Hutchinson, 1982); Ira Katznelson, *Black Men, White Cities: Race, Politics, and Migration in the United States, 1900–30 and Britain, 1948–68* (London: Oxford University Press, 1973); Robert Miles, *Racism and Migrant Labour* (London: Routledge 1982).

7. B. Carter, C. Harris, and S. Joshi, "The 1951–1955 Conservative Government and the Racialization of Black Immigration," *Immigrants and Minorities* 6, no. 3 (1987); B. Carter, C. Harris, and S. Joshi, "Immigration Policy and the Racialization of Migrant Labour: The Construction of National Identities in the USA and Britain," *Ethnic and Racial Studies* 19, no. 1 (1996); Ann Dummett and Andrew Nicol, *Subjects, Citizens, Aliens and Others* (London: Weidenfeld and Nicholson, 1982); Paul Foot, *Immigration and Race in British Politics* (Baltimore: Penguin, 1965); Zig Layton-Henry, *The Politics of Race in Britain* (London: Allen and Unwin, 1984).

8. Ira Katznelson, *Black Men, White Cities: Race, Politics, and Migration in the United States, 1900–30 and Britain, 1948–68* (London: Oxford University Press, 1973); Anthony M. Messina, *Race and Party Competition in Britain* (London: Clarendon, 1989).

9. Randall Hansen, *Citizenship and Immigration in Post-War Britain* (London: Oxford University Press, 2000); others who have employed an institutionalist approach (in different ways) include Gary Freeman, *Immigrant Labor and Racial Conflict in Industrial Societies* (Princeton, NJ: Princeton University Press, 1979); Erik Bleich, "Continuity and the Path to Change: Institutional Innovation in the 1976 British Race Relations Act" (paper presented to the British Study Group of the Center for European Studies, Harvard University, Cambridge, MA, March 15, 2002); Erik Bleich, *Race Politics in Britain and France* (Cambridge: Cambridge University Press, 2003).

10. Hansen, *Citizenship and Immigration*, 30.

11. Ole Wæver, "Societal Security: The Concept," in *Identity, Migration and the New Security Agenda in Europe*, ed. Ole Wæver et al.(New York: St. Martin's Press, 1993).

12. Rogers Brubaker, *Citizenship and Nationhood in France and Germany* (Cambridge, MA: Harvard University Press, 1992).

13. David Miller, "Reflections on British National Identity," in "British National Identity in a European Context," ed. B. Parekh, *New Community* 21, no. 2 (April 1995): 153–66; Richard Weight, *Patriots* (London: Macmillan, 2002); Linda Colley, *Britons: Forging the Nation, 1707–1837* (New Haven, CT: Yale University Press, 1992), 53–54.

14. Robin Cohen, *Frontiers of Identity: The British and the Others* (London: Longman, 1994).

15. Miller, "Reflections," 158.

16. Iain Hampsher-Monk, "Is There an English Form of Toleration?" *New Community* 21, no. 2 (1995): 227–40.

17. Liah Greenfeld, *Nationalism* (Cambridge, MA: Harvard University Press, 1992), 74.

18. Weight, *Patriots*, 7. See also Paul B. Rich, *Race and Empire in British Politics*, 2d ed. (Cambridge: Cambridge University Press, 1990), 13; Foot, *Immigration and Race*, 232.

19. See *The Norton Anthology of English Literature* (New York: W. W. Norton, 2003).

20. Gerold Krozewski, *Money and the End of Empire* (New York: Palgrave, 2001).

21. E. Zupnick, *Britain's Postwar Dollar Problem* (New York: Columbia University Press, 1957).

22. Weight, *Patriots*, 137.

23. Paul, *Whitewashing Britain*, 5 n. 22.

24. Layton-Henry, *Politics of Race*, 19.

25. C. Holmes, *John Bull's Island: Immigration and British Society, 1871–1971* (London: Macmillan, 1988), 210–14.

26. Quoted in David Cannadine, ed. *Blood, Toil, Tears and Sweat: Winston Churchill's Famous Speeches*, 1st American ed. (Boston: Houghton Mifflin, 1989), 151.

27. J. D. B. Miller, *Survey of Commonwealth Affairs: Problems of Expansion and Attrition, 1953–1969* (London: Oxford University Press, 1974), 13.

28. Arthur A. Stein, "The Hegemon's Dilemma: Great Britain, the United States, and the International Economic Order," *International Organization* 38, no. 3 (1984): 355–86.

29. Paul Kennedy, *Rise and Fall of the Great Powers* (New York: Vintage, 1989).

30. Deborah Welch Larson, *Origins of Containment* (Princeton, NJ: Princeton University Press, 1985).

31. Paul, *Whitewashing Britain*, 1.

32. P. J. Cain and Anthony G. Hopkins, *British Imperialism: Crisis and Reconstruction, 1914–1990* (London: Longman, 1993), 270.

33. Krozewski, *Money and the End of Empire*, 31–36.

34. Weight, *Patriots*, 136–37.

35. Patrick Gordon Walker, *The Commonwealth* (London: Secker and Warburg, 1962).

36. Robert F. Holland, *Britain and the Commonwealth Alliance 1918–1939* (London: Macmillan, 1981); F. H. Underhill, *The British Commonwealth: An Experiment in Cooperation* (Durham, NC: Duke University Press, 1956); H. V. Wiseman, *Britain and the Commonwealth* (London: Allen and Unwin, 1965).

37. Kennedy, *Rise and Fall*, 368.

38. Frank Heinlein, *British Government Policy and Decolonization 1945–1963* (London: Frank Cass, 2002).

39. Hansen, *Citizenship and Immigration*, 44.

40. Weight, *Patriots*, 137.

41. Ibid., 136.

42. Cooperation from sending states was more forthcoming from the countries of the subcontinent and West Africa. The Jamaican colonial government was more reluctant to apply de facto restrictions except in cases where applicants for travel documents were "fugitives from justice" or "lunatics."

43. Spencer, *British Immigration.*

44. Ibid., 45.

45. Layton-Henry, *Politics of Race*, 33.

46. Douglas S. Massey, *Economic Development and International Migration in Comparative Perspective* (Washington, DC: Government Printing Office, Commission for the Study of International Migration and Cooperative Economic Development, 1989).

47. International Labour Office, *International Migration* (Geneva: International Labour Office, 1959), 142, 169. Paul, *Whitewashing Britain*, 25.

48. Memorandum, "The Future of the UK in World Affairs," (PR (56) 3), Treasury, Foreign Office, and Ministry of Defense officials to Cabinet policy review committee, 1 June 1956. CAB 134/1315 (Public Records Office).

49. Stein, "Hegemon's Dilemma."

50. Heinlein, *British Government*, 107.

51. Weight, *Patriots*, 273–75.

52. Draft statement on colonial immigrants, August 3, 1955; see ibid., 84 n. 4.

53. R. B. Davison, *Black British: Immigrants to England* (London: Oxford University Press, 1966), 3.

54. Weight, *Patriots*, 294.

55. Edward Pilkington, *Beyond the Mother Country: West Indians and the Notting Hill White Riots* (London: I. B. Tauris, 1988).

56. Paul, *Whitewashing Britain*, 157.

57. Hansen, *Citizenship and Immigration*, 14.

58. Exceptions were made for persons born in the United Kingdom, CUKCs who held a UK passport, and those holding a UK passport issued in Great Britain or the Republic of Ireland.

59. Report of the Interdepartmental Working Party, September 26, 1961, 3, CAB 134/1469.

60. Spencer, *British Immigration*, 118.

61. Sheila Patterson, *Immigration and Race Relations in Britain, 1960–1967* (London: Oxford University Press, 1969), 18.

62. Patterson, *Immigration and Race*, 18 n. 3.

63. Ibid., 25.

64. Quoted in R. B. Davison, *Commonwealth Immigrants* (London: Oxford University Press, 1964), 7 n. 3.

65. Moreover, one thousand of these vouchers were reserved for Malta. See Zig Layton-Henry, "Britain: The Would-Be Zero-Immigration Country," in *Controlling Immigration: A Global Perspective*, ed. A. Cornelius, P. L. Martin, and J. F. Hollifield (Stanford, CA: Stanford University Press, 1994), 284.

66. Money, *Fences and Neighbors*, 86.

67. Spencer, *British Immigration*, 132.

68. Patterson, *Immigration and Race*, 30 n. 4.

69. See Paul Foot, *The Rise of Enoch Powell* (Baltimore: Penguin, 1969); Simon Heffer, *Like the Roman: The Life of Enoch Powell* (London: Weidenfeld and Nicolson, 1998); John Wood, ed., *A Nation Not Afraid: The Thinking of Enoch Powell* (London: Batsford, 1965).

70. Powell, *Reflections*, 379.

71. Race Relations Board, *Report of the Race Relations Board for 1966–67* (London: HMSO, 1967), 22.

72. See Bleich, *Race Politics*; D. T. Studlar, "Ethnic Minority Groups, Agenda Setting, and Policy Borrowing in Britain," in *Minority Group Influence: Agenda Setting, Formulation, and Public Policy*, ed. P. D. McCain (Westport, CT: Greenwood, 1993), 15–32.

73. Bleich, *Race Politics*, ch. 3; Bleich, "Continuity as the Path to Change," 7–14; Hansen, *Citizenship and Immigration*, 144–46.

74. Hansen, *Citizenship and Immigration*, ch. 7.

75. Money, *Fences and Neighbors*, 69.

76. Larry Grant and Pierce Gareth, "Immigration: The Screw Tightens," *Race Today* 5, no. 3 (1973): 94.

77. Cf. V. Bevan, *The Development of British Immigration Law* (London: Croom Helm, 1986); Satvinder S. Juss, *Immigration, Nationality, and Citizenship* (London: Mansell, 1993); Spencer, *British Immigration Policy*.

78. Spencer, *British Immigration Policy*, 144.

79. Walter Mattli, "Sovereignty Bargains in Regional Integration," *International Studies Review* 2, no. 2 (2000): 149–80.

80. Layton-Henry, "Britain," 288.

81. Hansen, *Citizenship and Immigration*, 207.

82. Spencer, *British Immigration Policy*, 147.

83. "British overseas citizens" was a category used primarily for Hong Kong.

84. Hansen, *Citizenship and Immigration*, 214.

85. Harry Goulbourne, *Race Relations in Britain Since 1945* (New York: St. Martin's Press, 1998), 54.

86. Joint Council for the Welfare of Immigrants, *Annual Report 1984/85* (London: Joint Council for the Welfare of Immigrants, 1985).

87. Cf. James F. Hollifield, *Immigrants, Markets, and States* (Cambridge, MA: Harvard University Press, 1992); David Jacobson, *Rights Across Borders* (Baltimore: Johns Hopkins University Press, 1996).

88. Christian Joppke, "Asylum and State Sovereignty: A Comparison of the United States, Germany, and Britain," *Comparative Political Studies* 30, no. 3 (1997): 283.

89. Ian A. Macdonald, *Immigration Law and Practice in the United Kingdom* (London: Butterworth, 1983).

90. Christian Joppke notes, however, that, "British asylum policy has been conditioned by its structural conflation with immigration control." Until legislation was passed in 1993 (Asylum and Immigration Appeals Act), no separate asylum rules existed, and asylum claims were processed pursuant to the Immigration Act of 1971. See Joppke, "Asylum and State Sovereignty," 285.

91. *Migration News* (January 1997).

92. Amnesty International, *United Kingdom: Deficient Policy and Practice for the Protection of Asylum Seekers* (London: Amnesty International, 1991), 4.

93. Joppke, "Asylum and State Sovereignty." See also Commission for Racial Equality (CRE), *Immigration Control Procedures: Report of a Formal Investigation* (London: Commission for Racial Equality, 1985).

94. Chris Randall, "An Asylum Policy for the UK," in *Strangers and Citizens*, ed. S. Spencer (London: Rivers Oram, 1994).

95. Layton-Henry, "Britain: The Would-Be Zero-Immigration Country," 279.

96. Joppke, "Asylum and State Sovereignty."

97. Ibid., 291.

98. *Migration News* (March 1996).

99. *Migration News* (February 1997).

100. *Migration News* (August 1998).

101. Ibid.

102. *Migration News* (May 2000).

103. Ibid.

104. Newspapers reported that many families who applied for asylum would first apply under the husband's name and, if rejected, appeal. However, rather than ending the process as intended by policymakers, those denied would then apply again under the wife's name, then again appeal if denied. Another approach utilized by some who were denied asylum was to report their children as lost, since authorities would not deport families who had missing children in the UK. See *Migration News* (May 2000).

105. Ibid.

106. *Migration News* (January 1997).

107. *Ibid.*

108. See Frank D. Bean and Michael Fix, "The Significance of Recent Immigration Policy Reforms in the United States," in *Nations of Immigrants: Australia, the United States, and International Migration*, ed. G. P. Freeman and J. Jupp (Melbourne, Australia: Oxford University Press, 1992), 55

109. *Migration News* (June 1997).

110. Demetrios G. Papademetriou, *Coming Together or Pulling Apart? The European Union's Struggle with Immigration and Asylum* (Washington, DC: Carnegie Endowment for International Peace, 1996).

111. Layton-Henry, *Politics of Immigration*, 231.

112. See Peter Andreas, "Old Walls, New Walls: The Shifting Function of Border Controls in the United States and Western Europe" (paper read at the Annual Meeting of the American Political Science Association, Atlanta, GA, September 1–3, 1999); Kitty Calavita, "Italy and the New Immigration," in *Controlling Immigration: A Global Perspective*, ed. Wayne A. Cornelius, Philip L. Martin, and James F. Hollifield (Stanford, CA: Stanford University Press, 1994); Wayne A. Cornelius, "Spain: The Uneasy Transition from Labor Exporter to Labor Importer," in *Controlling Immigration: A Global Perspective*, ed. Wayne A. Cornelius, Philip L. Martin, and James F. Hollifield (Stanford, CA: Stanford University Press, 1994).

113. Mattli, "Sovereignty Bargains," 149–80; Papademetriou, *Coming Together or Pulling Apart?*

114. Consistent with the "safe third country" doctrine. In June 2003, the British government added seven more countries to its list of "safe countries," bringing the total to twenty-four.

115. *Migration News* (April 2003).

116. *M2 Presswire* (December 2, 2002).

117. *Migration News* (July 2003 and October 2005).

118. *Migration News* (April 2003). See also Sarah Lyall, "Militants Use British Policy on Asylum to Plot Terror," *New York Times* (January 18, 2003).

119. *Migration News* (April 2003).

120. Ole Wæver et al., eds., *Identity, Migration and the New Security Agenda in Europe* (New York: St. Martin's Press, 1993).

121. "No to Rethink on British Identity," *BBC News*, October 11, 2000.

CHAPTER SEVEN

1. Myron Weiner, *International Migration and Security* (Boulder, CO: Westview, 1993), 3.

2. Generally, existing scholarship has not forwarded theories of policy formation emanating from this relationship, focusing instead on describing the existing and potential security implications that international migration presents.

3. Barry Buzan, *People, States and Fear*, 2d ed. (Boulder, CO: Lynne Rienner, 1991), 363.

4. Bill McSweeney, "Identity and Security: Buzan and the Copenhagen School," *Review of International Studies* 22 (1996): 85.

5. Samuel P. Huntington, *Who Are We? The Challenges to America's National Identity* (New York: Simon and Schuster, 2004), 24, 260; see also David M. Kennedy, "Culture Wars: The Sources and Uses of Enmity in American History," in *Enemy Images in American History*, ed. Ragnhild Fiebig-von Hase and Ursula Lehmkuhl (Providence, RI: Berghahn Books, 1997); Vamik D. Volkan, "The Need to Have Enemies and Allies: A Developmental Approach," *Political Psychology* 6 (June 1985);

Vamlik D. Volkan, *The Need to Have Enemies and Allies: From Clinical Practice to International Relationships* (Northvale, NJ: J. Aaronson, 1994).

6. Kennedy, "Culture Wars," 355.

7. Georgiy Arbatov, "Preface," in *Mutual Security: A New Approach to Soviet-American Relations*, ed. Richard Smoke and Andrei Kortunov (New York: St. Martin's Press, 1991), xxi; also cited in Huntington, *Who Are We?* 258.

8. Certainly, among the most provocative of these is Huntington's, *Who Are We?*

9. See, for example, Marc R. Rosenblum, *The Transnational Politics of U.S. Immigration Policy* (Boulder, CO: Lynne Rienner, 2004).

10. Cf. Nicholas Greenwood Onuf, "Sovereignty: Outline of a Conceptual History," *Alternatives* 16 (1991): 425–46; Jens Bartleson, *A Genealogy of Sovereignty* (Cambridge: Cambridge University Press, 1995); Thomas J. Biersteker and Cynthia Weber, eds., *State Sovereignty as Social Construct* (Cambridge: Cambridge University Press, 1996); Stephen Krasner, *Sovereignty: Organized Hypocrisy* (Princeton, NJ: Princeton University Press, 1999); Daniel Philpott, "Ideas and the Evolution of Sovereignty," in *State Sovereignty: Change and Persistence in International Relations*, ed. Sohail H. Hashmi (University Park: Pennsylvania State University Press, 1997); James A. Caporaso, "Changes in the Westphalian Order: Territory, Public Authority, and Sovereignty," *International Studies Review* 2, no. 2 (2000): 1–28; Giampiero Giacomello and Fernando Mendez, "Cuius Regio, Euis Religio, Ominum Spatium? State Sovereignty in the Age of the Internet," *Information and Security* 7 (2001): 15–27; Alan Cranston and Kim Cranston, *The Sovereignty Revolution* (Stanford, CA: Stanford University Press, 2004).

11. Mark W. Zacher, "The Decaying Pillars of the Westphalian Temple: Implications for International Order and Governance," in *Governance Without Government: Order and Change in World Politics*, ed. James N. Rosenau and E. Czempiel (Cambridge: Cambridge University Press, 1992); Gideon Gottlieb, *Nation Against State: A New Approach to Ethnic Conflicts and the Decline of Sovereignty* (New York: Council on Foreign Relations Press, 1993); Michael Ross Fowler and Julie Marie Bunck, *Law, Power, and the Sovereign State: The Evolution and Application of the Concept of Sovereignty* (University Park: Pennsylvania State University Press, 1995); Gene M. Lyons and Michael Mastanduno, eds., *Beyond Westphalia? State Sovereignty and International Intervention* (Baltimore: Johns Hopkins University Press, 1995).

12. David Harvery, *The Condition of Postmodernity* (Cambridge: Basil Blackwell, 1990); Susan Strange, "Wake Up, Krasner! The World has Changed," *Review of International Political Economy* 1, no. 2 (1994): 209–19; Susan Strange, *The Retreat of the State: The Diffusion of Power in the World Economy* (Cambridge: Cambridge University Press, 1996); Saskia Sassen, *Losing Control? Sovereignty in an Age of Globalization* (New York: Columbia University Press, 1996); Saskia Sassen, *Globalization and Its Discontents* (New York: New Press, 1998); James N. Rosenau, *Along the Domestic-Foreign Frontier: Exploring Governance in a Turbulent World* (Cambridge: Cambridge University Press, 1997).

13. On types of sovereignty, see Krasner, *Sovereignty*.

14. Andrew Linklater, "Citizenship and Sovereignty in the Post-Westphalian European State," in *Re-Imagining Political Community*, ed. Daniele Archibugi, David Held, and Martin Köhler (Stanford, CA: Stanford University Press, 1998), 114.

15. Ibid., 117; see also Yasemin Nuhoglu Soysal, *The Limits of Citizenship: Migrants and Postnational Membership in Europe* (Chicago: University of Chicago Press, 1995).

16. Miriam Feldblum, "Reconfiguring Citizenship in Western Europe," in *Challenge to the Nation-State*, ed. Christian Joppke (Oxford: Oxford University Press, 1998).

17. James N. Rosenau, *Along the Domestic-Foreign Frontier: Exploring Governance in a Turbulent World* (Cambridge: Cambridge University Press, 1997), 220; emphasis added.

18. Roxanne Lynn Doty, "Sovereignty and the Nation: Constructing the Boundaries of National Identity," in *State Sovereignty as Social Construct*, ed. Thomas J. Biersteker and Cynthia Weber (Cambridge: Cambridge University Press, 1996), 122.

19. David Jacobson, "New Border Customs: Migration and the Changing Role of the State," *UCLA Journal of International Law and Foreign Affairs* 3, no. 2 (1998): 443–62; see also Mathias Albert, David Jacobson, and Yosef Lapid, eds., *Identities, Borders, Orders: Rethinking International Relations Theory* (Minneapolis: University of Minnesota Press, 2001).

20. John H. Herz, "Rise and Demise of the Territorial State," *World Politics* 9 (1957): 473–93.

21. Benedict Anderson, *Imagined Communities* (London: Verso, 1983); Eric. J. Hobsbawm, *Nations and Nationalism Since 1780* (Cambridge: Cambridge University Press, 1990); Anthony D. Smith, *National Identity* (Reno: University of Nevada Press, 1991).

22. Christopher Rudolph, "Globalization and Territorial Borders in a Global Age," *International Studies Review* 7, no. 1 (2005): 1–20.

23. James F. Hollifield, *Immigrants, Markets, and States* (Cambridge, MA: Harvard University Press, 1992).

24. Krasner, *Sovereignty*.

25. On the condition of complex interdependence, see Robert O. Keohane and Joseph Nye, *Power and Interdependence* (Boston: Little, Brown, 1977).

26. See Douglas S. Massey et al., *Worlds in Motion* (Cambridge: Cambridge University Press, 1998).

27. Demetrios G. Papademetriou, "A Grand Bargain: Balancing National Security, Economic, and Immigration Interests of the U.S. and Mexico" (typescript), Migration Policy Institute (April 2002), 7. See also Bimal Ghosh, ed., *Managing Migration: Time for a New International Regime?* (Oxford and New York: Oxford University Press, 2000); Eytan Meyers, "Multilateral Cooperation, Integration and Regimes: The Case of International Labor Mobility," *Working Paper No. 61* (La Jolla, CA:

Center for Comparative Immigration Studies, November 2002); Rey Koslowski, "Possible Steps Towards an International Regime for Mobility and Security" (paper presented at the Annual Meeting of the International Studies Association, Honolulu, HI, March 1–5, 2005); Christopher Rudolph, "International Migration and Homeland Security: Cooperation and Coordination in North America" (paper presented at the Annual Meeting of the International Studies Association, Honolulu, HI, March 1–5, 2005).

28. John Ashcroft, "The War Against Terrorism: Working Together to Protect America," Testimony presented before the Committee on the Judiciary, United States Senate (March 4, 2003) (available online at http://www.globalsecurity.org/security/library/congress/2003_h/03-04-03_ashcroft.htm).

29. Canadian Embassy (Washington, DC), "Governor Ridge and Deputy Prime Minister Manley Issue One-Year Status Report on the Smart Border Action Plan" (press Release, October 3, 2003).

30. Rudolph, "International Migration and Homeland Security: Cooperation and Coordination in North America."

31. Quoted in Paul Wells, "We Don't Pull Our Own Weight: Manley," *National Post*, October 5, 2001, A6; also cited in Donald Barry, "Managing Canada-U.S. Relations in the Post–9/11 Era: Do We Need a Big Idea?" *Policy Paper on the Americas Vol. XIV, Study 11* (Washington, DC: Center for Strategic and International Studies, November 2003), 11.

32. Quoted in Steven Frank and Stephen Handelman, "Drawing a Line," *Time* (Canadian edition), October 8, 2001, 45; also cited in Barry, "Managing Canada-U.S. Relations in the Post–9/11 Era," 11.

33. *Conference Summary*, The Presidency Conference on Future European Union Cooperation in the Field of Asylum, Migration and Frontiers, Amsterdam Hilton, August 31–September 3, 2004, 2.

34. Koslowski, "Possible Steps."

35. See Kathleen Newland and Demetrios G. Papademetriou, "Managing Migration: Tracking the Emergence of a New International Regime?" *UCLA Journal of International Law and Foreign Affairs* 3, no. 2 (1998).

36. U.S. Department of State, "Highlights of U.S.-European Union Cooperation from July 2001 to June 2002," *Fact Sheet* (Washington, DC: Bureau of European and Eurasian Affairs, June 28, 2002).

37. Cresencio Arcos, "The Role of the Department of Homeland Security Overseas," *Heritage Lectures No. 840* (Washington, DC: The Heritage Foundation, June 2004), 1.

38. Koslowski, "Possible Steps," 20.

39. See Chalmers Johnson, *Blowback: The Costs and Consequences of American Empire*, 2d ed. (New York: Owl Books, 2004).

40. 9/11 Commission, *The 9/11 Commission Report: Final Report of the National Commission on Terrorist Attacks on the United States* (New York: W. W. Norton, 2004).

41. The White House, "Fact Sheet: Making America Safer by Strengthening Our Intelligence Capabilities," The White House (August 2, 2004). Downloaded June 22, 2005 at: http://www.whitehouse.gov/news/releases/2004/08/print/2004 0802-7 .html

42. See Amy B. Zegart, *Flawed by Design: The Evolution of the CIA, JCS, and NSC* (Stanford, CA: Stanford University Press, 1999).

43. Quoted at http://www.ucla.edu/spotlight/archive/html_2004_2005/stud 0904_zegart.html.

Index

amnesty program: and United States, 61, 64, 81; and France, 146
anti-immigration sentiment, 28, 65f, 104, 128, 148, 155, 167, 231
assimilation, 127, 182f

Bismarck, Otto von, 22, 86
Brubaker, Rogers, 21f, 86f, 99, 127f, 164, 169, 227

citizenship, 13, 21f, 29, 206f; and United States, 42, 83; and Germany, 86, 92f, 106, 111–113; and France, 126, 129f, 151–157 *passim*, 163f; and Great Britain, 173f, 179, 187, 195, 197, 206
civic nationalism, 127, 153, 168f, 201
civil rights, 54, 61, 63, 91, 185
collective action models, 17–20 passim
colonialism, 130f, 139, 143, 146, 151–154 *passim*, 176–180 *passim*, 186, 189
conservatism, 81, 87, 112, 119, 122f, 164, 175, 185, 201
constructivism, 25, 30, 39

demographic change and migration, 12, 26, 105, 113, 202
domestic political economy models, 15–21
Dublin Convention, 114, 148f, 158, 213

"E Pluribus Unum" (unity through diversity, United States), 41, 83
eugenics, 36, 42
European Coal and Steel Community (ECSC), 90, 130

European Economic Community (EEC), 130f, 143, 186

feedback loops, 32–36, 39, 56, 103
France: and Commission des Sages, 152–157 *passim*, 164; and French revolution, 127, 142, 163; and Le Pen, Jean-Marie, 149, 160, 164, 201; and National Front Party, 149f, 160; and National Planning Commission (CGP), 131, 133, 162; and Nationality Code, 151–157 *passim*, 164; and New York protocol, 146; and threshhold of tolerance, 128, 142; and *trente glorieuses*, 128, 137, 144; and Weil report, 156
—and French national identity, 126–128, 149–156 *passim*; civic nationhood, 127, 153f; ethnic nationhood, 128, 139, 141, 144, 149f, 153, 163ff; and liberalism, 127f, 131f, 138–158 *passim*, 162–165
—and immigration: labor recruitment programs, 127, 131f, 137, 154; and race, 127, 141; and laissez-faire approach, 131–142 *passim*; illegal immigration, 134f, 143–149, 156–160 *passim*; *arête de l'immigration* (immigration stoppage), 144–149 *passim*, 162; North African immigration, 141f, 150–156 *passim*, 5–32ff; voluntary repatriation of immigrants, 145
—and laws and accords: Evian accords, 130; Law of September 20, 130; Franco-Algerian Accord, 142f; Guigou Law, 156f; Pasqua Law, 155ff, 164

265